Pioneers of Critical Accounting

Jim Haslam • Prem Sikka
Editors

Pioneers of Critical Accounting

A Celebration of the Life of Tony Lowe

Editors
Jim Haslam
University of Sheffield
United Kingdom

Prem Sikka
University of Essex
United Kingdom

ISBN 978-1-137-54211-3   ISBN 978-1-137-54212-0   (eBook)
DOI 10.1057/978-1-137-54212-0

Library of Congress Control Number: 2016941857

Cover image © Christina Bollen / Alamy Stock Photo

Printed on acid-free paper

This Palgrave Macmillan imprint is published by Springer Nature
The registered company is Macmillan Publishers Ltd. London

To Thildy and the Lowe Family

Foreword

As one of his former graduate students whose entire academic career benefited from the foundations he laid, I am honoured to have been invited to contribute a Foreword to this *Festschrift* in recognition of Tony Lowe's major contributions to Accounting.

In 1971, when Ernest Anthony Lowe (1928–2014) was appointed as the first Professor of Accounting and Financial Management (his choice of title) at the University of Sheffield, Accounting was not taught in most universities in the UK, and much of the Accounting that was taught (not only in the UK) was based on the premise that **accounting is what accountants do.** In other words, it was seen by many that the technical aspects of accounting practice should provide the core under-pinning of the Accounting curriculum, and little thought was given to theorising about Accounting as a basis for:

- evaluating the adequacy of accounting practice as a step towards improving it;
- contextualising Accounting within organisational or societal frames of reference;
- considering the potentiality of Accounting (i.e., a critical assessment of what it might contribute within organisational and societal contexts);
- recognising that disciplines other than Economics (including Philosophy, History, Psychology, and Sociology) have significant roles

to play in generating novel insights into Accounting as a legitimate field of intellectual inquiry within the academy.

Tony initiated the development of a radical Accounting curriculum at Sheffield, and this spread through his engagement elsewhere as well as via the activities of those whom he mentored. But his endeavours went well beyond teaching-related issues. He was a pioneer in establishing (with a group of close colleagues who went to work with him in the 1970s) what became known as the "Sheffield School", the essence of which was recognising the need to use an array of inter-disciplinary and critical social science perspectives in seeking to understand Accounting in its organisational and societal contexts, along with a concern to bring about beneficial change.

In addition to his concerns over investing in human capital and extending the boundaries of accounting research, Tony was active in institution-building. For example, he played a major role in establishing what became the Management Control Association, and the *Interdisciplinary Perspectives on Accounting* (IPA) conferences. As chairman of the fore-runners (in the UK) of both the Committee of Departments of Accounting & Finance (1974–76), and the British Accounting & Finance Association (1975–76), he worked to promote networks, facilitate greater collaboration, and encourage the development of a culture characterised by increased rigour in accounting scholarship.

As a man, Tony Lowe could be difficult to get along with. He was often stubborn, not always inclined to give credit where it was due, less than perfectly consistent, not adept at organisational politics and, on occasions, rather less adaptive than one might expect from such a strong advocate of the power of adaptive systems! These characteristics meant that one had to reach out to him in order to appreciate his insights, and not everyone was willing to do this—to their loss.

Nevertheless, Tony Lowe made a huge contribution to the development of Accounting as a worthy discipline within universities worldwide. His legacy lives on through the ideas he nurtured and shared and which are now being passed on to successive generations by those who came directly under his influence. Further tributes can be found in Cooper (2014), Laughlin (2014), and Wilson and Sikka (2014).

This collection of essays by leading Accounting scholars from around the world is a fitting tribute to a pioneering scholar and an influential mentor:

Tony Lowe made a real difference

Richard M.S. Wilson
Business Administration
and Financial Management,
Loughborough University,
United Kingdom

References

Cooper, D. J. (2014). On intellectual roots of critical accounting: A personal appreciation of Tony Lowe (1928–2014). *Critical Perspectives on Accounting*, *25*(4/5), 287–292.

Laughlin, R. C. (2014). Tony Lowe and the interdisciplinary and critical perspectives on accounting project: Reflections on the contribution of a unique scholar. *Accounting, Auditing & Accountability Journal*, *27*(5), 766–777. [This tribute is included in the *Festschrift*—see pp. 1–18.]

Wilson, R. M. S., & Sikka, P. (2014, June). In memorium: Emeritus Professor E.A. Lowe. *British Accounting Review*, *46*(2), 213–214.

Contents

Biographies

David Cooper is Professor of Accounting at Alberta and Consulting Professor at Strathclyde. He obtained a BSc from LSE, a PhD from Manchester, three Honorary Doctorates and several other academic awards. David has written or edited nine books and 80 articles and chapters. He is an editor of *Accounting, Organizations and Society*, and Consulting Editor of *Critical Perspectives on Accounting*.

Jesse Dillard an emeritus professor at Portland State University, currently holds adjunct appointments at Victoria University–Wellington and the University of Central Florida. His published works include books, book chapters, and articles appearing in leading management and accounting journals. His teaching and research interests include the ethical and public interest implications of administrative and information technologies particularly as they affect social and environmental sustainability and accountability.

Mahmoud Ezzamel is Research Professor at Cardiff University, Cardiff, UK, and Professor of Management Accounting, IE Business School, Madrid, Spain. His research interests include the interface between accounting and social theory, with special focus upon organizational control and strategic performance measurement systems, accountability, corporate governance, accounting regulation in transitional economies, and accounting history. He has published widely in leading accounting and organizational theory journals and is a member of the editorial boards of eleven accounting and organization theory journals.

Michael Gaffikin is Emeritus Professor of Accounting and Finance at the University of Wollongong, Australia. His interests are in the political, philosophical and historical contexts of the development of accounting thought. He has served on several national and international academic and professional accounting bodies.

Rob Gray has recently retired as Professor of Social and Environmental Accounting at the University of St. Andrews. He has published widely— mainly on social and environmental accounting and sustainability. He founded The Centre for Social and Environmental Accounting Research in 1991 and for 21 years was its Director.

Jim Haslam was born in Bolton, 1960. Jim studied under Tony Lowe at Sheffield, 1978–81. A qualified accountant with a PhD from Essex, he has held positions at Aston, UCNW, LSE, Essex, Waikato, Heriot-Watt, Dundee, Durham and Newcastle. He returned to Sheffield in 2015 as Professor of Accounting, Governance and Society. He has held a number of international visiting positions, is on several editorial boards and is joint author of the book *Accounting Emancipation: Some Critical Interventions* (with Sonja Gallhofer).

Kerry Jacobs is Professor of Accounting at UNSW Canberra. He has over 25 years of experience in teaching and researching accounting in New Zealand, Scotland and Australia. Kerry's specialist teaching and research interests focus on public sector accountability, governance, audit, financial management and reform; particularly the relationship between accounting and politics. He likes asking annoying questions.

Richard Laughlin is Emeritus Professor of Accounting at King's College London, University of London. He was previously Professor at the University of Sheffield and the University of Essex, having started his academic career at the University of Sheffield and been appointed by

Tony Lowe. Richard is the founding Associate Editor of the *Accounting, Auditing and Accountability Journal* and the *Journal of Accounting and Organizational Change*. In 2005, he received the British Accounting Association's Distinguished Academic Award.

Cheryl R. Lehman is Professor of Accounting at Hofstra University (NY), publishing and presenting her research in diverse venues. Serving on the Board of the Institute for Women's Policy Research (IWPR) and the Warsaw based Network of East–west Women (NEWW), her advocacy on gender, race, and class is well known. She is general editor of *Advances in Public Interest Accounting*, and on the Editorial Board and reviewer for a dozen journals. She recently received her License in Clinical Social Work (LCSW), interning with incarcerated youth, examining immigration, prisons, and gender-class-ethnicity premises. She continues to be on the forefront of social justice and unconventionality in her research.

Alan Lowe has recently accepted a position at RMIT, Melbourne. His research has included accounting control systems, ERP and Internet reporting using case studies and interpretive methodology. Recent projects include due diligence in private equity, control systems in a food oil refinery and an international recruitment group based in The Netherlands and UK.

Aideen O'Dochartaigh recently completed her PhD at the University of St. Andrews and currently holds an IRC Postdoctoral Fellowship at University College Dublin. Her research interests are in the areas of sustainability accounting, social enterprise and alternative organisational forms.

Winnie O'Grady is a lecturer at the University of Auckland. Her research addresses the integrated operation of performance management and control systems and uses the viable system model and management control system package as framing devices. The research has examined traditional and beyond budgeting approaches to performance management and control.

Clemence Rannou is a lecturer in accounting at the University of Laval. Her primary interests lie in the interface between management accounting and sustainability—the subject of her PhD studies which she is conducting at the University of St. Andrews.

Robin Roslender is Professor of Accounting and Finance at Dundee University. He was previously Professor in Accountancy at the University of Heriot-Watt and has held an academic post at the University of Stirling. His current interests are in the intellectual capital field, the fate of interpretive sociology in accounting research and human capital reporting. He has acted as a senior academic adviser for the UK Commission for Employment and Skills. He is editor of the *Journal of Human Resource Costing and Accounting* and is a member of the editorial board of *Critical Perspectives on Accounting*.

Prem Sikka is Professor of Accounting at the University of Essex, UK. His research on accountancy, auditing, tax avoidance, tax havens, corruption, corporate governance, money laundering, insolvency and business affairs has been published in books, international scholarly journals, newspapers and magazines. He holds the Working for Justice Award from the Tax Justice Network, Accounting Exemplar Award from the American Accounting Association and the Lifetime Achievement Awards from the British Accounting and Finance Association and *PQ Magazine*.

Jeroen Veldman is Senior Research Fellow at Cass Business School, City University, London. He has held a visiting professorship at UPMF, Grenoble and has previously held appointments at Cardiff Business School and the Utrecht School of Governance, Utrecht University. His research addresses the historical development of the public limited liability corporate form and how this corporate form currently functions in and between organization studies, management, company law, economics, finance, accounting, politics, and corporate governance.

Geoffrey Whittington is currently Emeritus Professor of Financial Accounting at the University of Cambridge, a Life Fellow of Fitzwilliam College, a Senior Associate of the Judge Business School, in the Centre for Financial Analysis and Policy, and an Honorary Professor at the University of Sussex. From 2001 to 2006 he was a full-time member of the International Accounting Standards Board.

Hugh Willmott is Professor of Management at Cass Business School, City University, London and Research Professor in Organization Studies, Cardiff Business School, UK. He has held visiting professorships at Copenhagen Business School and the Universities of Uppsala, Lund, Innsbruck, Sydney and the University of Technology, Sydney. He co-founded the International Labour Process Conference and the International Critical Management Studies Conference. He currently serves on the board of *Academy of Management Review, Organization Studies, Journal of Management Studies* and is an associate editor of *Organization*. He has contributed to a wide range of management and social science journals and has published over 20 books.

Richard M.S. Wilson has devoted his career to boundary-spanning (on a disciplinary basis, a geographic basis, and between the academy and professional practice). He came under Tony Lowe's lasting influence when he was a graduate student and worked in association with him for almost 20 years thereafter.

Introduction

Tony Lowe was a pioneer of critical accounting who transformed our thinking about accounting by locating it in broader social and political contexts. His interdisciplinary approach to accounting enabled us to see accounting as a moral, social and practical technology that affects a wide variety of stakeholders. Whilst it is too early to make any definitive claims about Tony's legacy, those who met and interacted with Tony have a particular appreciation of how he inspired scholars and students to question the established modes of thinking. Like most human beings, Tony was a complex person, but his work was of praxis: commitment to engagement so that all human beings can live fulfilling lives.

This book begins with reflections on Tony, the person, academic, scholar, organiser and the person. The insights are provided by Richard Laughlin, a former colleague from Sheffield University who worked closely with Tony in what eventually became known as the 'Sheffield School'. The chapter captures some of the complexities of Tony, the person, and also records his lifelong commitment to critique and empowering others to see the world through different lenses.

Kerry Jacobs recalls his earliest encounters with Tony Lowe and his relentless insistence on interdisciplinary critique and questioning conventional wisdom. Such engagements can be unsettling, but those travelling beyond the conventional saw richer possibilities of personal awakening and emancipatory social change.

Tony's earlier thoughts about management control systems (MCS) were informed by cybernetics and their influence and possibilities are explored in the chapter by Winnie O'Grady and Alan Lowe (not related to Tony). O'Grady and Lowe indicate how Tony's articulation of principles of MCS design, integrating the law of requisite variety, challenged conventional work. They suggest that contingency theory's development somewhat displaced cybernetics from MCS academic discourse (and more recently they note the prevalence of Simons' levers of control, or LOC)—but they indicate parallels in these theories. They suggest, somewhat controversially, that Stafford Beer's work reflected a markedly greater appreciation of uncertainty and controllability and an approach flexible enough to accommodate contingency theory and LOC.

The chapter by Rob Gray, Aideen O'Dochartaigh and Clemence Rannou sees in Lowe's work an opportunity to look afresh at social accounting and accounting in general, underlining Lowe's commitment to uncovering how accounting and control could be developed to better serve organizations, well-being and a more benign vision of industrial and post-industrial society. At the same time, Gray, O'Dochartaigh and Rannou note that an implied radical re-structuring of economy and society is scarcely—explicitly—explored in Lowe's work.

The contribution by Robin Roslender acknowledges that Lowe, given his significant role in the development of interdisciplinary and critical accounting research, helped him realize that his sociological imagination might find an unexpected outlet in the critical and social analysis of accounting. Roslender sees Lowe's key emphasis in a stepping outside of the prevailing methodology of accounting research. He concludes with an insightful view of the possibilities in critical research.

Jesse Dillard, in a personal perspective on critical accounting's sustainability, highlights Lowe's concern to broaden out and open up accounting and those involved and implicated therein. He sees means by which Lowe's legacy manifests in terms of radicalising accounting for the improvement of the human condition and as a contributor to and expression of a more democratic governance system. Dillard's text provides an excellent reflexive construction of the critical accounting project today, linked to Lowe's intervention, and promotes an 'agonistic dialogic accounting'.

Michael Gaffikin, reflecting on his personal interactions with Lowe, places emphasis on what he sees as Lowe's interdisciplinary enterprise and his concern to explore accounting via methodology and methods from a social science perspective. The theory, methodology and methods that Gaffikin discusses in this context reflect developments in social and political theory as seen by Richard Bernstein. Gaffikin positions a vision of accounting for a more efficient and fairer society in a critique of neo-liberalism.

Jim Haslam suggests the significance of Lowe's influences beyond his published writings, whilst acknowledging the latter's contribution. He emphasises critical possibilities and dimensions of Lowe's early interest in systems theory and cybernetics, seeing continuity in Lowe's work in terms of an engaged commitment to bettering the world. He suggests that Lowe had an interest in Habermas that may have reflected Habermas' interest in a rational reconstruction of systems. Further, he points to Lowe's interest in radical possibilities in post-modernism, if perhaps more to refine a critical modernist position. He links this here to a post-Marxist working of 'emancipatory accounting'.

Cheryl Lehman sees Lowe's concerns to think differently, strive for a better state and actively participate in change as complementing feminist-intersectionality research that is aimed at eradicating prejudice and re-configuring meaning. Lehman especially links Lowe to the feminist-intersectionality research she advocates in elaborating Lowe's view that the creation of power differences as a social phenomenon is not inevitable.

Geoff Whittington makes reference to Lowe's earlier work in systems and cybernetics in elaborating the development of the IASB as an adaptive institution that has responded to social and economic pressures and changed its policies accordingly. He demonstrates the importance of social and political influences on the IASB but also points to positive potential in the IASB's development of a conceptual framework, its transparent system of oversight and due process and its increased representation of and accountability to the world it is meant to serve.

David Cooper and Mahmoud Ezzamel go beyond a focus on technical aspects of the design and usage of the Balance Scorecard (BSC) to give more attention to an evaluation of its implied approach to managing and organizing. Following Lowe and others, they suggest that a discussion of values needs to be an integral part of the choice of control systems: if the BSC's emphasis of managing based on evidence and facts has some merit, the authors are concerned to highlight the problematics of such managing. They also point to how BSC can be used differently—promoting dialogue and debate and possibilities for more democratic organizational processes.

Willmott and Veldman argue that few issues in organization studies are more critical than understanding the modern corporation. Their contribution echoes Lowe's concern to highlight the problematic ethics of the corporation and aspects of it such as limited liability. Their chapter looks at embedded legal, economic and political imaginaries—intertwined, mutually re-inforcing but contradicting one another. The political imaginary indicates the centrality of the economic imaginary in the systematic excluding of voices other than shareholders and directors in corporate governance.

What might be called the political economy of tax advice was a particular area of interest of Lowe. Prem Sikka's contribution reflects Lowe's advocacy of engagement, including with the large accountancy firms, and his indicating of opportunities for critical academics to intervene in public affairs. He draws attention to publicly available evidence to show that Big Four accountancy firms are engaged in anti-social practices. The evidence is provided by drawing attention to their addiction to crafting tax avoidance schemes. Such developments pose serious questions about the status of the firms as ethical and professional entities. Sikka notes that many erstwhile tax avoidance schemes have been deemed illegal by the courts; the firms rarely face any sanctions by the professional bodies.

Jim Haslam
School of Management
University of Sheffield
South Yorkshire, United Kingdom

Prem Sikka
Essex Business School
University of Essex
Colchester, United Kingdom

List of Figures

List of Tables

Tony Lowe and the Interdisciplinary and Critical Perspectives on Accounting Project: Reflections on the Contributions of a Unique Scholar

Richard Laughlin

1 Introduction

Ernest Anthony Lowe, Emeritus Professor of Accounting and Financial Management at the University of Sheffield, died peacefully in Sheffield on 5 March 2014 aged 85. Tony Lowe, a quite unique accounting scholar, was unquestionably the "father figure" of what has come to be

Reflective obituaries, like the one that follows, are invariably personal and inevitably selective in covering the contributions of complex scholars. However, the author would like to thank Jane Broadbent and David Cooper for their helpful, detailed and thoughtful comments on a previous draft. David Cooper has also written a reflective obituary for *Critical Perspectives on Accounting* (CPA) (Cooper forthcoming). Cooper and the author each worked on contributions completely independently and only commented on the other's piece when both were almost finished. Further insights about Tony Lowe can be found in a reflective obituary to be published in the British Accounting Review. The author would also like to thank James Guthrie and Lee Parker, editors of the *Accounting, Auditing and Accountability Journal*, for their comments. However, the following, with all its selectivity and omissions, is entirely the author's responsibility.

R. Laughlin (✉)
School of Management and Business, King's College London,
University of London, London, UK

© The Author(s) 2016
J. Haslam, P. Sikka (eds.), *Pioneers of Critical Accounting*,
DOI 10.1057/978-1-137-54212-0_1

1

known as the "Sheffield School" where he was Professor of Accounting and Financial Management from 1971 to 1985. He has also been seen as one of the key founders of what Roslender and Dillard (2003) and Broadbent and Laughlin (2013) label the "Interdisciplinary and Critical Perspectives on Accounting (ICPA) Project[1]".

The concept of a "Project"—taken from Roslender and Dillard's (2003) historical analysis of the emergence of ICPA—gives a sense of intentionality and something that is ongoing and incomplete, which captures well the research insights of the now global community that has been concerned with not only understanding, but also calling for critique and often change in the role of accounting in organisations and society using a range of perspectives drawn from diverse social sciences.

Beginnings are always difficult to determine with accuracy, but it is largely uncontentious that Tony Lowe was the "father figure", leader and enabler of a group of colleagues, associates and students in Sheffield who became scholars of distinction in their own right and leading contributors to the ICPA Project. Referring to this group as the "Sheffield School", however, needs some clarification. Equally to claim that Tony Lowe was also one of the key founders of the ICPA Project needs careful analysis. The sad death of Tony Lowe provides a unique opportunity both to say something about him, his life and his many contributions as well as to provide some reflections on the "Sheffield School" and how Tony and others associated with him in Sheffield contributed to the development of the ICPA Project. This paper, therefore, should certainly be read as an obituary to Tony Lowe, to celebrate his many contributions, but, as befits the complex and extraordinary man that he was, this will not be a traditional obituary.

The following is divided into two sections followed by a brief conclusion. The first section looks at Tony Lowe, his life and his work and the formation of what has subsequently come to be known as the "Sheffield School". This is taken further in the second section where the institutional space to allow the ICPA Project to develop is explored and its linkages to those associated with Tony Lowe during his time in Sheffield is explored.

2   Tony Lowe and the "Sheffield School"

2.1   An Unconventional Beginning

Tony Lowe's journey into higher education was unconventional. At the age of 19, in 1947, he joined the army with the Royal Signals to fulfil the requirement at that time following the Second World War for all young men to undertake two years of National Service. After leaving the army he became an Articled Clerk with a firm of Chartered Accountants, qualifying as a Chartered Accountant (in 1952) and a Chartered Secretary (in 1953). He then set up a small firm of Chartered Accountants and was in practice before starting an undergraduate degree in 1954 in Economics, specialising in accounting, at the London School of Economics and Political Science (LSE) from which he graduated with a first class honours degree in 1957.

His undergraduate degree, coupled with his qualification as a Chartered Accountant and a Chartered Secretary were the only formal qualifications he had when in 1957, immediately after graduating from the LSE, he was appointed to his first lectureship at the University of Leeds. He stayed at Leeds for nine years until 1966 and during the 1962–1963 academic year he took leave of absence to hold visiting appointments in the USA as Sloan Faculty Fellow in MIT, Ford Foundation Research Fellow at Harvard Business School and Visiting Lecturer at the University of California in Berkeley.

He left Leeds in 1966 and moved initially to take up a Senior Lecturer position in the University of Bradford (from 1966 to 1968) and then moved to the Manchester Business School (MBS) (from 1968 to 1971), again as a Senior Lecturer. Anthony Hopwood was at MBS at the same time. Together, they set up a control research project with Tony Tinker and Tony Berry as researchers. This was the only time that Anthony Hopwood and Tony Lowe were in the same institution and the only time they collaborated. Whilst sharing an increasing intolerance towards the dominance of economics, in all of its many forms, to inform an understanding of the nature of accounting they were different in many ways making it difficult for them to work together. Yet, as Roslender and Dillard (2003), Baker (2011) and Broadbent and Laughlin (2013) argue, both Anthony Hopwood and Tony Lowe were key, if not the key, founders of the ICPA Project despite the difference in their respective contributions.

2.2   The Management Control Workshop Group

It was in MBS that the thinking and values that would become hallmarks of his time in Sheffield started to emerge through the formation of the Management Control Workshop Group (MCWG). Tony Lowe's interest in systems theory and management control systems, formed whilst he was at Leeds and Bradford, started to become clear and apparent in a range of significant publications that appeared towards the end of his time at MBS (cf. Lowe 1971a, b; Lowe and McInnes 1971). But what was apparent to him was how much more needed to be analysed and understood. For Tony, the MCWG was to provide a forum for this understanding to develop. Initially the MCWG was a Manchester-based group involving Tony Lowe, Tony Tinker and Tony Berry (who were part of the original research team at MBS) along with David Otley, who was also a doctoral student at MBS at the time. When Tony Lowe moved to Sheffield, followed by Tony Tinker, and David Otley moved to Lancaster, the MCWG became a northern England-based network and involved a range of others, including David Cooper who took up a lectureship at the University of Manchester in 1972. The MCWG continued to expand its membership over the years and metamorphosed in 1988 into the Management Control Association (MCA), now with an international membership and continues, in good Tony Lowe tradition, as an intellectual space and network of discovery in the broad area of management control systems. The significance of this intellectual space can be judged by the numerous publications that have come out of the MCA and its changing and expanding membership over the years. To give a flavour of the quality and significance of this work and link it back to Tony Lowe, we need go no further than the highly significant National Coal Board study undertaken just before one of the most bitter industrial relations disputes the UK has ever experienced. The research came out of the MCWG and the researchers were mostly from either the Universities of Manchester or Sheffield, some of whom have already been mentioned above whilst others feature below, and were led by Tony Lowe. The publications from this study (e.g. Berry et al. 1985) and the impact that it had politically at the time remains of considerable significance and has continued to be a key reference point for all those engaged in and actively involved in the ICPA Project over the years.

2.3   The Formation of the "Sheffield School"

In 1971 Tony Lowe took up the first Chair in Accounting and Financial Management at the University of Sheffield and was to remain in this position until his early retirement in 1985.[2] It was during this time that he gathered around him a number of young inexperienced staff members, part-time staff, undergraduate, masters and doctoral students who have become significant internationally recognised scholars in ICPA research. Within the first two years of Tony Lowe's appointment he had, in turn, appointed Tony Tinker, Dick Wilson, Tony Puxty and Richard Laughlin as Lecturers in Accounting and Financial Management. None of this group had doctorates at the time—although Tony Tinker's was close to completion having been Tony Lowe's doctoral student in MBS—and in all cases these individuals were young, eager to learn yet inexperienced given this was their first full time lectureship position. Trevor Hopper joined the staff in 1980 following an early and quite extensive engagement with the MCWG. David Cooper was also closely involved with Sheffield and from 1975 until 1981 was a part-time lecturer at Sheffield.[3] Despite his part-time status David Cooper played a full part in the academic debates that were occurring at Sheffield during this time. Undergraduates during Tony Lowe's time in Sheffield are too numerous to list but two stand out—Jim Haslam and Wai Fong Chua—both graduating with outstanding first class honours degrees. Masters students are again too numerous to list but Jan Mouritsen and Jane Broadbent[4] stand out. There were also a considerable number of doctoral students but, again in the context of future leading figures in the ICPA Project, a number stand out including those already mentioned (Tony Tinker, Tony Puxty, Richard Laughlin, Wai Fong Chua,[5, 6] and Prem Sikka).

Naming names is always a bit invidious since it is so easy to omit someone of note[7] but the reason for doing this in this case is for two reasons. First, to indicate the significance of those named in the context of those associated with and contributing to and advancing the current work of the ICPA Project[8] and the very fact that all of them started their careers in different ways at Sheffield. Second, to make clear that given the diversity of these individuals that what has come to be known as the "Sheffield School" is not some simple set of identical look-a-likes. The characteristics of the individuals listed, if they constitute a "School", can be best understood by a set of shared academic and political values that were nurtured and influenced by the values of Tony Lowe.

2.4   The Values of the "Sheffield School"

Three values stand out[9] and are embodied in the idea of a "community of practice", in a sociological sense, that Tony Lowe created in Sheffield.[10] The literature on communities of practice is considerable and diverse but it is worth highlighting that a "community of practice" constitutes:

> Groups of people who share a concern, a set of problems, or a passion about a topic, and who deepen their knowledge and expertise in this area by interacting on an ongoing basis. (Wenger et al., 2002, p. 4)

This definition captures well the community that Tony Lowe created initially in the MCWG and then in Sheffield. It was a group who shared a "passion about a topic" with a belief that it was through close and intense interaction that understanding developed. Tony Lowe, as the leader of this group, created the intellectual space for these interactions to occur. He did not determine the outcome of these interactions and what should constitute knowledge, but he did create the underlying values that should guide these various interactions.

The first of these values that Tony Lowe imbued in the thinking of the Sheffield "community of practice" was that knowledge about the nature and functioning of accounting in organisations and society was inadequate and in need of fundamental reshaping through a range of social science perspectives. The 1970s saw a global re-emphasis within accounting research, which Mattessich (2008, p. 193) typecasts as a move away from a more "normative a priori" accounting research to an emphasis on "empirical research in accounting". Tony Lowe not only shared this move but was part of the revolution that was calling for change. What he did not share, and stood strongly against, was the developments that were underway, particularly in the USA, to fill this lack of understanding by an intensification of the use of various forms of financial economics as the only discipline and set of theories that could fill this move to an empirical understanding. Tony Lowe and his colleagues in Sheffield rejected the view that financial economics should be regarded "[...] as more rigorous and scientific, thus deserving privileged treatment" (Roslender and Dillard, 2003, p. 327). What was needed was not a call for one way to discover empirical insights and spurious claims to scientific "truth", but the need to look to other social sciences, beyond financial economics, to provide new insights into the empirical nature of accounting in organisations and society. He also stood against the claim that these discoveries could be regarded as absolute truths, which again he saw financial economics doing.

The epistemology espoused by Tony Lowe was not a call, however, for relativism and an "anything goes" approach to discovery. It required having conviction about the social science approach adopted and the resulting understanding but being open to challenge and other perspectives. Tony Lowe never doubted the power and relevance of systems theory to provide new insights into accounting within organisations and societies. This was reinforced and developed through working with Tony Tinker on the latter's doctorate and their insightful and significant joint work on systems theory and cybernetics that not only informed their understanding of accounting but shed new light on these theoretical priors (cf. Lowe and Tinker 1976a, b). Despite this conviction, Tony Lowe did not expect that all should become systems theorists and cybernetricians. What he valued and imbued was a rejection of the dominance of financial economics and the need for a wide engagement with all social sciences, clear choice, conviction of choice and open critical discourse to defend discoveries.

The second of these values was the importance of teaching and learning for everyone and the necessity to see this as a two-way process. To Tony Lowe the degree programmes that were taught and the consequent learning assessment schemes at Sheffield were as important as the research and writing. Not to see teaching in this light was unacceptable. Teaching should always be social science based, critical in nature and always stretching students to their limits from the first to last day of any course on any degree, involving minimal "spoon feeding" and maximum self-discovery through extensive reading and writing. Assessment was also important since it helped to judge learning but could not and should not be seen as the only ways to make this judgement. Teaching, however, was to be a two-way dynamic process. Tony Lowe was of the view that the taught could teach the teachers new insights that they had not seen before and not to be open to this was unacceptable. This spirit of two-way learning driven by self-discovery also applied to the academic development of the teaching staff. Tony Lowe did not value any contemporary, formal models of mentoring of younger staff. They were thrown in at the deep end to find their own way even though he was always available to debate (and challenge) discoveries and through such processes allow both his own learning and that of those he mentored. In sum, teaching and learning was highly valued in Sheffield but not in a simple traditional one-way teacher to taught sense.

Those who were associated with the teaching programmes in Sheffield were imbued with this ethos and many, with Tony Lowe's strong approval, took this ethos further. A flavour of these developments are recounted in Laughlin et al. (1986) but perhaps it is Dick Wilson's initiative to develop new and innovative first-year undergraduate textbooks in financial accounting, managerial accounting and financial management that captured more fully the new approach to teaching and learning that was emerging in Sheffield. So in 1984 it was decided to produce three very different textbooks. Five of the six authors came from Sheffield, with the sixth, Rob Gray, although not a Sheffield staff member, known well by the Sheffield colleagues. The books finally appeared in 1988 (Wilson and Chua 1988; Puxty and Dodds, 1988[11]; Laughlin and Gray 1988). All these books were dedicated to Tony Lowe and contained a considerable amount of his insightful work into systems theory. These books remain revolutionary first year texts which, whilst being successful across the world and greatly appreciated by the students, stumbled in the longer term since not enough teachers were willing to make the changes needed to their teaching programmes. This stress on innovative teaching and learning has been taken forward by many in many ways over the years but perhaps most noticeably by Dick Wilson in his work with the British Accounting and Finance Association and through the *Accounting Education: An International Journal*, which he established and of which he was the founding editor for many years.

The third of these values was the importance of critique and the need to be open to pursue progressive change in both ideas as well as in accounting and management practices. Tony Lowe believed in constant critique about virtually everything. The logic was clear: if ideas or practices did not survive critical analysis they were weak and/or inappropriate and should be changed. The operationalisation of this, even for those who understood what was occurring, was not easy but for those who weathered the storm and could justify their ideas the end result was greater confidence in their understanding. Equally for those whose ideas did not survive this critique but listened and learned, there were rewards of new levels of understanding that could be defended. However, for those new to this set of challenges and for those in a managerial relationship to Tony Lowe—such as senior university managers!—such behaviour was invariably seen as completely inappropriate and led to considerable difficulties. What also was key in this valuing of critique was that understanding the nature of accounting in organisations and society was never the end of the research process to Tony Lowe. Critique of this understanding to test its viability was, as already indicated, vital but critique had to encompass possible change for the better in the roles of accounting that were being discovered.

3   The "Sheffield School" and the Start of the ICPA Project

These three values were the major attributes of all those listed above who could be seen as the "community of practice" that constituted the "Sheffield School". They were values that remain central to the thinking of these individuals albeit expressed in sometimes rather different ways than Tony Lowe would have expressed them himself. Now I want to return more directly to the ICPA Project and show how the early developments in this project can be seen as an outgrowth of what was happening in the MCWG and in Sheffield and was driven by the above "community of practice" values.

It will be recalled that the first and third of these values that Tony Lowe held relates to the vital importance of creating intellectual spaces for debate and interaction to allow understanding to emerge and change to occur through the adoption of a variety of social science perspectives. These values summarise well the entire purpose of the ICPA Project.

In the 1970s many of those associated with Tony Lowe were of the view that the space needed for new discoveries to be made through the adoption of a wide range of social science perspectives was inadequate. What was deemed to be needed was the creation of institutional spaces beyond the MCWG and Sheffield on a much wider global footing. Also, whilst Anthony Hopwood had taken an early and vitally important initiative in 1976 to create Accounting, Organizations and Society (AOS) to provide a publication outlet for research that now would be seen as under the umbrella of the ICPA Project, there were growing doubts about the capacity of AOS to capture fully what was starting to emerge. This was somewhat exacerbated, as Baker (2011) indicates, with AOS being at pains to maintain the legitimacy of the journal to the Americans and keep them involved in AOS. This laudable objective at one level led to greater space given in the journal to papers that were sympathetic to the interests of the US academic community, which, to many, and certainly those associated with Sheffield and Tony Lowe, seemed not the way to proceed.

Rather than tolerate the perceived growing intolerance and the seeming intellectual imperialism of certainly some US thinking, Tony Lowe, Tony Puxty and Richard Laughlin decided to confront this thinking directly. The opportunity for this came when Watts and Zimmerman (1979) published their "market for excuses" paper in *The Accounting Review* (TAR). Lowe, Puxty and Laughlin wrote a critical commentary on this paper and submitted it to TAR for publication in the hope of opening a wider discussion in this journal about alternative social science perspectives on accounting research. The details of this far from successful engagement have been discussed elsewhere[12] but suffice to say this commentary was not published in TAR but finally appeared in extended form in another American journal—the *Journal of Accounting and Public Policy* (Lowe et al. 1983). The closure of debate that this commentary was actually meant to open up and how this occurred is well captured in Tinker and Puxty (1985) under the telling and accurate title of *Policing Accounting Knowledge: The Market for Excuses* Affair.

This "Affair" is introduced at this juncture partly because of the centrality of Tony Lowe in what happened but also because it convinced both Tony and his Sheffield and Manchester associates of the urgent need to create additional alternative intellectual spaces to allow the embryonic ICPA thinking to flourish. With the American journals largely intolerant to this thinking[13] and AOS being the only outlet for publications in the area and the discursive spaces of the MCWG and in Sheffield and Manchester becoming less than was needed, the need to create more intellectual spaces became a priority. It was with this priority in mind that in 1985 David Cooper (who was at UMIST at this time) and Trevor Hopper (who had moved to the University of Manchester from Sheffield in 1983) organised the first Interdisciplinary Perspectives on Accounting (IPA) Conference.[14] AOS was never formally involved with the first IPA Conference or subsequent ones even though it published special editions of papers from the conference in 1986 and 1987. Tony Lowe was a very strong supporter of the IPA Conference and its organisers and presented a paper co-authored with Richard Laughlin, which was subsequently published in a book, entitled Critical Accounts, drawn from selected conference papers (Laughlin and Lowe 1990). Tony Lowe's hallmark challenging and intense debating style strongly influenced the way the IPA Conference was conducted, with one and a half hour sessions for a single paper led by discussants rather than the author, where all participants were expected to have seriously read the paper presented and to engage in extensive discussion about the contents

James Guthrie and Lee Parker already had in mind the development of a new journal—originally called *Accounting, Auditing and Accountability* (AAA)—to supplement the publication spaces available through AOS. This idea had come out of James working with Reg Mathews on editing the Australasian *Social Accounting Monitor* (SAM). SAM had come to the notice of MCB Press in Bradford, which approached James to see whether he would be interested in setting up a new journal in the broad area covered by SAM. In 1986 James approached Lee to co-edit AAA with him. Even though this was clearly an Australian initiative, James and Lee were keen to link into the ICPA Project developments that were apparent in the first IPA Conference. In 1986, following consultation with Wai Fong Chua, James asked me to become an Associate Editor of the new journal. I was initially rather reticent to accept this invitation but David Cooper persuaded me to do so and convinced me of the need for a new journal. So in February 1987 I agreed to act as one of the two[15] founding Associate Editors of what has become the *Accounting, Auditing and Accountability Journal* (AAAJ). The first edition of *AAAJ* appeared in 1988. From this time the ICPA Project had now an alternative publication outlet to AOS.

This expansion of the publication possibilities increased further with the launch of *Critical Perspectives on Accounting* (CPA) in 1990. The founding Editors were David Cooper and Tony Tinker, both with strong connections to Tony Lowe and Sheffield. One of the four initial Associate Editors was Trevor Hopper, again with similar connections to Sheffield.

The three core journals[16] [16] (*AOS, AAAJ* and *CPA*) that are most associated with the ICPA Project were therefore in place by 1990 and in different ways can be seen as connected to, and influenced by, Tony Lowe and his associates at Sheffield. Whilst the associations with *CPA* are clear[17] those with *AAAJ* and *AOS* are not as obvious. Certainly the early links with me and *AAAJ* are clear and it was only from the beginning of 2014 that I ceased being an Associate Editor. But the current Associate Editors include two others with Sheffield connections—namely Jane Broadbent and Jeffrey Unerman—although Jeffrey's connections to Tony Lowe are considerably less than Jane's having completed a Sheffield doctorate many years after Tony Lowe's time there. AOS is more complex. *AOS* has always been associated with Anthony Hopwood who was always rather distant from Tony Lowe and his colleagues. However, *AOS*, the home of many seminal ICPA papers, did have David Cooper as one of its first Associate Editors until 1990 when, with Tony Tinker, he started *CPA*. However, following Anthony Hopwood's retirement as Editor-in-Chief and his subsequent untimely death, David Cooper, Wai Fong Chua and Peter Miller, all with connections to Tony Lowe and Sheffield, were appointed editors under a new Editor-in-Chief, Chris Chapman.

It was not just journal outlets that were important for Tony Lowe but also the discursive forums to generate the networks and ideas needed were also of vital importance and these too have occurred. The IPA Conference, which started in 1985, became a triennial conference.[18] The intervening years were then filled by the Critical Perspectives on Accounting (CPA) Conference, which started in 1993, followed by the Asia-Pacific Interdisciplinary Research in Accounting Conference (APIRA) in 1995 both, unlike the non-aligned IPA Conference, closely linked to CPA[19] and AAAJ, respectively. These three conferences now work together in a three-year cycle with the next CPA Conference in July 2014, followed by the next IPA Conference in 2015 and the next APIRA Conference in 2016.

These discursive forums along with the journals that are now available across the world are not only spaces of which Tony Lowe approved but they are in part influenced by his values imbued in those associated with him in Sheffield who played a major part in their initial formation.

4   A Concluding Thought

Throughout Tony Lowe's long and distinguished career he believed in the power of creating "communities of practice" where critical interactive debate could occur and from which understanding could be generated. He also believed in the importance of going beyond understanding to critical engagement with this understanding leading to possible change for the better in the role of accounting in organisations and society. He also placed a high priority on teaching and learning in a two-way process between the taught and the teacher to accompany rigorous research. He never tired on these priorities or lost sight of them as key values to drive quality research and quality learning. They are values that are the core foundation of the ICPA Project and Tony Lowe would turn in his grave if he felt that as heirs to this intellectual space that has been created we fill it with mindless discussion that does not concentrate on the use of a wide range of social science perspectives to understand and change the role of accounting as practised in organisations and society.

Notes

1. Whilst Roslender and Dillard (2003, p. 327) distinguish between the "interdisciplinary" and the "critical" they see "[…] the latter being a subset of the former" and this distinction and interconnection is maintained when referring to ICPA. Roslender and Dillard (2003, p. 332) also make clear the links between the "Sheffield School" and the early developments of the ICPA Project. As they point out: "Between 1981 to 1984…The UK was confirmed as the home of the project with the Sheffield School continuing to play a major role in its development and wider diffusion".

2. Tony Lowe subsequently took up a research position at the University of Manchester Institute of Science and Technology (UMIST) followed by full-time positions at the University of the South Pacific (1990–1993) and the University of Waikato (1993–1995) interspersed with a range of part-time positions at Trent Polytechnic (as it was called at the time now Nottingham Trent University), University of Southampton, Manchester Metropolitan University and finally at Heriot-Watt University, Edinburgh. It is difficult to be precise as to when he finally retired but it was probably 2003 or 2004. During the first few years after his first "retirement" in 1985 he worked closely with David Cooper, Tony Puxty, Hugh Willmott, Keith Robson, Prem Sikka, Jim Haslam and Sonja Gallhofer on a range of important critical research studies into accounting regulation and the accounting profession (cf. Puxty et al. 1987; Sikka et al. 1989; Lowe et al. 1991; Willmott et al., 1992). However, a more detailed explication of this research and his many other activities past his official "retirement" in 1985 from Sheffield must await for another time and place.

3. Other part-time lecturers at Sheffield included David Otley and Andy Stark, neither of whom would probably see themselves as

committed to the thinking that was starting to unfold with the full-time staff. However, they were exposed to and part of the rather novel teaching and assessment programmes and practices and the wider debates that were occurring in Sheffield leaving some level of influence over their thinking.

4. Jane Broadbent undertook the Sheffield MA part-time during the academic years 1986/1987 and 1987/1988 following an invitation by Tony Lowe and Dick Wilson to apply to take the degree. In September 1988, towards the end of the taught part of the master's programme, Jane was appointed as a Lecturer in Accounting and Financial Management and completed her MA and then her doctorate as a staff member.

5. Wai Fong Chua, following the completion of her undergraduate and doctoral degrees in Sheffield, became a Junior Research Fellow (in 1979) and was then appointed to a lectureship (in 1981) and remained in this position until 1983 when she moved to the University of Sydney.

6. David Cooper and Jim Haslam should be mentioned as those completing PhDs even though neither of them were formally registered at Sheffield. Both would, however, acknowledge an intellectual debt to Tony Lowe for active supervisory assistance from him on their respective doctorates.

7. In this regard Peter Miller should be mentioned since he was a Lecturer in Accounting and Financial Management at Sheffield from 1985 to 1987. He had been appointed by Tony Lowe even though by the time Peter started Tony had just retired. This was Peter Miller's first accounting lectureship and he acknowledges that his thinking was influenced by Tony Lowe and his Sheffield colleagues.

8. All those listed, apart from Tony Puxty who sadly died very prematurely in February 1995, are still active scholars and academics albeit a number of them no longer hold full-time academic positions. None of them are based in Sheffield any longer—the last of those mentioned to leave were Richard Laughlin and Jane Broadbent in 1995. However, the ethos and values that had been so much a part of Sheffield for over 20 years did not die out in 1995 and continued

through a range of new staff that were appointed or were, like Peter Armstrong, already on the staff.

9. The broad nature of these values were touched on in a eulogy given to Tony Lowe by Richard Laughlin (2001) when, in April 2000, Tony received the British Accounting Association's Distinguished Academic Award for his outstanding contribution to the development of accounting knowledge.

10. This understanding of what has come to be known as the "Sheffield School" as a "community of practice" is thanks to Jane Broadbent. Whilst Broadbent and Laughlin (2013) more than hint at these connections, it was only after the book was completed and after further reflection Jane could see these linkages more clearly.

11. Colin Dodds was on the staff at Sheffield in 1984 and whilst not mentioned to date was very sympathetic to what was happening under the leadership of Tony Lowe. But Colin kept a distance certainly from many of the extensive research debates that were occurring at that time.

12. See the summary in Broadbent and Laughlin (2013) for those interested, which includes a range of relevant and related references.

13. It is worth pointing out that the only paper that tried to open up the wider—rather than the specific critique of the "market for excuses" paper, which was partly addressed in TAR through Christenson (1983)—that Lowe, Puxty and Laughlin intended, appeared in 1986 when Wai Fong Chua (1986) succeeded in her publication of a paper on alternative approaches to research. Since then the pages and interest have been silent.

14. This was to be called the Critical Perspectives on Accounting Conference but the sponsors preferred the seemingly rather less challenging title of Interdisciplinary Perspectives on Accounting. With the idea of the ICPA Project the interdisciplinary and critical are back together again, which is where they always should have been.

15. The other was Barbara Merino from North Texas State University who was also involved in the 1985 IPA Conference.

16. These are core but clearly not the only journals publishing ICPA research—notable other outlets are *Accounting Forum* edited by Glen Lehman and *Advances in Public Interest Accounting* edited by Cheryl

Lehman. And as Roslender and Dillard (2003, p. 335) point out there are numerous other journals that now publish ICPA research without making this a dominant focus.

17. David Cooper and Tony Tinker remained co-editors until 2008. David Cooper remains the Consulting Editor for CPA whilst Tony Tinker has started a range of new outlets for ICPA work notably the *International Journal of Critical Accounting*.

18. Interestingly, the second IPA Conference in 1988 was organised by Trevor Hopper, Richard Laughlin and Peter Miller all with Sheffield and Tony Lowe connections.

19. Whilst Tony Tinker ran a number of conferences from his base in New York in the late 1980s and early 1990s, the 1993 start date of the CPA Conferences was the date when the specific links to the CPA journal were made clear.

The Man Who Always Asked Why!
The Reflexive Accounting of Tony Lowe

Kerry Jacobs

1   Introduction

Beyond his role as a researcher, writer and educator, Tony Lowe was always ready to challenge and question the individual, society and the practice of accounting. In this chapter I will reflect on the practice of Tony Lowe as an example of what Pierre Bourdieu called reflexivity through an exploration on how I encountered and experienced Tony. There is a danger that as the critical or interdisciplinary literature develops, it loses its reflective edge and therefore needs to reengage with Tony Lowe's persistent challenge and not simply reproduce but question and challenge society and ourselves.

This paper begins with a somewhat personal description of my own encounters with Tony Lowe as an example of practices of reflexivity.

K. Jacobs (✉)
School of Business, University of New South Wales (UNSW), Canberra, NSW, Australia

© The Author(s) 2016
J. Haslam, P. Sikka (eds.), *Pioneers of Critical Accounting*,
DOI 10.1057/978-1-137-54212-0_2

19

I then extend my experience into a broader discussion of notions of reflexivity, particularly as developed in the work of Pierre Bourdieu. I then discuss how the biographical positioning and academic project of Tony Lowe could be understood as a celebration of notions of reflexivity and the power of the position of the embedded outsider. As a post script I attempt to turn this practice of reflexivity back on ourselves to ask if critical accounting remains self-critical.

2   An Encounter with Tony

I remember the first time I met Tony Lowe. It was at a critical accounting workshop run in Manchester in 1996. Somehow I got invited to join an extended group which was coalescing around Tony and was heading off to dinner. Sitting next to Tony, we fell into conversation about my work and my PhD study on accounting and public sector reform. Tony asked me why I was doing what I was doing—and I found that a quick or simple answer would not be accepted. Rather, I was challenged to explain and justify why I was doing what I was doing. When asked yet again 'why', I replied in something akin to desperation 'so I can be a professor'. Then, quick as a shot, Tony asked me why I wanted to be a professor. I was left speechless, dumbfounded and shocked. Tony's questions had pushed me beyond my answers and I simply had nothing more to say. For nearly a year I struggled with these questions—until at last when I thought I sorted it out I ran into Tony again—at one or other of the UK-based accounting conferences (most likely the 1997 Interdisciplinary Perspective on Accounting conference in Manchester) quite ready to trot out my latest answer and certain that this would be sufficient to satisfy Tony's 'why' challenge. My poor naive and innocent self was clearly not up to the power of Tony's questions about how I know what I was doing was research and how it would benefit society. I fell at the first stage. Obviously my answers were totally inadequate and I retreated, terrified, with my intellectual tail between my legs. I gathered myself (or at least the pieces I could find) and set about yet another process of self-examination and reflection. However, this time I was more tentative with my conclusions and answers and well aware that I was less than prepared for my next Tony Lowe encounter. Strangely it was this sense of humility (or perhaps humiliation) which formed the basis of my next conversation with Tony and which gave me the ability to reflect on the process. Asking difficult questions was just what Tony did (and perhaps perturbing academics both young and old)—and the questions he raised could never be answered in an absolute sense. But rather his questions were a challenge to reflect on my choices and goals in my career and in my life more generally.

This encounter with Tony was something of a surprise as there was a generosity, welcome and personal interest that I never expected. I had conceived of Tony as a distant figure, like some kind of tribal patriarch, encountered through his writings, and as a supervisor of many of the academic grown-ups I had met. Yet what I experienced from Tony was an intense (and somewhat overwhelming) interest in me as a person and as an academic and a challenge to move beyond my taken for granted and unquestioned assumptions to become more reflective about my society, about accounting and about myself.

The best term I can use to describe Tony's practice of challenging and questioning is reflexivity. Tony demanded reflexivity of himself, of those around him, of those he worked with and of those who read the papers he was part of. In that sense the early critical research in accounting and the researchers in this field can be seen as characterising that reflexive practice and carrying it into their own work.

What is fascinating when considering Tony's practices as a mentor, which is sometimes lost when just reading the papers he authored, is the double nature of his reflexive practice. It is clear that the papers and projects that Tony was involved in challenged the academic (and the broader) community to question the taken for granted privileges and interests in society. However, the real and perhaps most fundamental contribution of Tony Lowe was to force us to question and challenge our own taken for granted self-deceptions.

3   Notions of Reflexivity

There is no doubt that Tony's approach to education and mentoring could be characterised as a Socratic path to critical thinking with constant, probing and disturbing questions. As both dialogical and dialectical, this form of questioning is intended to illuminate assumptions and illogic whereby those questioned recognises the flaws of their own position. One of the major defences offered by Socrates at his trial was that the unreflective life was not worth living. Therefore, reflectivity has often been seen as a core concern and an essential hallmark of reason and, therefore, of the academic (see for example Kant's 'What is enlightenment').

Notions of reflexivity have been a key and persistent theme in the work of Pierre Bourdieu (who also invokes Kant). Bourdieu (1990, p. 187) argues that a key part of the work of sociologists [and social researchers more generally] is to face what is not hidden in an absolute sense but what is taken for granted or what those in positions of power refuse to recognise. It is this underlying process of collective self-deception that Bourdieu calls us to challenge and explore as researchers and offers the conceptual 'navigation aids' of habitus, doxa, field and capital to help us to challenge and resolve the problems of self-deception (Wacquant 1992, p. 31). However, the problem of reflexivity cannot be limited to the external and Bourdieu (Bourdieu and Wacquant 1992, p. 68) argues that we must turn this reflexive gaze on ourselves as a process of sociological epistemology. In that sense we are a product of our intellectualist space (and its own struggle for states and interests) in addition to our personal biography encoding certain taken for granted tastes and preferences in our habitus. From this perspective we read observed social behaviour according to the bias of our own social origins (class, gender, ethnicity etc.) and according to the agenda (and privileged position) of our academic field. However, perhaps most dangerous is the intellectualist bias, where we see the world as a spectacle, a process to be understood and explored rather than a problem to be solved This intellectualist approach risks rupturing the connection with the logic of practice and collapsing practical logic into scholastic logic (Wacquant 1992, p. 39).

It is this very practice of self-reflexivity that characterises both Bourdieu's inaugural lecture at the College de France (23 April 1982,

Bourdieu 1990 p.177) and his final lecture (Bourdieu 2007). In his inaugural 'lecture on the lecture', he argues that researchers (scientists [sic]) should turn their reflective tools on themselves and question that taken for granted realities (and that those responsible for the theological and terroristic use of canonical writings might awaken from their dogmatic slumber to put their work to test in practice). Bourdieu (1990, p. 181) challenges his academic colleagues to move beyond their struggle over the monopoly of the legitimate representation of the social world to a reflexivity that recognise and documents the nature of that struggle. From his perspective all social activity is understood as social struggles over specific capital within a given social space (field). Because of those who are caught up in the game (illusio) find it difficult to recognise the illusory nature of the struggles, stakes and profits and it is only from the standpoint of the impartial spectator who invests nothing in the game or in its stakes that the nature of the self-deception and the mechanisms of violence and domination become evident (Bourdieu 1990, p. 181). From a methodological perspective, the only true researcher (or scientist in Bourdieu's language) is the person willing to adopt the mental (reflexive) position of outsider and question what everybody else (the insiders) takes for granted.[1] As such it is our embodied and unquestioned sense of self (habitus) which fits us to our social space and allows the enactment of practical logics, is also the aspect that blinds us to the nature of our activities, misrecognising the socialised and taken for granted (doxa) as inherent and invariant. From this perspective the reflective act disenchants, it breaks the spell and draws our attention to the very things which are forgotten in the act of doing (Bourdieu 1990, p. 197). Therefore, reflexivity is seen as the way whereby research (social science in particular) can take itself for its object, and use its own weapons to understand and check itself (Bourdieu 2004, p. 89). Untimely the purpose of this is to reveal the implicit social constraints that bear on research as they do on all human activities (Bourdieu 2004, p. 90).

The position of the outsider was fundamental to Bourdieu's sense of self and to his understanding of how reflexivity is to be practiced as a key element of research method. In this way, the position of the outsider is the normal position of critical and reflective work (while recognising that researchers are required to turn their own reflexivity on themselves (or at least their own taken for granted norms) (Bourdieu (2004, p. 89). Bourdieu's challenge of the system in which he prospered and his criticism of the consecration action performed by educational institutions is obvious in the first chapter of *Homo Academicus* (Bourdieu 1988) entitled 'a book for burning'. In his epilogue Craig Calhoun (Bourdieu 2010, p. 280) directly relates Bourdieu's notions of reflexivity, habitus and doxa to Bourdieu's experience as an outsider on the inside within the field of French intellectual elite. Calhoun (Bourdieu 2010, p. 280) argues that Bourdieu's estrangement from the institutions within which he excelled propelled his critical analysis of French academic life and of the state and capitalism more generally. From a methodological perspective Bourdieu normalised his own position as an outsider and argues that for research (science) it is necessary to adopt a reflective stance. It is interesting that Bourdieu's contemporaries Jacques Derrida and Michael Foucault shared a certain horror of the dominant culture of the Ecole Normale and this informed their struggle to what conventional struggles obscured (Bourdieu often reminded listeners that Foucault attempted suicide as a student) (Bourdieu 2010, p. 280).

Conceived starting from this last lecture at the College de France Bourdieu's *Sketch for Self-Analysis* (Bourdieu 2007) can be seen as an application of his notions of reflexivity to himself. In outlining the path that led him from rural Béarn to education as a philosopher in the elite Parisian institutions, he reinforces the points made by Calhoun (Bourdieu 2010) by positioning himself as an outsider. This is related to his biographical upbringing, social class and intellectual setting. This is particularly evident when he notes educational background, academic mentors and institutional setting (including their positions in the Collège de France) that he shared with his friend and colleague Michel Foucault (Bourdieu 2007, p. 79).

4   Practicing Tony Lowe

It is this position (or at least the mental position) of being the outside which was evident in Tony Lowe and is shown most clearly in one of his favourite stories of how he became an accountant. His entry into the accounting profession was not simple or inevitable as he came from working class roots. His mother was the cleaner in a local chartered accounting firm and was encouraged to bring her son to meet the senior partner (whose office she cleaned) upon completion of his National Service obligations. He was so impressed with a young Tony Lowe that the partner agreed to accept him as his 'articled clerk'. While there were no specific fees at this point, the clerks were not well paid. However, Tony was not paid at the clerk's rate but at the same level as more qualified and experienced people. Although Tony's experience and description of this partner was grateful and affectionate, this did have the effect of placing Tony both as an insider and an outsider within British society. Despite being qualified as a chartered accountant and a chartered secretary, with a first class honours degree in Accounting from the London School of Economics, he also remained aware of his own working-class background and of the fact that he never really fitted in the academic field that he found himself located in. Perhaps it was because of this dissonance that the position as the first Professor of Accounting & Financial Management at the University of Sheffield was such a welcome opportunity and that under his leadership the accounting faculty at Sheffield became so novel and distinctive for its critical and reflective approach (Laughlin 2014).

It was this annoying and persistent form of reflexivity so characteristic of Tony's interrogative style which became the distinctive hallmark of the Sheffield School and of the early work that came from the school and it was Tony's self-identity as an outsider on the inside which was the basis of this collective practice. Laughlin (2014, p. 772) reflects this when he describes Tony Lowe's "challenging and intense debating style", his commitment to critical interactive debate and an approach to education which involved challenging and stretching students (and staff) beyond their limits.

Laughlin (2014, p. 771) neatly encapsulates Tony's approach to critique and challenge by suggesting that this was the third core value associated with the Sheffield School (under Tony's leadership).

> Tony believed in constant critique about virtually everything. The logic was clear: if ideas or practices did not service critical analysis they were weak and/or inappropriate and should be changed. The operationalization

of this, even for those who understood what was occurring, was not easy but for those who weathered the storm and could justify their ideas the end result was greater confidence in their understanding. Equally for those whose ideas did not survive this critique but listened and learned, there were rewards of new levels of understanding that could be defended. (Laughlin 2014, p. 771)

Laughlin (2014) goes on to describe conflicts between Tony and senior university managers who clearly did not welcome or relish Tony's reflective and critical questioning or the notion that other people's ideas and suggestions might actually be better than their own. However, implicit in these comments is an observation that while Tony's questions were helpful and powerful, they were not always enjoyable.

One of the most confusing things about considering Tony's academic papers is that almost all of them were jointly written with one (and quite often more) co-authors. So it is difficult to decode from a reading what Tony's role was within that process. However, it is possible to identify what Tony was not. He was not an individual researcher as every paper was aimed at the development and enhancement of a broader "Community of Practice" (see Laughlin 2014, p. 775). Clearly Tony recognised that reflexivity was not an individual exercise but exists as a collective exercise practiced within a community (Wacquant 1992, p. 36).

Although Tony's early work was based on systems theory and management control, and this remained a constant theoretical tool throughout his career (see Laughlin 2014, p. 770), he was constantly open to new and different theoretical approaches to assist in understanding and critiquing the role(s) and influence of accounting in society. On the surface, this early systems theory and management control work does not appear to be particularly critical or reflexive, reflecting a structuralist and functionalist perspective. However, a deeper reading reveals both critical and reflective elements in these papers. Lowe (1971) can be understood as a response to the somewhat narrow economic approach to organisations and decision making and as an argument for a larger and more holistic approach to enterprises drawing on a range of organisational, social and behavioural disciplines (Lowe 1971, p. 2). As such, Tony argues that there is a need to move beyond idealised and functionalist the notion of what happens in the realm of management planning and control to draw on behavioural and social variables to explore what does happen. In effect his 'why' question is prefigured even and this stage and he goes on to make an important argument that perspective of the academic economist on business activity (academic logic) is not necessarily shared by those actually involved in the business (practical logics) (Lowe1971, p. 8). Extending this logic, Tony was also willing to criticise accounting for providing little insights into the 'subtle input–output relations within the organisation' (Lowe 1971, p. 4). The general theme of the need to recognise the importance of human working relationships and human performance characteristics in the area of management control was also present in this early work (Lowe and McInnes 1971).

Issues of critique, engagement and reflexivity are more evident in subsequent publications. His growing critique of the restrictive influence of 'economic logic' was a driver for what Tinker and Puxty (1995) called "the market for excuses affair". This represented the attempt by Tony and colleagues to bring the tribal brand of reflective questioning to the growing dominance of neo-classical economic thinking represented by US accounting researchers more generally and by the 1979 paper by Watts and Zimmerman on accounting theories. Ultimately published as Lowe et al. (1983) the paper was critical of Watts and Zimmerman's (1979) use of a [neo-classical] economic framework, simplistic approach to research design and the quality of their empirical evidence. From this perspective, the reflexive 'why' was presented to this part of the academic accounting community and firmly rejected (at least in terms of the ongoing dominance of the issues that Watts and Zimmerman (1979) were criticised for). From this perspective, Tony's willingness to adopt the position of the outsider and to challenge the dominant within the field has been shared with the wider community associated with Sheffield and the emergent interdisciplinary perspectives on accounting group. The nature and development of this community of practice is evident in Laughlin's (2014) listing of the large number of key thinkers in the accounting literature who were directly associated with Tony.

Within the published papers it is clear that it was never an exposition of theory for its own sake, but rather the theoretical always served the purpose of understanding accounting and critical engagement with practice. Combined with the empirics, the theoretical was a tool for reflecting on what accounting was, what it had done and what it could be. Yet Tony's commitment to a given theoretical position was neither doctrinaire nor relativist. It was clearly based on his reflexive practice and it is certain the every student, co-author, colleague and collaborator was persistently challenged to defend their theoretical approach by Tony's 'why' questions.

This is illustrated in the paper (Berry et al. 1985) relating to the UK National Coal Board (NCB), conducted at a time of high industrial and political conflict yet also built on Tony's concerns about economic logic, his systems perspective on control and the need for both a structural and people-focused perspective. While being centrally focused on understanding management control systems in practice, this paper raising many of the themes (such as visibility, legitimacy, loose coupling and ambiguity) which were fundamental to subsequent work in the critical accounting literature. The analysis also provided the tools to understand the broader conflicts relating to the NCB and a clear critique of the role of neo-classical economics within the change process. As critique of the role of the finance function in driving change this paper was a response to the progressive closure of the UK collieries and the 1984–1985 miners' strike and a radical positioning of accounting research on the side of workers rather than management. It seems highly likely that this positioning was influenced by Tony's reflective questioning of the status-quo and his own working-class roots and brought both Tony and the other authors into direct conflict with PwC who were advising the NCB and the government who were advocating the use of accounting as a tool of economic efficiency and mine closure.

The relationship between the academic analysis and the practical/political engagement was also evident with the involvement of Tony Lowe, Hugh Willmott and Prem Sikka with the parliamentary passage of the Companies Act 1989. This group brought their brand of reflective question to the UK parliament through a series of seminars on the social and political role of accounting for the Labour party's frontbench spokespersons on trade and industry (Wilson and Sikka 2014, p. 214). Clearly Tony's difficult questions were not limited to his friends and colleagues.

5   Postscript

Many of the flames that Tony lit burn still today. Sikka et al. (1995) call for accounting academics to transcend their academic, professional and institutional fields to engage in broader public and social debates where accounting is increasingly deployed as a wider tool of truth and politics. Sikka et al. (1995) present Kenneth McNeal, Abraham Briloff and Edward Stamp as examples of academics that embody this form of social engagement and critique. But Tony Lowe could easily be included in that community. Likewise Sikka and Willmott (1997) present a number of strategies by which critical accounting academics might disseminate alternative discourses around accounting in the public space. In particular, they highlight the power of alliances with politicians, meetings with officials, mobilising practitioners and other accounting academics. However, external engagement must start from a position of internal awareness and self-critique which requires the exercise of reflexivity.

Tony's radical approach of asking 'why' as a path towards reflexivity offers a clear and approachable path to those who wish to continue the critical project by participating in broader social and societal debates by providing an awareness of the assumptions an limitations of existing systems. However, the critical project cannot end with questioning social assumptions; we must also turn the tools on ourselves to question our own assumptions. Otherwise we will never escape the illusio of our own academic game/field and find the courage to turn our back on our own games of status and recognition.

It is interesting to note that the German term for a PhD supervisor is doctorate father/mother. From this perspective, those who were directly (and significantly) supervised by Tony were his academic children. Laughlin (2014) clearly documents many of the individuals who were supervised by Tony (while noting that there were also others where the relationship was not so formal). Many of us who came later were supervised by these and, in turn, have supervised our own PhD students. As human families share a common characteristic, physical and behavioural traits I like to think that the academic family (and in effect the wider critical and interdisciplinary accounting community) share Tony's characteristic to constantly ask ourselves and the world around us the difficult (and irritating) question of 'why'. The danger is that as time passes Tony's annoying but insightful voice could easily recede into the background and the field of critical and interdisciplinary accounting research could easily lose this practice of reflexivity. In many ways critical and interdisciplinary research has become a new status-quo and the contemporary members of this community may have become too settled and comfortable where the once radical voices are the new taken for granted (Molyneaux and Jacobs 2005). The challenge remains as a community of scholarship is to question even our founding fathers, to examine our taken for granted and to continue to ask the 'why' questions of ourselves, of accounting and of the society which we are a part.

Note

1. It is acknowledged that it is impossible to be 'impartial' or an outsider in the true sense. Yet it was the very effort to question what others take for granted which Bourdieu presents as the goal of reflexivity. In this way he can be seen as normalising his own sense of being an outsider (Bourdieu 2007).

Management Control: The Influence of Cybernetics and the Science of the Unknowable

Winnie O'Grady and Alan Lowe

1 Introduction

Systems and cybernetic concepts are evident throughout Tony Lowe's early work (Lowe 1971a; Lowe and McInnes 1971; Lowe and Tinker 1976a, p. 258, b; Tinker and Lowe 1978). Tony made considerable effort to explore how systems and cybernetic concepts could advance our understanding of management control systems. There is no doubt he was well acquainted with key themes developing in general systems theory and cybernetics, and regularly invoked concepts from these disciplines in his work. This article considers two systems and cybernetic themes present in Tony's work, namely the design or structure of control systems and the law of requisite variety.

W. O'Grady
Department of Accounting and Finance, University of Auckland, Auckland, New Zealand

A. Lowe (✉)
RMIT, Melbourne, Australia

© The Author(s) 2016
J. Haslam, P. Sikka (eds.), *Pioneers of Critical Accounting*,
DOI 10.1057/978-1-137-54212-0_3

A review of selected publications reveals the fundamental systems ideas underpinning Tony's work. His thinking was underpinned by the idea that control systems should be designed so that organisations can manage their relationship with the environment; should integrate strategic, management and operational control processes; and require both feedback and feedforward information in order to function. He argues that the fundamental role of control systems is to manage the organisation's relationships with its environment. This view is consistently maintained throughout his work. Early statements argue that effective control systems are those that can manage the critical enterprise-environment relationship (Lowe and McInnes 1971) while, later, Lowe and Puxty continue to assert that control "is predicated on an understanding of the necessary relationship between an organisation and its environment" (Lowe and Puxty 1989, p. 22).

Tony (Lowe and McInnes 1971; Lowe and Puxty 1989; Lowe & Tinker 1977) argued for a holistic view of control systems and challenged Anthony's view (1965) of: a three-way distinction between strategic, management and operational control; strategic control and strategic planning as the domain of senior management; strategic planning as a precedent to management control with the latter's role simply to implement those plans and; management control as efforts to influence individual behaviour to ensure strategic plans are achieved. Tony consistently advocated for the adoption of control systems that integrated both planning and control, and focused on control of the organisation rather than the individual. He argued that "being able to ensure that the managers controlled do as the plans require is a very different concept from being able to ensure that the organisation adapts…to its environment" (Lowe and Puxty 1989, p. 22).

Tony also advocated for a broader view of control than that achieved through simple feedback processes. He argued that 'control' depends on both time-lagged feedback information and feed-forward information (Lowe and Puxty 1989). He took issue with the traditional conceptualization of feedforward information as a product of periodic planning processes, operating independent of management control processes. Lowe and Puxty argue that planning must take place continuously, at all levels of the organisation. Continual planning processes operating at multiple levels help the organisation foresee its next move in relation to its environment and anticipate which actions will minimise disruptions caused by changes in the environment (Lowe and Puxty 1989, p. 20). Planning is thus considered the aspect of control that introduces feedforward information into the control system.

Tony's work on planning and control reflects his efforts to develop a framework that integrated a broader view of control than was apparent in the literature at the time. A particular feature was his insistence on the importance of feedback and feedforward information flows. His proposed framework incorporated the organisation and its environment, integrated strategic, management and operational control processes and included both feedback and feedforward information flows used for control (Lowe and Puxty 1989, p. 21).

In the remainder of the chapter we first examine selected aspects of the cybernetic ideas incorporated into Tony's work. In the next section we review the influence of cybernetics as seen through Tony Lowe's work. This is followed by a discussion of Stafford Beer and his development of the viable system model. Following this we analyse the VSM and its contribution to management control to provide a more situated understanding of Tony's insights and to consider their apparent limitations. We next offer a comparison between cybernetics and contingency theory prior to some thoughts on the demise of cybernetic enquiry as research interests in management control switched very strongly at first to contingency theory and subsequently to Simons' levers of control. Finally, we provide concluding thoughts and brief suggestions for further research.

2   Early Research on Management Control: Tony Lowe and the Contribution of Cybernetics

In this section we outline some of the significant ideas that cybernetics has contributed to management control and planning systems. Initially, we describe Tony Lowe's cybernetics-inspired framework of control that sought to integrate different dimensions of control with feedback and feedforward information flows. He argued that such a framework was the only way to achieve a holistic understanding of how control processes fit together and interact to achieve organisational control (Lowe and Puxty 1989, p. 21). This framework is briefly summarized in the following section.

2.1   The Rrelude to Control: Information Gathering

Tony approached the problem of control system design from an information processing perspective with the aim of creating a model of business decision-making. He described management control as "a system of organisational information seeking and gathering, accountability, and feedback designed to ensure that the enterprise adapts to changes in its substantive environment" (Lowe 1971b, p. 5). He conceptualized the organisation as a bounded collection of five elements, namely information centres and decision centres, linked by information flows, guided by decision rules, synthesized within the management decision system. These components provided the base for his model of control for business enterprises. Here Tony depicted the enterprise-environment relationship as an input–output transformation taking place in an open system. Inputs and outputs were interpreted as "a large and diverse collection of human needs and values" (Lowe and McInnes 1971, p. 222). The internal structures were the arrangements required by organisations to relate and adapt to their dynamic external environments (Lowe 1972; Lowe & Tinker 1977) and consisted of three interacting sub-systems, labelled the decision and control, funds flow and operating systems, linked by feedback and feedforward information flows. The model is depicted in Fig. 1 and further explained below.

The organisation being managed is presented in the centre of Fig. 1. It operates within its substantial[1] environment. The structure of the enterprise as a system refers to the relationships of the elements within the enterprise and also with the behaviour of the enterprise, as a whole, in relation to its environment (Lowe and McInnes 1971, p. 218). An organisation's interactions with the substantial environment involve receiving informational, financial and physical inputs from it and returning trans-

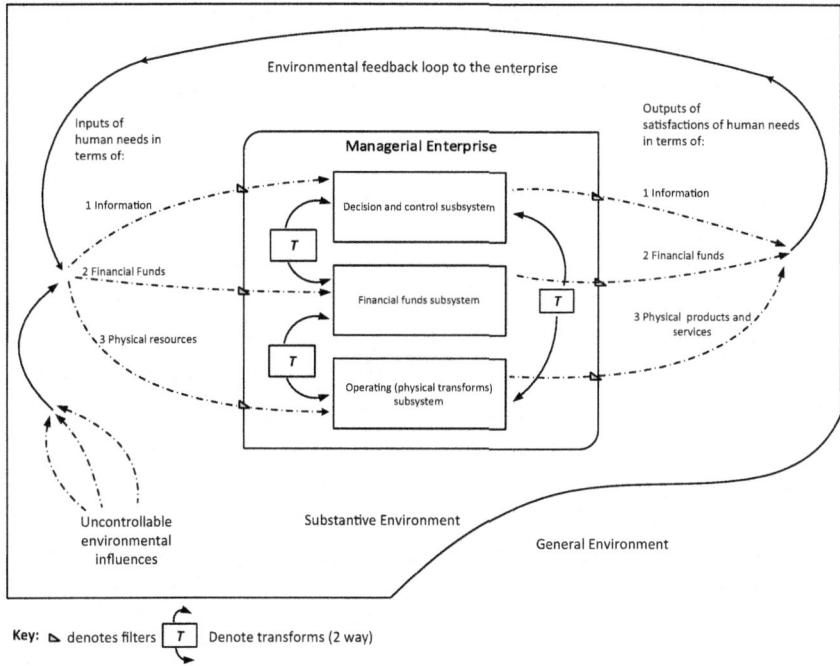

Fig. 1 The business enterprise as a financial-economic system (Lowe and Tinker 1977, p. 178)

formed informational, financial and physical outputs to it. The outflows from the organisation can be used to influence the substantial environment in ways that favour the organisation (Lowe and McInnes 1971, p. 114) and consequently reduce the organisation's need to adapt to it.

The components of the internal structure are the decision and control, financial funds and operating (physical transformation) sub-systems. The decision and control sub-system is comprised of a predictive model of future possible states and a choice model. This sub-system manages the existing transformation process and also anticipates the future by searching for new opportunities and threats, and imagining their consequences for the three sub-systems.

An organisation manages its interactions with the substantive environment to influence its performance in terms of its selected performance criteria. Successful organisations are able to match conditions in the substantive environment with their internal organisation (Lowe and Tinker 1977 p. 175) either by increasing their ability to respond to changes in the environment or by exerting influence to minimize the impact of those changes. As environmental conditions change, organisations learn and adapt, making changes to, for example, their decision models, transformation processes, performance criteria or objectives in order to achieve their expected performance.

The internal structures must be capable of controlling both routine, repetitive input–output processes and innovative and imaginative processes required for longer term viability and adaptability (Lowe and Tinker 1977 p. 174). Accordingly, internal structures must have the ability to manage uncontrollable factors in the substantive environment that can impact organisational performance. Controlling these factors is achieved by acquiring additional information about them and anticipating their likely impact on performance. The decision and control system thus integrates strategic control alongside management control by supporting "management's 'imaginative faculty', for speculation and anticipation, involving both search for new opportunities and the reduction of hypothetical states to the consequences for the three sub-systems" (Lowe and Tinker 1977 p. 179). Thus the interactions between the organisation and its environment reflect both operational and strategic issues.

A second system-based theme evident in Tony's work is the law of requisite variety, as discussed next.

2.2   The Law of Requisite Variety

A second system's concept drawn on in Tony's work is Ashby's (1958) law of requisite variety (LORV). Basically, the law states that effective control depends on the regulator having a range of responses (variety) that matches the range of conditions (variety) that it has to manage. Accordingly, Lowe and Tinker (1977) argue that for organisations to control performance, internal structures must be able to produce the range of responses (variety) required to match the variety being generated in the substantial environment. Furthermore, management's control capability is influenced by the quality of information supplied to it and decision rules embedded in the decision system. Existing decision rules are applied by lower level operating programmes until dynamic environments require the decision system to generate new responses (variety). Modifications to decision rules and operating programmes are made by higher order programmes referred to as monitors. Ultimately, the variety of the response repertoire available to performance programmes is predicated on the monitors governing their behaviour. The LORV determines the extent of adaptation and innovation capacity required in the organisation's problem solving mechanisms (decision models or programmes).

Tony recognized the importance of devising internal structures that promote organisational control by establishing requisite variety between the organisation and its substantial environment. The logical progression of this work would be to synthesize these concepts within a single model. A further extension of Lowe's view of organisational control would be to disentangle the information and decision centres comprising the decision and control system, and their associated information flows including the communication underpinning them. This challenge was not taken up in the management accounting literature. In the next section, we consider how Tony's model could have been extended from the work of Stafford Beer.

3 Stafford Beer and the Viable System Model

Beer's work (1981, 1985, 1995) centred on the development of the viable system model (VSM). In the VSM Beer sought to design an internal structure through which the organisation could satisfy the law of requisite variety. The internal structure in the VSM is comprised of five components, labelled systems 1–5,[2] and the communication channels and information flows connecting them. The key systems are briefly described in Table 1.

The systems listed in Table 1 do not align precisely with the internal elements identified by Lowe, but nonetheless address the same issues. Systems 1 Implementation of the VSM are equivalent to Lowe's physical transformation system. The remaining systems can be equated with

Table 1 Systems of the viable system model

System	Commonly labelled	Description
5	Policy	Maintains organizational values, rules, norms and identity; chooses future directions; creates organizational structures
4	Intelligence	Monitors the external environment for opportunities and threats and develops proposals for adaptation and change
3*	Monitoring	Gathers information directly from Systems (1) via ad hoc inquiries to confirm information provided to System 3 and extend System 3 understanding of conditions impacting Systems (s) 1 performance
3	Cohesion	Manages System(s) 1 for efficiency, synergy and cohesion. It allocates resources, ensures accountability and implement policies set by higher systems
2	Co-ordination	Coordinates activities of System(s) 1 to ensure they function smoothly and adhere to consistent set of standards
1	Implementation	Is composed of a collection of self-managed operational sub-units which undertake value adding activities via exchanges with their local environments. Typically, multiple operational units co-exist within System 1

the decision and information centres sitting within Lowe's decision and control sub-system and indicate where specific functional decisions are made. Systems 5, 4 and 3[3] collectively form a 'meta-system' for regulating system 1. This distinction between regulator system and meta-system reflects Lowe and Tinker's distinction between operating programs and higher order monitor programs. They observe that "monitors…exist to control…lower order performance programs" (Lowe and Tinker 1976a, p. 148).

Each element of the regulatory system performs a specific function. System 3 Cohesion encompasses Lowe's financial funds subsystem (and Anthony's management control role). It functions are to promote efficiency of operations, allocate resource and maintain accountability. System 4 Intelligence has a role similar to Lowe's 'imaginative faculty' and Anthony's strategic planning. System 5 has a policy role which neither Lowe nor Anthony refer to. Finally, system 2 encompasses the organisation's formal information systems. This aligns with Tony's concept of information centres (Lowe 1971b).

Each VSM role is supported by particular information conveyed in specific communication channels. In Tony's model, all information types are labelled as generic information flows attached to the decision and control sub-system. The VSM more clearly delineates these information flows, specifying the types of information linking specific functions via particular communication channels. These channels and the information they convey are listed and briefly described in Table **2**.

Furthermore, the VSM more clearly distinguishes the operational, management and strategic dimensions of control and shows how they

Table 2 Information channels in the viable system model

Channel	Name	Linking	Description
A	Command	S1–S3	Information to communicate and manage compliance to legal and corporate requirements and cultural norms
B	Resource bargaining and accountability	S1–S3	Information to support negotiations about action programs and resourcing and convey accountability information
C	Anti-oscillation or Coordination	S1–S2–S3	Information to communicate common standards and conventions through guidelines, and maintain routine information systems
D	Audit	S1–S3*–S3	Information about specific aspects of operational performance on an ad hoc basis
E	S3-S4 homeostat	S3–S4	Information to establish a balance between the requirements of existing operations (as represented by S3) and the anticipated demands of the future environment (as represented by S4) through intense interaction and debate
F	Policy intervention	S5–S3–S4	Information to communicate vision, mission, identify and to guide the operation of the S3-S4 homeostat
G	Algedonic	S1–S5	Information to quickly report incidences of emergency or failure in the (S2-S3*–S4) management system (an organizational 'override' channel)

are integrated via the information they exchange. The VSM's systems identify the functions responsible for specific types of decisions while its channels clarify the types of information required by each. The VSM thus extends the model proposed by Lowe and Tinker (1977) by unbundling the dimensions of control implicit in the decision making and control system and separately identifying the types of information flows.

The VSM is typically presented in diagrammatic form, as shown in Fig. 2. The diagram clearly indicates how components of the control sys-

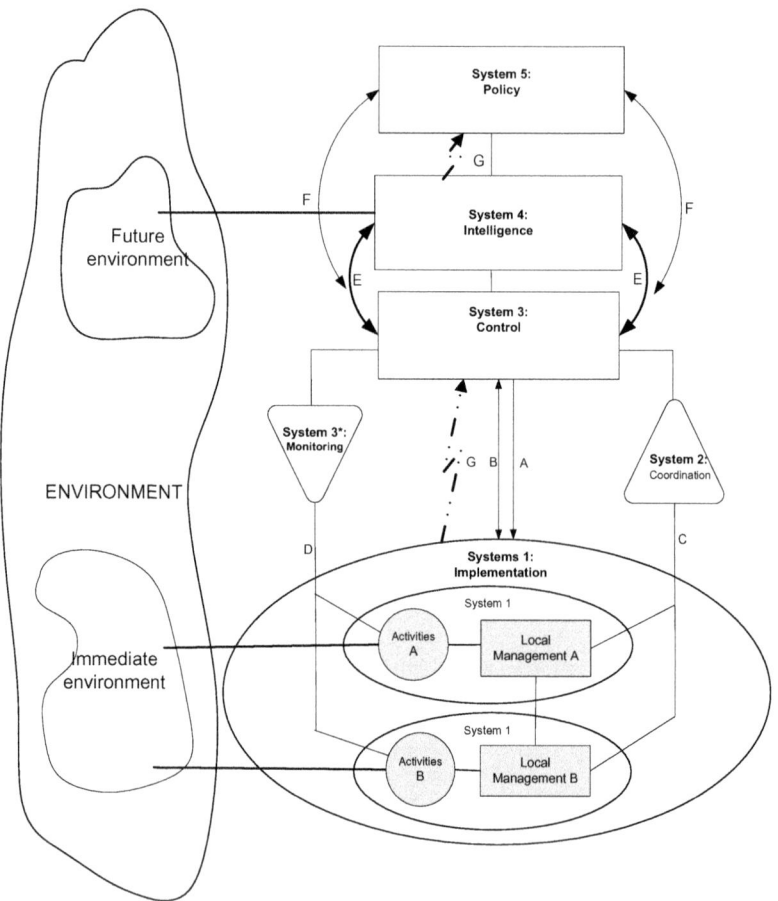

Fig. 2　The viable system model (Adapted from Beer 1981, pp. 130–31)

tem are intended to interact with one another via the specified communication channels. The systems and channels are labelled in the diagram to correspond with the functions and channels identified in Tables 1 and 2, respectively.

The VSM is also notable for being recursive, meaning each set of systems 1 to 5 nests within a higher level set of systems, a little like Russian Babushka dolls. The recursive aspect of the model directly relates to the observations made by Lowe and McInnis (Lowe and McInnes 1971, p. 214) about the usefulness of different levels of resolution or hierarchy. They state that "a careful and constant use of the idea of resolution levels will greatly assist analysis in the development of MCS". The use of resolution levels implies the enterprise control problem can be consistently decomposed by adopting the relevant focus. "In each case, the system being analysed is a somewhat different one, but each can be consistently related to the others in terms of the overall analysis of the MCS problem for the whole enterprise" (pp. 215–216). While the VSM can be used to depict multiple levels of recursion in a single diagram, the detail in the resulting model is not easily assimilated. The relevance of the VSM concepts of meta-system, system and recursion are presaged in Lowe and Tinker's comment that "indeed a whole hierarchy of decision processes, each operating on the one below may be envisaged" (1976a, p. 148).

4   The VSM and Its Contribution to Management Control

The preceding summary reveals that the VSM offers a more elaborate depiction of the systems and cybernetic concepts incorporated into the work done by Tony and his collaborators. The model identifies a structure which would allow organisations to achieve requisite variety and maintain performance in the face of changing environmental conditions. Nonetheless, there is a fundamental difference in the approach of the VSM and that adopted by Tony and his co-authors.

The premise underpinning Tony's work would fit with what Pickering describes as a world perceived as a regular law-like place that can be known more or less exhaustively. While unknowns are acknowledged to exist, they are something to be conquered and drawn into the world of the known (Pickering 2004, p. 30). This fundamental belief is evident in, for example, Lowe and Tinker's discussion of operating programmes into which decision rules and processes are embedded, and where the role of monitor programmes is seen to be establishing decision rules and determining when they need to be modified or changed. In contrast, the VSM reflects Beer's belief that exceedingly complex systems, which occur in social contexts, are unknowable and we have to learn how to cope with, rather than control, them. Complexity requires mechanisms that are capable of self-regulation,[4] meaning they can respond to situational perturbations, even those that have not been anticipated, in a way that maintains dynamic homeostasis. Furthermore, these mechanisms, referred to by Beer as homeostats, allow for continual learning and updating of decision routines and goals. A key differentiating feature here is that the self-regulation envisaged by the VSM is achievable within the system at each level of recursion, without the necessity for intervention from outside the system. The system or sub-system must have the ability to self-regulate thus limiting the issues to be managed outside the system, by a higher level regulator, to those that cannot be resolved at this current level of recursion.

The potential of the VSM to inform management control research has been explored in only a handful of studies to date. The VSM specifies the necessary and sufficient components of control systems, as indicated by cybernetic principles. One such application of the VSM for this purpose is provided by Bititci et al. (1999). As part of a wider study of best practice in performance measurement, the authors sought to identify a universally applicable business structure within which to position practices that promoted agility. They suggest that a synthesis of the VSM (Beer 1979, 1981, 1985) and business process thinking (Childe et al. 1994; Hammer 1990) could produce structures that organizations could use to maximize their ability to respond to rapidly changing operating environments. The researchers applied the VSM to assess the structure of their case organisations and concluded that a "viable business structure is cybernetic and is true for all businesses" (Bititci, et al. 1999, p. 197). The authors do note, however, that "our research...is not [able]...to provide objective data on the actual agility, responsiveness and performance of organizations using the viable business structure" (Bititci, et al. 1999, p. 198). More recent research provides some evidence of this link, as discussed next.

Morlidge (2010) drew on cybernetic principles to model financial performance management systems (FPMS). The VSM provided the framework for situating the principles within an organisational context (Morlidge 2010, p. 85). He proposes twelve structural principles that aligned with the systems and communication channels identified in the VSM. His eleven informational principles reflected the nature of the information required for regulation and the eleven regulatory principles addressed the processes used to support and update the decision rules and predictive models employed by the regulatory system. Having created a questionnaire based on the 34 principles, to measure the 'cybernetic health' of organisations, Morlidge applied it to two organisations. In a second stage analysis, he considered the relationship between the cybernetic scores and indicators of financial performance. In one assessment, he measured the cybernetic health of Unilever Poland before and after a major reorganisation involving changes to its organizational structure and practices. Morlidge (2010) found Unilever Poland's cybernetic score increased after the change and its revenues subsequent to the reorganisation were less volatile and grew more steadily in contrast to the volatility and steady decline prior to the changes. He concluded that cybernetic structure and organisational performance are linked.

Researchers in various disciplines are considering the potential of cybernetics and the law of requisite variety. Examples of recent studies include Ojha et al. (2013) who use the law of requisite variety to investigate the relationship between manufacturing flexibility and operational performance. They develop a requisite variety construct that matches manufacturing flexibility (internal variety) with demand variability (external variety). They find that manufacturing flexibility, interpreted as the ability to vary timing (using equipment flexibility), quantity (using volume flexibility), and output variety (using product-mix flexibility), enables the organisation to regulate work flow to match changing levels of demand variability. Godsiff and Maull (2011) explore sources of variability and the strategies adopted to manage it through the analysis of a case study based on a commercial laundry. They identified that the main source of variety was the volume component of demand and that the management system was designed to provide the capability to respond to it. Vogus and Sutcliffe (n.d.) investigate whether requisite variety allows organizations to notice more, develop a broader repertoire of responses, and be more adaptive over time. They develop a model to test the effects of requisite variety on risk detection (noticing), innovation (responding), and firm performance (adapting). They have yet to report the results of an application of their model to a sample of 174 IPO software firms. These and other studies indicate that cybernetics researchers are seeking ways to operationalize the LORV.

5   Cybernetics and Contingency Theory

A part of the argument we offer in this chapter concerns the relative neglect of cybernetic theory and the associated law of requisite variety in contingency based perspectives of control. The LORV offers interesting ways of extending and augmenting insights derived from contingency research in a management control system context. Contingency theory argues that the appropriate form of organisation varies according to contingent factors arising in the environment.

The LORV offers a more nuanced perspective of the relationship between environmental complexity and organisational structure. The law of requisite variety defines the qualities a regulator must possess, expressed in terms of variety, to achieve a desired outcome or goal set (Ashby 1958; Morlidge 2010). This means the goal set impacts the variety required of the regulator. For example, the options available to regulators trying to achieve multiple, precisely specified (tight) goals are more constrained than those available to regulators pursuing fewer, less specific (loose) goals. While contingency research considers the relationship between the environment and the organisational structure, it has not fully considered the influence of the goal set on the structure of this relationship. This more precise articulation of Ashby's law recognizes a three way relationship between the varieties of the environment, the regulator and the goal[s]. For effective control, the net variety of the regulator and its goal set must at least match that of the situation being controlled. This distinction between regulator and goal set allows for the development of hypotheses that offer significantly greater correspondence to the context than those presented by the more conventional and limited concepts that define contingency theory. Despite the limitations acknowledged in the contingency approach (Chenhall 2007; Otley 1980, 2015) the findings from this stream of research do not contradict the relationships suggested by cybernetic theory or the LORV as discussed next.

Morlidge (2010) reviews the findings of contingency research, as summarized by Chenhall (2003), from the perspective of cybernetics and req-

Table 3 Comparing contingency and cybernetic understandings of organisational control

Findings of contingency theory	Insights from cybernetics/LORV
Environment	Situations of high environmental
The more uncertain the external environment, the more open and externally focussed the MCS	uncertainty increase variety (open and external control systems) required of regulator
When tight financial controls are used in uncertain environments, they are associated with the simultaneous use of flexible, interpersonal interactions	The use of tight (low variety) goals in high variety (uncertain) settings increases use of mechanisms that increase regulators ability to respond (flexible interpersonal interactions) to changing conditions
The more hostile and turbulent the environment, the greater the reliance on formal controls, including traditional budgets	Unclear how to interpret this finding. For an organisation with a low variety control system, any form of environmental turbulence is 'hostile'
Technology	Low situational variety (standardised,
Technologies characterised by standardised and automated processes rely more on traditional MCS (including budgets) and there is less incidence of slack	automated processes) reduces the variety required of the regulator; no need to enhance variety via budget slack
With higher task uncertainty, there is less reliance on standard operating procedures and accounting performance measures, but higher incidence of participation, broad scope MCS and greater use of personal controls such as clans control	High situational variety (task uncertainty) increases use of mechanisms that enable regulator to respond to wide range (high variety) of conditions
Higher levels of process interdependence are characterised by the use of more informal controls, more frequent interaction and greater use of aggregated and integrated MCS	High situational variety (process interdependence) increases use of mechanisms that enable regulator to respond to wide range (high variety) of conditions

Adapted from Morlidge (2010)

uisite variety. He considers whether contingency findings are congruent with what one would expect given Ashby's law. Table 3 summarizes some of his analysis which compares the contingency findings with respect to environment and technology factors to expectations based cybernetics principles.

The conclusion Morlidge (2010) draws based on his comparisons, is that the findings of contingency research broadly reflect the expectations about organisational control derived from cybernetics and Ashby's Law.

Cybernetics and the LORV offer the potential to develop a theoretical framework that is currently lacking in contingency theory. Cybernetic theory can accommodate the wide range of attributes currently addressed by contingency theory, such as tight/loose goals noted above, and synthesise them within one overarching framework. Many of the dichotomies found in extant research, such as formal/informal control and bureaucratic/cultural control, would simply be viewed as different ways of achieving requisite variety in the regulatory system. Furthermore, the concept of variety allows the thinking behind contingency theory to be formulated in a much more rigorous way.

6   Discussion: The Displacement of Cybernetics by Contingency Theory and LOC

Our evaluation of the contribution of Tony Lowe to management control has sought to show how the systems principles he, and allied authors, worked with were theoretically well founded. Their research was an important step forward that offered a valuable counterbalance to earlier ideas on planning and control (Anthony 1965). Unfortunately the line of research which Tony and his co-authors developed was then rather neglected in the management control domain. The application of cybernetics ideas, in the management control literature, was overtaken by an increasing focus on contingency theory research. Contingency offered an apparently fruitful avenue to researchers who preferred the apparent advantages of remote collection of quantitative data over fieldwork. At the same time, although the highly simplistic models (Carenys 2010) underpinning contingency research suited data analysis and publication, they often related poorly to real world systems and contexts (Otley 2015). More recently, Simons' levers of control framework—another simple model of organisational control—has gained currency in management control research. Consequently, conventional management accounting control theory is dominated by research informed by contingency theory and the levers of control (LOC) framework [and in some cases a combination of the two].

We have suggested above that a return to a more realistic image of the complexity of organisations as systems could contribute important insights. The only approach that clearly offers such a framework is that of cybernetics and the VSM. The VSM is sufficiently flexible to accommodate both the levers of control framework (O'Grady et al. 2010) and, as argued above, a contingency approach. We offer below a very limited comparison of the key concepts of cybernetics in comparison to contingency theory and LOC in Table 4. While a more sophisticated comparison might separate some differences between contingency theory and levers of control our focus is on what cybernetics offers. Consequently we will not go further here save to suggest that the comparison might best be characterised in the following manner: (i) The cybernetic/LOC comparison is primarily about the inner structure of the control system whereas (ii) The cybernetic/contingency comparison hinges primarily on the degree of concern attached to achieving an appropriate match between the control system and its environment. Cybernetics is about self-regulation whereas conventional management control (and certainly conventional management control research tends to be about the control of others assuming a relatively hierarchical environments.

Tony Lowe and others in accounting have often noted the backward looking nature of much accounting information. The contrast between the cybernetic approach and the historic orientation typical of traditional accounting information systems is also noted by Beer who suggested that we should 'look straight ahead down the motorway while you are driving flat out [rather than as] most enterprises are directed with the driver's eyes fixed on the rear-view mirror' (Ibid., 1972, p. 199, as cited in Pickering 2004). This observation recognizes that there are severe limits to the

Table 4 Alternate control approaches

Cybernetic	Levers of control/contingency
Control is a property that emerges from the operation of the system; the system enables the organisation to be in control	Control is exerted over the organisation
Control depends on managers establishing structures that enable self-regulation supported by the provision of appropriate information	Control relies on managers being in charge and exerting control over and influencing the behaviour of others
Control is dispersed and there are multiple loci of control—although there is still some upward reporting, it is designed to be minimal	Control resides at apex of hierarchy
Strategic control is effected via strategic planning arises at multiple levels	Strategic control is enacted through plans almost exclusively assumed to be developed at the top of hierarchy
Proactive control through the continuous integration and balancing of strategic and operational concerns	Less active control through periodic interactions when senior management invokes interactive control
Control is about achieving requisite variety	Control is about achieving the plan

ability of conventional information systems to provide novel and real time information to deal with unexpected circumstances. A further limitation associated with traditional approaches to control is related to the information processing limitations or bounded rationality of individual or groups of managers commonly associated with information overload.

According to Pickering (2004) there is a bigger problem than the ability to process data. This is the error of assuming analysis of the past can be used to fully anticipate the future. He considers that this leaves the information system detached from the action and therefore unable to offer useful decision support (see also Beer 1985):

> …conventional informatics…is all about the accumulation of data and knowledge. One might eventually want to draw on that knowledge for action. *The information system is, as it were, detachable from the action* (Pickering, p. 30, emphasis added)

We believe Tony remained committed to the need for information systems which could be comprehensively designed to enable the organisation to deal with any problems facing it. On the other hand, Beer's central idea is that organisations need adaptive systems to deal with complex and unknowable changes in the environment in real time. Pickering (2004) again notes that:

> ...all Beer's projects can be understood as specific instantiations and workings out of a cybernetic ontology of unknowability and becoming: *a stance that recognizes that the world can always surprise us and that we can never dominate it through knowledge. The thrust of Beer's work was thus to construct information systems that can adapt performatively to environments they cannot fully control.* (Ibid., p. 29, emphasis added)

We think that Tony sought to assimilate ideas from cybernetics into management accounting control while maintaining a relatively conventional perspective. Despite their grounding in different paradigms, similarities to the VSM are apparent, especially in the priority given to the external environment: the economy, competitors, the market and customers. Here Tony and his colleagues were relatively open to looking outward in contrast to the much more closed system view of contingency theory at the time.

7   Conclusion

We have briefly outlined in this chapter the cybernetic developments of both Ashby and Beer which went beyond the work that Tony and others developed in management accounting. The LORV and VSM which we briefly describe earlier are instantiations of these ideas about coming to terms with levels of complexity in the environment that neither Tony nor other later writers in the conventional literature on management control have addressed in a systematic manner. This is a surprising oversight that indicates the possibility of considerable scope to advance our understanding of what we can and cannot control. The working through of these cybernetic ideas on complex control systems ought to be enticing for management control researchers. Such cybernetic approaches to control might also be better supported in an environment where computing power is much cheaper and more readily available.

The further investigation of these ideas could also offer a synergy with qualitative and interpretive field work that was largely absent when Tony began his investigations into complex control systems. Such a move could pick up more directly on Pickering's conception of the unknowable, or the unknowability of complex systems, much more strongly. Interpretive research would tend to accept the notion that there are severe limits to what we can ever know of human social interactions. Researchers using a broadly Interpretive lens are much more likely to appreciate that the contributions of their research to the understanding of control systems may only ever be transitory. Such research offers us the opportunity to seek explanations of context based events that ought to serve as important clues on the limits of existing control systems. Such understandings help us to appreciate what controls cannot achieve rather than continually promoting the idea that a more sophisticated system and better implementation is always just a step away. Here there are important linkages in research and management accounting practice that offer performative frameworks for understanding control practices at the micro level (Nama and Lowe 2014; see also Jorgensen and Messner 2008; Lowe and Koh 2008). Interpretive practice-based approaches would accept fully the ideas on unknowability that Beer and his cybernetic-based ideas highlight. The attempts to build ever greater responsiveness into complex control frameworks to deal with environmental perturbations was something that Tony Lowe clearly also struggled to represent. This latter research would offer a somewhat different but potentially complementary perspective to a thoroughly cybernetic approach.

Notes

1. The substantial or substantive environment is defined to be that subset of the general environment which affects the organisation's performance.
2. There is also a system 3*, read "3 star".
3. Including its supporting systems 2 and 3*

4. The ability of a system to monitor and correct its own behaviour using information communicated from the environment. Self-regulation mechanism can be simple of complex. Complex self-regulatory devices include those geared to respond to conditions which anticipate a loss of control and make an adjustment before this happens, and those that have sufficient flexibility to respond to unanticipated conditions (Leonard 1990/revised 2004, p. 52).

Organisational Effectiveness and Social and Environmental Accounting: Through the Past Darkly

Rob Gray, Aideen O'Dochartaigh, and Clemence Rannou

1   Introduction

Revisiting work that is as deeply embedded in the lexicon as is that of Tony Lowe, can prove to be a salutary experience. Here are ideas one had forgotten, ideas one had come to take for granted, even ideas one had over-looked. More substantially, revisiting the Lowe *oeuvre* offered

We are very pleased indeed to be able to acknowledge the considerable advice, support and encouragement from Richard Laughlin on an earlier draft of this chapter. Thanks are also due to Sue Gray for her suggestions and comments.

R. Gray (✉)
School of Management, University of St Andrews, St. Andrews, Fife, Scotland

A. O'Dochartaigh
University College Dublin, Dublin, Ireland

C. Rannou
University of Laval, Québec City, Québec, Canada

© The Author(s) 2016
J. Haslam, P. Sikka (eds.), *Pioneers of Critical Accounting*,
DOI 10.1057/978-1-137-54212-0_4

an arresting opportunity to look afresh at both accounting and social accounting. This chapter is a response to that opportunity.[1]

There were several broad, albeit related, issues which arose in this reconsideration of Tony Lowe's contribution. The first reaction was the striking reminder that scholarship—despite its inevitable historical debts and echoes—is principally a product of its time and context. This is hardly a contentious suggestion but it does remind us that understanding and evaluating that scholarship requires some degree of sensitivity to, some empathy with perhaps, that time and context. And what a different time it was, illustrating many of the things that have been lost in academe (as elsewhere) over a relatively short time.

One such loss is illustrated by the long term commitment that Lowe gave to developing an edifice of normative reasoning. A substantial portion of his work was based on a combination of speculation based upon careful reasoning that sought to explore how organisational accounting and control systems could be developed to better serve a more benign vision of industrial and post-industrial society. Such careful and committed speculation with an explicitly moral and political purpose would be very rare these days and not much encouraged.[2]

Relatedly, one could not but be struck by the optimism that informed so much of the work. Throughout his writing, there is a striking assumption that reason and good scholarship—albeit informed by a moral and democratic sensibilityare worthy in and of themselves and, further, that such may lead to improved organisations. This, indeed, was a time when (however naively) it really did seem to be possible—as well as desirable—that firms might actually become both potentially responsive to society's needs and subject to society's control. The raw brutality of neo-liberalism and the overwhelming ubiquity of financial markets and multi-national corporations had yet to become quite so obvious, overwhelming and intrusive. Indeed, much of the work appears, in retrospect, strangely conservative, rationalist, contractarian and (dare one say it?) almost pluralist with a predominantly management (managerialist?) focus. The work, in its faith in and commitment to communication and democracy, is optimistic and/or naïve.[3] But one can only be encouraged by this peek into a history in which it was perfectly reasonable to explore the possibilities of organisations embedded in and supporting a society. It is difficult not to yearn for a time when it was less than outrageous to imagine managers constructively and humanely engaged with their host society. Lowe's work speaks to us of the empowering nature of visions of possibility (see also Gallhofer et al. 2015).

That aside, what really stands out as one re-reads Lowe's work is the diverse, fundamental and interdisciplinary scholarship which was itself focussed around real social purpose. The work draws from, *inter alia*, systems theory, philosophy, politics, management and organisational theory and cybernetics and is remarkable for its willingness to speculate, to explore possible avenues and to develop intellectual edifices that might speak in articulate ways to man's condition and the social sciences in general. How strangely old-fashioned such a fundamental insistence on scholarship seems: the absence of a self-referential obsession over "getting published" or "identifying our contribution" would strike so many of the current denizens of our colleges as mystifying and beyond comprehension. Indeed, it is the very breadth of reading and thought that commends so much of Lowe's work to us... and by implication, suggests that there may be real benefit to be had from some critical self-reflection on the increasingly narrow focus of so much of the academy's current research.

Probably the central motif in Tony Lowe's work is that of "organisational effectiveness": a novel, if often under-specified, notion that bore, at its heart, concepts of organisational life derived for and focussed upon the well-being of society. Accounting, in all its forms, was (or should be) designed to enable and ensure that organisations were effective in the pursuit of their goals—goals held for them by all stakeholders. And such an optimistic and liberating vision was predicated largely upon the idea that the conflicts between stakeholders needed to be exposed and, ultimately, that they could be, to a reasonable degree, resolved. Accounting, control and accountability were at the centre of such an attempt at resolution (That such resolution might require radical re-structuring of society and the economy was rarely explicitly explored in Tony's work however. But see Tinker 1985).

Such a vision resonates interestingly with much of (the admittedly reformist orientated) social accounting literature. It offers a challenging opportunity to re-frame the social accounting project(s) as something more like accounting and control in support of organisational effectiveness; where organisational effectiveness is understood as embracing social justice, stability, environmental probity and, ultimately sustainability. It is an attempt to briefly explore this possible re-visioning that informs this chapter.

The chapter is organised as follows. Section 2 revisits accounting whilst Sect. 3 explores organisational effectiveness. In Sect. 4 we start the process of relating Lowe's work to social accounting and then, more explicitly in, respectively, Sects. 5 and 6, we seek to draw out some themes on the issues of first management control and social accounting and then effectiveness and sustainability. Section 7 contains a few tentative conclusions.

2   Accounting and Beyond?

It seems we should start with 'accounting' for two important reasons. First, for better or worse, a considerable body of the social accounting literature and practice still draws from and reflects many aspects of (what could be conventionally recognised as) its accounting roots. (Whether social accounting becomes a series of 'new' accountings or remains the ideal to which (all) accountings should aspire to develop, is another matter entirely, Gallhofer et al. 2015: especially p. 852). Second, despite Tony Lowe's polymath affinities and his close empathy with management control, it was with accounting (often as conventionally understood) that he was principally and most obviously concerned.

Tony Lowe and the "Sheffield School" as it was (and is) widely known, most notably set about examining the roots of accounting, exposing the empty instrumentalism of much accounting "reasoning" and offering alternative, more nuanced, interpretations of what accounting is and what it could be. A relatively early piece exposed accounting's unexamined *"… presupposition… that in "the beginning" there was earth, fire, water, air and accounting, [and consequently that it] completely fails to recognise the particular social conditions and needs that gave rise to and sustain accounting as an activity"* (Lowe and Tinker 1977a, p. 266). That paper essentially argued that it would seem that accounting has no awareness of the need for *"a guiding theory of community, national or even global social welfare"* or even, it seems, for any theory of power (p. 263). Accounting was, its advocates seemed to suggest, a technology independent of and unrelated to any sense of human or social well-being. (And this critique continues to remain so very apposite in both the mainstream accounting profession and its North America academy.)

Simultaneously—and with no apparent sense of irony on the part of the accounting profession—this absence of any overt awareness of accounting's inherent ideology seemed to be employed to restrict other accountings from emerging. New accounting possibilities (such as those suggested in *The Corporate Report*, ASSC 1975) seem to survive or fail only through some abstruse market test rather than via any explicit argument as to how such innovation may or may not advance the public interest which the profession claims to serve. The irony being, obviously, that this is of itself adherence to a particular theory of power and societal well-being—albeit one the community of accounting resists making explicit (Sikka et al. 1989).

In the light of this sort of (absence of) reasoning it should probably come as no great surprise that early and "respectable" excursions into social accounting should rest on the same evasive and ill-considered foundations (Solomons 1974) and that other, more grounded notions of, social accounting would not be permitted to flourish.[4] One striking implication of the work of Tony Lowe and his colleagues is that had the accounting profession chosen to develop their musing from a well-examined basis in control and accountability, then the profession might well have found itself embracing *The Corporate Report* in a much more active and constructive manner. It is sobering to recognise that if the profession had directly explored the problematic relationships between accounting and social well-being, it would probably have found itself on a collision course with the more brutal elements of free market ideology (Gallhofer et al. 2015). That is, it is salutary to realise that had the *"management control problem [been] explicated in terms of maintaining a relationship between the enterprise's structure and its environment."* and if that relationship had been understood in terms of socio-economic responsibilities (Lowe and Tinker 1977b pp. 173–174) then many of the problems that social accounting has emerged to try and address might never have been necessary. That is, however fanciful a notion it might be, were current systems of accounting properly designed to accommodate, support and explore an organisational effectiveness based in social, economic and environmental terms, then they might well have made social and environmental accounting as a separate field, redundant.

3   Organisational Effectiveness

Whilst the academy may be replete with attempts to explain how organisations behave and why they behave in the ways they do, normative reflection on what an organisation is _for_ remains all too rare. Or, more precisely, in the absence of explicit consideration, it is too often assumed (to badly paraphrase Keynes) that the purpose of organisations is to maximise shareholder wealth or some other purely narrow and economic analogue. Furthermore, it still seems fairly rare to see much careful and systematic attention paid to the economic, social, environmental and ethical claims and justifications for corporate activity as we currently know it, (see, for example, Jacobsen 1991; Thielemann 2000; Mansell 2013). Given the increasing dominance of the multi-national corporation on the one hand, the assault on the non-profit sector on the other, and the struggling emergence of the social enterprise and cooperatives in between, this is all the more remarkable. It is in this context that the notion of organisational effectiveness may still have important traction.

A key element of Tony Lowe's project was the examination of what a socio-economic organisation actually should look like, how we might understand it and how accounting, accountability and control systems might seek to maintain its complex effectiveness, (see, for example, Lowe and McInnes 1971). Not only was this building from a substantial and applied notion of systems theory but it laid the foundation for so much else that was to follow. To understand organisations as open systems and to envision and explore them from different levels of resolution, brings such matters as conflict and the actual, claimed and/or potential contribution (sic) of the firm to society to the very heart of the design and maintenance of accounting and control, (Lowe and Soo 1980). A vision of firms which are not simply oppressive vehicles for shareholder greed and irresponsibility opens up a range of liberating possibilities: possibilities that have the audacity to conceive of a world in which economic activity is not the sole *raison d'être*, in which economic pursuit is not so destructive (in societal, ecological and Schumpeterian senses) and in which economic pursuit does not need to (however implausibly) scrabble to justify its existence through claims to societal and environmental beneficence (Lowe and Soo 1980).

To dare to ask what an organisation is for, whether such a purpose can be justified, and then explore how accounting, accountability and control might be used to resolve our concerns is a visionary and liberating notion to which we might well pay attention. Its spoor is evident in early examples of Lowe's writing (see, for example, Lowe and Shaw 1968), is key to the heart of his project (see, for example, Lowe and Soo 1980; Lowe 1981) and whilst the onslaught of neo-liberalism severely dented the optimism of the vision it never quite disappeared it seems (Puxty et al. 1987). Indeed, whilst pragmatism may counsel the constraining of possibilities under difficult circumstances, there is no academic reason why such a change of context need suppress a morally liberating vision.

But perhaps the most telling influence this line of reasoning had on how we might understand social accounting actually lay in the very foundations of how we might understand accounting itself that Lowe laid down across his career. Over a period of something like 20 years (see, for example, Lowe and McInnes 1971; Laughlin and Lowe 1990), the integration of systems thinking, organisational effectiveness, management control and accounting systems produced a unique articulation of accounting. This articulation is given fuller expression in the conception of accounting that underpins Laughlin and Gray (1988). We would suggest that the view of accounting that Laughlin develops there, principally, from Lowe's work, provides an unusually clear basis from which it becomes possible to articulate coherent relationships between costing and bookkeeping, financial/management accounting practice *and* accounting theory *and* provide a coherent basis for seeing social accounting as an inevitable and essential component of any broader and more societally orientated accounting. Without these foundations, social accounting (at least as it often understood) probably would not have been possible (Gray et al. 2014).[5] Unfortunately, Lowe never developed these ideas himself (although see Tinker and Lowe 1980 for some hints of the possibilities).

4   Social and Environmental Accounting

Whilst one of the recurring themes in Lowe's work (explicitly in conversation, more implicitly in the written word) was to erode the distinction between financial (i.e. external) and management (i.e. internal) accounting and reporting (see, for example, Tinker and Lowe 1980; Laughlin and Lowe 1990), this has always seemed one of the less essential of his arguments. The different power structures governing the two activities and the different roles that they play empirically, although similar in the broadest principle, are very different in their detail. The distinction between the two has been common in social accounting and, one might contend, has become increasingly important. It is a distinction we choose to maintain for the purposes of this chapter: however utilitarian that might be.[6]

To read a great deal of the social accounting literature one might be forgiven for inferring that the primary function of external social and environmental reporting was to assist short-term investors in their gambling assessments of risk, reputation and management competence in order to aid them in their pursuit of yet another extra dollar. This may, indeed, be a possible explanation of why companies voluntarily produce such disclosure. But if this is the primary motivation for studying social accounting we may as well bundle up what is left of this emergent field with governance and investor studies and, packing up the tents in which societal, environmental and sustainability accountings have been nurtured and explored, move along to some more fruitful activity motivated by a wider understanding of planetary and social need.[7]

The principal moral basis for external social reporting has typically been offered as that of the discharge of a wide-ranging accountability and, in particular, holding the increasingly large and rapacious entities of modern financial capitalism to account for their claims to (variously) social responsibility and sustainability. Equally, such an accountability should help to inform society about the extent to which organisation are (or more likely are not) satisfying the purposes for which stakeholders would wish to hold them responsible (Mintzberg 1983). So much of social and environmental accounting, ideally, is designed to expose or redirect the worst excess of organisations which are supported and motivated through a rapacious and strictly partisan accounting and control system. In essence the purpose of what we tend to know as social and environmental accounting is ideally, as Tinker and Lowe note, to expose the conflicts inherent in managing economic, social and environmental expectations. In Lowe's terms, the role of external social accounting and accountability can be understood as an attempt to expose organisational *ineffectiveness*.[8] That is, to thereby encourage a greater and much broader interaction between organisations, society and the natural environment in a way which might ensure that firms (especially) were pursuing a broader notion of organisational effectiveness. Such an effectiveness (to quote Tinker and Lowe 1980) at a minimum would meet *"society's desire to override the market imperative with social and humanitarian goals"* (p. 1). We would be looking for nothing less than a fuller intertwining of society and the entity (p. 13). Such notions are relatively easily conceived of with regard to external social and environmental reporting. They do not seem to be so easily imagined with respect to internal (management) accounting, (see, for example, Norris and O'Dwyer 2004; Durden 2008).

Laughlin and Lowe (1990) see their project as an attempt to articulate accounting information systems—both financial and management accounting as conventionally understood—not as closed systems but, rather, as ones reflecting and influencing their societal context. However, it seems to remain inevitable that the potential for management accounting to reflect a wider notion of society (wider than (say) a simple economic dominated system such as capitalism) is greatly constrained and a good deal more than a change of accounting is likely to be necessary. That is, management accounting does reflect society—but only insofar as profit seeking organisations reflect a particular emphasis in society. Whilst it is possible, and entirely desirable, to imagine an internal accounting which will better reflect notions of societal and ecological wellbeing, it seems likely that only at the margins might the accounting itself be able to stimulate any such change, (see, for example, Power 1991, 1994). The problem seems to be that current management accounting deeply and profoundly reflects a dominant hegemonic view of society and that this, in turn, influences society, further driving out (what Thielemann 2000; calls) the market alien values such as justice, reasonableness, social relationships and so on. The idea behind much of the *external* social accounting was to create new accounts which would reflect and demonstrate the nature of conflicts between conventional business pursuit and the changing faces of society—whether this be inequality in pay, the treatment of employees, the challenges of human rights or the ecological devastation caused through unnecessary consumption and production. In management accounting, as Laughlin and Lowe (1990) demonstrate, the problems are more acute: that is, to what extent, if at all, might management control systems change to reflect a change in society? The answer unfortunately is probably not at all unless the management (and *their* financial masters) deem it to be in their interests as they currently understand that notion. As organisations become apparently *more* economically and performance focused, inevitably there is less room for manoeuvre for any socially-orientated innovation in management accounting.[9] (Unless, that is, one buys into the misdirection of "ideas" like "creating shared value" and such like, Crane et al. 2014).[10] So, it seems, we are likely to see management control as more and more oppressive—more and more driving out market alien values and less and less responsive to social and environmental necessities—*except in so far* such response meets the economic needs of a small elite group (Sikka et al. 1989, p. 61).

5   Management Control and Social and Environmental Accounting

Seen in this way, through the lens of Tony Lowe's project (see especially Lowe and Tinker 1977a, b), management accounting's response to social and environmental issues—despite appearing to be strangely disorientated, partial and disconnected—is perhaps less surprising. Management accounting has experienced attempted and actual innovations. There has been seriously substantive work done in accounting and labour relations; much might have been expected from the significant if frequently somewhat puzzling explorations of human asset/resource accounting; the brief experimentation with energy accounting was promising; many have expressed excitement over the exploration of intellectual and other capitals; and there has clearly been widespread enthusiasm for "new" techniques such as balanced score cards and corporate community investment. But despite (or because of?) these initiatives it is far from clear that either management accounting itself has changed especially or that such changes as have managed to embed themselves have had much substantive influence on how firm effectiveness is managed and judged. There are so many lost opportunities here (but that is a matter for another day).

And, equally, the social accounting literature (as generally understood) has responded to only parts of the attempts of management and cost accounting to offer information and control options for greater organisational effectiveness.[11] In this respect, it is salutary to recall Jones' (1990) insightful exploration of social accounting's difficulties in the face of a more determined capitalism: despite adopting an uncharacteristic reformist mantle, he plausibly forecast that a social-management accounting was likely to make little progress—and this has been broadly the case for the last 25 years.

So whilst there has been a relatively widespread interest in some aspects of an "environmental" accounting, closer inspection reveals that this apparent success of environmental management accounting will serve to illustrate how the appearance of activity and change can be misleading when nothing substantive is actually happening.

Very broadly, the possibility of developing an environmental management accounting has been long mooted in the literature (Dierkes and Preston 1977) and the considerable possibilities for new information systems and methods of measuring and controlling to ensure a more environmentally effective organisation have been well recognised and explored (see, for example, Power 1991; Ditz et al. 1995; Gray and Bebbington 2001). Few have sought out innovation and proselytised the possibilities of environmental management accounting more than Stefan Schaltegger and colleagues in the Environmental Management Accounting Network (EMAN) (see, for example, Schaltegger and Burritt 2000; Schaltegger et al. 2008; Bennett and James 1999). EMAN's work is replete with examples of innovation and with ideas and possibilities in which management accounting and costing systems, investment appraisal and management performance measurement offer organisations ways of controlling their enterprises in more ecologically-sensitive ways and yielding 'wins' for both the entity and the natural environment. This work has been ably supplemented by optimistic field work which seeks to tease out and explore the evidence of advances in management understanding and awareness—and consequently in management performance measurement (see, for example, Spencer et al. 2013).

A story of success and innovation can indeed be told (Schaltegger et al. 2008) and there is no question that management accounting has increasingly interacted with the growing number of environmental management systems, is implicated in helping organisations develop more eco-efficient opportunities, develop more imaginative business cases and think more constructively about the environmental implications of capital budgeting decisions. However, one would look in vain for alterations in the way in which nature is understood within the accounting or for a more pluralistic and democratic understanding of management decisions. It is far from apparent that these changes have actually altered the substance of management accounting and control practices or indeed management performance (Spencer et al. 2013). The broader evidence seems to suggest that the inroads environmental awareness has made to the accounting profession and its practitioners have not substantially changed over 20+ years. And the data is clear that *organisational* engagement with the environment has not altered in any substantive way (Randers 2012). And despite the considerable societal and ecological evidence of a need for substantial change in ways of organising and controlling, relatively little substantive change in management accounting practice (and theory perhaps) itself has developed. Such responses as there have been, are only first order changes (Laughlin 1991); the design archetype and interpretive schema—of the firm or of management accounting—has remained untouched.[12] The effectiveness of the organisation is still measured by its profit seeking, the environment has simply been factored in as another element of risk and reputation management and the considerable innovative possibilities have simply been watered down or side-lined.

Not that one would hear this story from the profession itself where tales of heroic change abound. The point is, following Lowe's work further, that the challenge offered by sustainability to management accounting is still being looked at in narrow technical ways with no holistic view of the planet and its species. But perhaps the most remarkable aspect of this—and the one which seems to proffer some substantial support for the foregoing point of view—is the relatively low volume of social and environmental accounting research that focuses on the management accounting and control systems of organisations. There is some, of course, but compared to the work on external reporting it is a tiny proportion. One obvious—and compelling—conjecture would be that perhaps researchers are inclined to think that as nothing has changed there is nothing to find? Perhaps academe sees management accounting and control orientated research into social and environmental issues in organisations as frequently 'uninteresting'—or at least insufficiently interesting to be worth overcoming the inevitable problems of research access?

Lowe and Tinker (1977b)[13] recommended that we look, not at a "social management accounting" or an "environmental management accounting" but at a larger "management accounting problem" which is all about seeing management control as maintaining relationships between an organisation and its environment but where neither the organisation nor the environment are seen in restricted, purely economic, neo-liberal ways. Thus does "management accounting and control", seen in this manner, automatically embrace such matters as the social and the environmental. This offers us a normative basis for critique of management accounting practice and perhaps that is the turn that the literature needs to take; it is, we would argue, certainly the only sensible route when social and environmental issues are raised to the overwhelming challenge of sustainability.

6   Organisational Effectiveness for Sustainability?

The principal challenge that mankind faces—and one which the species, the accounting profession, academe and business (*inter alia*) seem especially ill-equipped to address—is that of re-directing human activity to reduce its rabid un-sustainability. The preponderance of argument and evidence suggests that firms—especially the large dominant multinationals—are extremely effective in promoting *un-sustainability*. This is clearly madness by any reasonable notion of social-economic desirability: highly *ineffective* in Lowe's terms. A growing body of work has emerged that seeks to demonstrate this contention (Whiteman et al. 2013; Tregidga and Milne 2006; Milne et al. 2009) and, increasingly, to demonstrate the impediments to a more desirable form of organisational effectiveness, (Lowe and Soo 1980; Barter and Bebbington 2010; Young and Tilley 2006; Lamberton 2000; Stubbs and Cocklin 2008; Kearins et al. 2010; Zollo et al. 2014). A key argument in some of the work on external reporting for sustainability has been that substantial—as opposed to the currently vacuous—external accounting for (un)sustainability would demonstrate the extent to which organisations are intrinsically *ineffective* in their contribution to sustainability, (Owen 2008). Indeed, it is in such approaches where one can often see the holistic and inter-relationship bases of accounting that Lowe's work encouraged and presaged. Despite the continuing refusal of both organisations and the professions to develop and report anything approaching substantive accounts of un-sustainability, there is relatively little academic work, it would seem, that adopts an appropriately analytical stance to this question (for some exceptions see, for example, Bebbington and Gray 2001; Bebbington et al. 2001; Gray and Bebbington 2000). Certainly there is work here which starts to develop normative ideas about how accounts of un-sustainability might be envisaged, works out the practicable issues and then addresses organisations with the proposals. This approach has, as yet (?), proved unsuccessful in gaining any purchase in organisations, in the profession or in the mainstream of academe (Bebbington et al. 2007; Mitchell et al. 2012; Gray 2010).

The normative work in management accounting regarding sustainability-relevant issues has, one might contend, been more self-disciplining and (as we touched upon above) more inclined to explore potentials that firms might be willing to adopt rather than possibilities that an effective and sustainable planet actually requires. Important exceptions to this general statement exist (see, for example, Bebbington 2007) but what it seems is still missing is the concerted and imaginative project that Tony Lowe might have encouraged which would systematically address the kinds of accounting that a sustainable enterprise needs to function and become effective, (see also Gray and Laughlin 2012).

There is something of this wider call for imaginative work in Bebbington and Larrinaga (2014) but we remain quite some way from a speculative and explicitly normative approach to management accounting for sustainability.

Sadly, it is probably the case that a significant proportion of this failure might be laid at the doors of academe itself. It is perfectly apparent that much of the work that is carried out in the profession and in industry under the banner of "sustainability" has virtually nothing to do with sustainability (see, for example, Milne and Gray 2013). This is not entirely surprising and reasonable explanations for such behaviours can be found (Bebbington and Gray 2000). What is far more bewildering is the extent to which academe seems content to be acquiescent in this capture and hollowing out of a demanding empirical category like "sustainability"... academe is actively complicit in the process of turning "sustainability" into an empty signifier: at which point debate, research and experimentation is about business-as-usual, not an imaginative and holistic notion to which a considerable proportion of human activity needs to be directed (Sikka et al. 1995).

Rather than conclude on a note of pessimism perhaps we might try and draw some cautious optimism from more recent developments within the organisation studies literature. In particular, we might point to much of the recent work in *Organisation and Environment*, and the re-orientation of that journal, championed by, among others, Starik and Hoffman (e.g. Starik and Kanashiro 2013; Starik 2013). These authors call for management scholars to engage more substantively with sustainability at a systems level, and to challenge the "unsustainable status quo" (Haigh and Hoffman 2014; see also Starik and Turcotte 2014).

In this vein, Hoffman has explored the potential of what he calls "hybrid organisations", defined as "organisations at the interface of the for-profit and non-profit sectors" (Haigh and Hoffman 2014). This also speaks to some of the more radical work in the emerging field of social entrepreneurship, where scholars have begun to consider what a more sustainable, or less unsustainable, (more *effective)* form of commercial activity might look like (e.g. Nicholls 2010; Emerson 2006). The wider organisation studies field is also beginning to produce some interesting explorations of what sustainability might mean at an organisational level (e.g. Battilana and Dorado 2010; Valente 2012) and to re-engage with the ecological roots of sustainability "theory" (e.g. Jermier 2008; Whiteman et al. 2013). While this is far from a substantial body of work, what these examples illustrate is that we as scholars cannot shrug that "there is nothing new to find"; new theories are emerging by which we can begin to creatively explore the possibilities of organisational effectiveness for sustainability. The sustainability field is, perhaps belatedly, starting to embrace what Lowe would recognise as the need for explicitly normative speculation in scholarly work. Although Lowe never quite reached this point, careful and systematic study of organisational effectiveness would, in all probability, encourage us to move in just this, highly desirable, direction.

7   Conclusions?

Is there a conclusion to be drawn from this short fantasy on what Tony Lowe might have had to say about the current state of accounting with respect to social, environmental and sustainability issues? It would seem that there has been a failure within the academic community to fully embrace the vision that Lowe offered us for imagining and developing new emancipatory accountings. Equally disturbing, Lowe's very proper commitment to education and the transformative possibilities of real education (see, for example, Laughlin et al. 1986; Chabrak and Craig 2013) seem naïve in the light of the realisation that it is the educators themselves who are most complicit in the suppression of the conflicts and tensions necessary to generate accountings for effective organisations. Do researchers and educators any longer deserve warranty in this connection?

As Tinker and Lowe (1984) say (if we might permit a little mis-quoting) *"[Accounting] has lost much of the vitality and vision it had a decade ago". It languishes in a morass of technical specialization; it lacks overall coherence, and direction…the literature elevates a "technocratic rationality" and neglects "social rationality"* (see also Tinker and Lowe 1982). What we are left with is one of the most telling quotations which is (probably?) associated with Tony Lowe[14] that these days accounting and firms are "doing well, that which they shouldn't be doing at all" (see, for example, Machin and Lowe 1983). Fiddling whilst Rome burns hardly seems the half of it.

The final thought is an entertaining one to take away from this re-visiting of the past and this trying to retrospectively engage with a thoughtful, awkward, iconoclastic, scholarly and (add your own adjectives) colleague: just as Tom Gladwin brings (the idea of) a fish and a peasant into every meeting he has discussing sustainability and business, wouldn't it be entertaining if we brought the idea of Tony Lowe into every meeting where accounting was discussed? We would never be bored again.

Notes

1. It is probably difficult for younger academics to appreciate that the influence of Tony Lowe relies at least as much upon his personal support, his initiatives, his conversations and his ideas as it does on his publications. He was never an especially prolific writer but, more importantly, he was laying down the foundation for our discipline(s) at a time when the helter-skelter pursuit of publications was simply not an issue—and would have been seen clearly as the absurdity that it is. Tony Lowe resigned from his full time position at Sheffield University in 1985—that was 30 years ago. Consequently, essays such as this one inevitably rely in part upon one's memories of his influences. Equally, it is inevitable that any interpretation of his writings must recognise that they appeared at a time when many of the current anxieties and preoccupations of academe might have seemed less acute.

2. The reasons for this turn away from the self-consciously moral deductive reasoning are various and probably include *inter alia*: the dominance of North American "positivism" and the pursuit of the allegedly scientific; the intrinsic difficulty of normative reasoning and one's consequential vulnerability to academic attack; perhaps a growing lack of moral and intellectual courage; perhaps even the abandonment of moral judgement that seems such a consequence of misreadings of the postmodern turn.

3. It often seems as if a commitment to optimism requires some degree of (what may be unkindly thought of as) naivety.

4. In addition to the *Corporate* Report, there have been many attempts to articulate various new accountings explicitly derived from and/or as manifestations of dominant accounting discourse. None has succeeded in breaking into the autopoietic core of conventional accounting practice and profession, (see, for example, Gray et al. 2014).

5. We are grateful to the editors for pointing out that such insights probably did not originate with Tony Lowe and that, indeed, these notions might be found in Bentham's work (Gallhofer and Haslam 1993).

6. This somewhat cavalier dismissal of the argument that current accountings are more similar than different is made primarily on the grounds of practice and the pragmatic potentials for change. In doing so it ignores, *inter alia,* the constitutive and ideological roles of conventional economic accountings and the dominant roles of capital—from which perspectives, of course, accountings are more similar than different.

7. It is genuinely concerning that new scholars might come to the study of a subject like social accounting (whose substance is explicitly entirely dependent upon interpretation and context) with only a narrow reading from a few selected journals. To make sense of (what Lowe and Tinker refer to as) the relationship between accounting and society requires a breadth of vision. Ideally social accountants need to bring to their study some understanding of society and politics; some awareness of ecology and psychology; and some sense of ethics and the foundations of knowledge. Without such a context, social accounting is a truly trivial activity and/or area of study. One certainly won't gain this view from reading only a selection of accounting journals and having only the sketchiest sense of the core literature itself.

8. Where *"effectiveness"* is the gap between what an organisation *is* doing and what it *should be* doing (Lowe and Soo, (1980), we might suppose *ineffectiveness* to be the corollary—the extent to which it is not doing that which it should.

9. The arguments around external accountings have been different not least because additional accountings are demonstrably possible: either as issued by the company itself (as the largely trivial GRI reporting is) or as part of an enforced external social accountability constructed by non-market entities like NGOs and pressure groups.

10. The "creation of shared value" joins a long list of spurious attempts to suggest that societal, environmental goals are entirely commensurate with the pursuit conventional economic goals. Crane et al.'s article explicitly exposes the explicit and implicit assumptions underlying such attempts and shows them to be essential empty.

11. Although there is a relatively substantial corpus of *environmental* accounting research, it is, predictably, managerialist in emphasis. The social accounting literature viewed more broadly includes very little work directly examining *social* issues and the possibilities for management accounting. Notable exceptions include Norris and O'Dwyer, (2004) and Durden, (2008).

12. It is apposite to point out that our interpretation of this level of change material differs with that of Richard Laughlin and this remains a matter of some entertaining debate. Basically, though, there may be superficial changes (such as including of different cost categories and the allocation of overheads in more nuanced ways), there is no substantive change (in, for example, use of discount rates, long-term projections and/or the attempted inclusion of externalities).

13. We should note again that this work is not explicitly concerned with "social" accounting, (see also Lowe and Soo 1980).

14. The original source is elusive but we also have seen it attributed to Peter Drucker, Kenneth Boulding and Paul Ehrlich!.

Thinking About Critical Methodology

Robin Roslender

When the editors invited me to contribute an essay to this collection I had little difficulty in identifying a topic, one that I am sure had crossed Tony's mind on many occasions. As an incomer to the emerging tradition of interdisciplinary and critical accounting research in 1985, a tradition that owes an immense debt to Tony, I soon recognised that my sociological imagination, initially configured in another Yorkshire university, had maybe found a hitherto unexpected outlet. In a couple of early contributions to the literature of interdisciplinary and critical accounting, I shared some of my understanding of the nuances of sociological theory, something I happily continue to the present time. But I was always conscious that, as exciting as social science theory and theorising are, Gouldner had long ago identified the lure that a "pilgrimage" to "a holy place" had for sociologists as they "grow old[er]". Throughout my career I have taught my students about research methods and methodology, although never as much as I find myself doing these days. And, of course, I am not as

R. Roslender (✉)
School of Business, University of Dundee, Dundee, Scotland

© The Author(s) 2016   **73**
J. Haslam, P. Sikka (eds.), *Pioneers of Critical Accounting*,
DOI 10.1057/978-1-137-54212-0_5

young as I once was, so the time had come to actually write something about this topic. For Gouldner, it was the need to recognise the myth of a value-free sociology. For Tony, it was about stepping outside of the prevailing methodology of accounting research. For me, it is about what I think critical methodology encompasses.

1   Setting the Scene

Even for those readers who have experience of teaching modules on research methods and methodology in accounting, the term *critical methodology* is likely to be relatively unfamiliar. At the same time, however, they are likely to have broached the subject in some way or another, usually informed by insights first gleaned over thirty years ago from Burrell and Morgan's seminal text *Sociological Paradigms and Organisational Analysis*. The normal procedure is to rehearse their arguments about the way in which the interpretive turn in sociology in the mid to late 1960s, and thereafter the sociology of organisations, allowed sociologists to develop a more genuinely social scientific approach to their endeavours than was possible within the prevailing functionalist paradigm, with its positivistic underpinnings. The discovery of a second sociology, to borrow Dawe's 1970 imagery, promised to release a younger generation from the constraints imposed by continuing to ape the natural sciences, and implicitly the physical sciences, in attempting to fashion a science of society. Suddenly a varied prospectus of extant minority sociological ways of seeing, invariably linked in some way to the thinking of the most renowned of sociologists, Max Weber, became available to researchers. In due course, a small group of accounting researchers were to enthusiastically replicate the interpretive turn in sociology during the 1980s (Roslender 2015).

   With the benefit of hindsight, Burrell and Morgan were in a position to recognise that sociology, and again the sociology of organisations, had experienced a second, parallel turn. They identified this as constituting the development of a generic sociology of radical change, which differed from both functionalist and interpretivist sociologies, now designated as the sociology of regulation. The sociology of radical change was defined by a commitment to make use of sociological insights to promote radical social change towards a better social order. In the same way that Weber was recognised to be the principal inspiration for interpretive sociologies, Karl Marx was cast to play a parallel role within the realms of radical sociology. Once again a plethora of minority radical sociologies was quickly explored within the study of organisations, to great effect, a process that a slightly larger group of accounting researchers also replicated during the 1980s.

Within the sociology of radical change Burrell and Morgan drew attention to the existence of important distinctions, organised around the idea of structural and humanistic Marxism. They were very explicit that both designations incorporated significant variety, and at the margins, as captured on page 29 of the text, the differences might be argued as being very limited. Nevertheless, they were comfortable to emphasise the structural/humanistic dichotomy, identifying the former with contemporary Marxist social theorists such as Althusser and Coletti, while within the humanistic ranks were members of the Frankfurt School, including its then (and now) dominant theorist, Jurgen Habermas.

At this juncture it is useful to take a step backwards and recall how Burrell and Morgan constructed the other axis of their celebrated 2×2 matrix, as set out in the short opening chapter of their text. A continuum between subjective and objective social sciences is identified, being constituted by four sub-continua labelled: ontology; epistemology; human nature and methodology. Within this schema, "methodology" is asserted to be concerned with ideographic and nomothetic approaches to scientific explanation, perhaps best understood to refer to the formulation of particular explanations and law-like propositions respectively. As a consequence, the message that Burrell and Morgan are usually understood to provide to researchers is that when embracing a humanistic Marxist perspective the researcher is also rejecting a positivistic standpoint. By implication, those more attracted to structural Marxisms are less worried by the suggestion that their emphases may attract the pejorative positivistic label. Indeed it might be argued that the ends justify the means—social betterment through robust scientific enquiry.

Returning to our point of departure, to the extent that the notion of critical methodology has any meaning within Burrell and Morgan's tool box, it can refer either to radical positivism or radical interpretivism, or indeed some variant between these two extremes. If you think about it, not really very good guidance!

2   Looking for Clues?

In one of the first papers to commend the development of a tradition of critical accounting research, Lowe and Tinker (1977) asserted that accounting, understood as both theory and practice, manifested an ideological blindness that they encouraged like-minded researchers to document. In doing so, they use the terms "accounting methodology" and "intellectual emancipation" in such a way as to impress upon readers that it was highly unlikely that continuing to research in accounting employing its prevailing positivistic methodology would challenge this ideological blindness and that it was now necessary to step outside of that methodology (= the project of intellectual emancipation) in order to do so. In other words, there was a need to fashion a critical methodology. Lowe and Tinker had come to recognise the negative consequences that a continued acceptance of the intellectual hegemony that married positivism, functionalism and conservatism would have for those who, like themselves, sought to develop a more socially and politically progressive accounting praxis.

Although in the next years Burrell and Morgan's text would provide members of the Sheffield School, among others, with many valuable insights towards progressing these objectives, Gallhofer et al. (2013) identifies the rather less widely cited text by Bernstein (1976) as also being influential in this process, with both Laughlin and Chua extensively informed by him. Bernstein's "critical theory of society" approach is heavily skewed in the direction of Habermas and Critical Theory, which aligns with humanistic Marxism in Burrell and Morgan's taxonomy, and is thereby to be recognised to encompass a firm rejection of positivism and strong reservations about the interpretivist alternative. However, in common with Burrell and Morgan, Bernstein is largely silent on the detail of the methodological aspects of the preferred radical (critical) alternatives.

Taken together, despite their key role in furnishing the initial foundations of the critical accounting research tradition, neither Burrell and Morgan nor Bernstein provide little actual insight as to the substance of the alternative methodology that Lowe and Tinker (1977) identify as being necessary to accomplish the desired intellectual emancipation from the prevailing ideological blindness of accounting theory and practice. More significantly, however, although close to forty years later we have an appreciation of what critical methodology *is not*, namely positivism or interpretivism, both of which, to invoke Marx's own dictum, provide the means only to understand the world but not to change it, there remain relatively few clues about what critical methodology *is*, beyond the aforementioned suggestion of a continuum of variations involving radical positivism and radical interpretivism. While this may not appear to have significantly compromised the development of a rich portfolio of critical accounting insights during the intervening years, a compelling case for returning to first principles exists.

There is widespread consensus around the idea that methodology is concerned with the philosophy of (research) methods. It identifies and examines the various underpinnings of the many research methods or techniques that are available to researchers, as well as the issues associated with knowledge, knowing and the knowable. As a consequence, methodology is intimately associated with epistemology and ontology. At its simplest epistemology is concerned with the study of knowledge, or more specifically with questions about how we can know and what it is possible to know. The growth in interest within the social sciences, and particularly in sociology, with epistemological issues evident from the 1960s reflected a recognition that it was desirable for every researcher to have a necessary degree of awareness of the hidden underside of their practices, rather than leaving such matters to those colleagues who had elected to explore these hitherto abstract and arcane matters. Much the same motivations explain the parallel interest in ontology, understood to be concerned with that which is to be known, and more specifically the nature of being itself. While epistemology and ontology are readily understood to be complementary problematics, it is the latter that might be considered to be of marginally greater importance, on the grounds that it is important to know about what it is you are seeking to know about, prior to embarking on understanding the limits and possibilities of knowing. In this regard it is too easily forgotten that as recently as 50 years ago the predominant ontology informing social scientific enquiry held that there was no need to worry about whether what is to be known by either natural or social scientists is significantly different. As a consequence 'positive knowledge', the deliverable claimed by those who advocated a positivistic methodology, was a taken for granted. In this regard, the emergence of a viable alternative, in the guise of interpretivist methodology, always had significant implications beyond the social sciences.

This, of course, returns to Burrell and Morgan's own opposition within the sociology of regulation, functionalist versus interpretivist approaches to organisational analysis. At the extreme, the former incorporates a realist ontology and a positivist epistemology, in contrast to intepretivism's nominalist (constructionist) ontology and hermeneutic (rather than an "anti-positivist") epistemology. It also provides us with some general clues about what critical methodology might encompass, namely a critical epistemology coupled with a critical ontology. Although this might seem to be a fairly simplistic assertion, it has the merit of taking the discussion beyond the position that within the sociology of radical change it is possible to identify a continuum of such methodologies that reflect the same within the sociology of regulation.

In order to proceed, it is preferable to begin by considering the notion of a critical epistemology. At its simplest such an epistemology would be characterised by an acceptance of the need to accomplish the pursuit of social betterment. In this respect, a critical methodology consciously eschews the idea that knowledge might be understood in terms of objectivism and subjectivism, instead substituting the dismantling and abandonment of knowledges that justify and contribute to the reproduction of the status-quo. What this assertion is not to be understood to imply is that it is possible to construct a true knowledge that serves to underpin some ultimate set of social arrangements. A critical epistemology might, therefore, be understood to be a negative epistemology, although once again not the polar opposite of a positive/ist epistemology. Critical epistemology seeks to promote what might be rather than what is, thereby being underpinned by an alternative vision of what ought to be, a characteristic it also shares with the prevailing hegemony. Critical epistemology's negativity is, therefore, a radical negativity, since the knowledge it provides is at odds with that which currently holds sway.

Critical ontology is concerned with the nature of what exists, or more precisely, the contestable nature of what exists. Unlike 'uncritical' ontology, which incorporates a large measure of metaphysics and is characterised by a similar degree of abstractness, critical ontology focuses on the undesirable aspects of what is, as these are shaped by the prevailing hegemony. Critical ontology substitutes the debate about the existence of a real world 'out there' or the constructionist position that focuses on how that world is constructed through action, including research enquiry, with the observation that these two views are best understood to be reinforcing and, more significantly, give rise to highly contestable outcomes that critical social science seeks to reveal and disseminate in the form of emancipatory knowledge, i.e, knowledge that is consciously designed to promote social betterment. It is not that debating the merits of realism and positivism are without value, rather that what is to be recognised is that the constructed reality in its various manifestations does not serve the interests or the ends of the vast majority of those who construct, inhabit and reproduce it.

Informed by these fundamental insights on the purview of critical epistemology and ontology, and thereby critical methodology, it becomes possible to identify a number of ideas that are already familiar to many critical accounting researchers and that merit being designated as aspects of critical methodology.

3 Immanent Critique

The long established notion of immanent critique, or "immanent criticism" as it is sometimes referred to, provides a valuable point of departure. For commentators such as Held (1980) and Antonio (1981) immanent critique sits at the very heart of Marx's method of analysis. Horkheimer, the writer from within the Marxist tradition who was to do as much as anyone to promote immanent criticism, said of it in *Eclipse of Reason* (1947) that it confronts "the existent, in its historical context, with the claim of its conceptual principles, in order to criticize the relation between the two and thus transcend them" (quoted in Held 1980, p. 183). Held continues by commenting that following Marx, "Horkheimer argued that there is a contradiction between the bourgeois order's ideas and reality, between its words and deeds" (p. 183). Horkheimer is usually identified as being very firmly in the ranks of Critical Theory, serving as the Director of Institute of Social Research from 1930 until 1953, overseeing its relocation to the USA in the 1930s and it subsequent re-establishment at the University of Frankfurt in 1950. He is also identified as providing the widely influential characterisation of critical as opposed to "traditional theory":

> [C]ritical theory in its concept formation and in all phases of its development very consciously makes its own that concern for the rational organization of human activity which is its task to illumine and legitimate. For this theory is not concerned only with goals already imposed by existent ways of life, but with men and all their potentialities. (Horkheimer 1937, in Connerton 1973, p. 223)

Over time the precise detail of Horkheimer's notion of immanent critique evolved, in some part as a consequence of his on-going collaboration with Adorno whose thinking on it was shaped by his own preferred research foci. Habermas, the principal inheritor of the legacy of the Frankfurt School also contributed to our understanding of the notion of immanent critique.

Despite a very evident affinity between immanent critique and Critical Theory, it would be a great mistake to conclude that it should be understood to be somehow uniquely associated with it. The key observation is the assertion that immanent criticism sits at the very heart of Marx's method and not simply Critical Theory. Earlier a distinction was made between Critical Theory and those Marxisms that are designated as being more structurally focused, i.e, between radical humanism and radical structuralism in Burrell and Morgan's taxonomy. However, it is easy to overlook the observation that this distinction is principally adopted for analytical or taxonomic purposes. It is based on the differing emphases within the Marxist canon between the ideational and philosophical Marxist theory that is most readily evident within Critical Theory and the more materialistic and economistic emphases of associated with political economy, Burrell and Morgan's contemporary Mediterranean Marxism, labour process theory, etc. In truth, while scholars tend to place great emphasis and significance on differences, some of which are arguably quite fundamental, there is much that the broad categorisation of Marxist theory shares in common. In this regard it might be remembered that, quite early in the development of critical accounting, Chua (1986) appeared comfortable utilising a single "critical" designation, echoing Hopper and Powell's earlier identification of the emerging critical accounting research tradition as straddling both elements of Burrell and Morgan's earlier opposition (Hopper and Powell 1985).

Horkheimer's own focus on contradiction, identified by Held, confirms this. For many the concept resonates more readily with structural Marxism where it is often linked with that of over-determination, the pair being employed in tandem to explore the working through (out) of the ultimate unsustainability of the prevailing social order and its attendant distorting ideological justifications. A more Critical Theory-oriented interpretation of the power of ideology emphasises the ways in which those whose interests it promotes, and seeks to represent as 'the truth' (or reality), are somewhat more robust than might otherwise be apparent. It is only by painstakingly applying the method of immanent critique, with its ultimate objective of securing a better or more open, egalitarian social order, that individuals will come to realise, through heightened self-awareness, as opposed to the more widely canvassed class consciousness, the fundamental shortcomings and constraints of the order that surrounds them. Neither emphasis is sufficient on its own, with immanent critique providing the critical theoretic glue that binds together the different but overlapping conceptual frameworks that a radical intellectual interventionism or theoretical practice has evolved.

Immanent critique problematizes what is, subjecting the prevailing order, and those knowledges that have been devised to justify it, to scrutiny, through a process of dismantling (rather than deconstruction). No specific alternative order or knowledge is privileged, however, since there can be no ultimate state that will inevitably be achieved. Rather, immanent critique entails an exercise in analysing what exists by subjecting it to the claims that it makes for itself, while coming to understand what might be. In this respect, immanent critique is an exercise in coming to an awareness of the partiality of what exists, which in turn exists to be reconfigured through the process of resolving the inherent contradictions that lie at the core of the is of the capitalist social formation.

4   Laughlin's Operationalisation of the Critical Theoretic

An early engagement with the notion of critical methodology is found in Laughlin's widely cited 1987 "Accounting, Organizations and Society" paper on studying accounting systems in organisational contexts. A member of the Sheffield School from its earliest days, Laughlin remains a central figure in promoting a Critical Theory perspective in accounting research, particularly the value of the work of Habermas, on which he draws in this paper. Laughlin is unequivocal that any attempt to employ Critical Theory in accounting research entails not only understanding how accounting functions. Such understandings are simply a precursor to change ("transformation") for the better ("improvement"), an attribute that is not necessarily present in the alternative ways of seeing that had become increasingly commonplace in critical accounting research in the recent past. Laughlin's brief introduction to the different approaches to Critical Theory identifiable with four of its key exponents—Horkheimer, Adorno, Marcuse and Habermas—confirms that in their own ways they all sought to contribute to a better world for the humans who inhabit it, the generic project of social betterment that continues to motivate not only Critical Theorists but all those who subscribe to the practice of engaged enquiry.

On page 485 Laughlin refers to Habermas holding "a seemingly less radical perspective" to his three predecessors. This is certainly at least a contestable assertion, although there is a considerable body of evidence to support the view that Habermas may have become personally less radical over his own lifetime. At the same time, Laughlin seems to be attracted to a more moderate radicalism, something that is subsequently clearly evident in two papers on accounting methodology published in 1995 and 2004 (see Roslender 2013 for a discussion of Laughlin's middle range thinking). Equally contentious is Laughlin's translation of the precepts of Critical Theory, among which immanent critique is fundamental, to the level of an organisation or an accounting system, thereby fashioning a persuasive methodology. Laughlin asserts that this is not a problem for any of the aforementioned theorists, least of all Habermas whose model, in his view

> …has the greatest potential both as a methodological approach for understanding and changing accounting systems design and for investigating social phenomena more widely. (Laughlin 1987, p. 485)

On balance perhaps, it is necessary to make a start somewhere.

Laughlin's account of Habermas' methodology is based on insights that are to be found in the latter's introductory essay to the fourth edition of his text *Theory and Practice,* originally published in 1971 and republished in an abridged form in 1974. Habermas' insights are expanded by Laughlin to produce an operationalised methodological approach designed for the purpose of understanding and changing accounting in organisational contexts. The methodology is constituted by three stages (or four if the "quasi-ignorance" stage is included). Having gained access to an organisation, researchers are challenged to develop a working knowledge of how it currently functions, hence the term quasi-ignorance. Through a systematic process of exploration and enquiry, in which particular emphasis is placed upon looking beyond the observable reality, and via a process of discussion, the researcher seeks to identify what would appear to be the critical research questions or "critical theorems" to be pursued, as well as to develop an initial understanding of possible, progressive solutions to these questions. At this point, the researcher should be sufficiently well apprised of the present organisational reality to move to the process of enlightenment stage. In essence this is the equivalent of the generic data collection stage, although of necessity very different. Reflecting Habermas' broader commitment to promote a democratic mode of discussion designed to result in significant individual enlightenment, i.e., the ideal speech situation, the researcher and the researched engage in a lengthy period of discussion, designed to verify the former party's informed assessment of the prevailing social arrangements and how these might be enhanced for the benefit of the researched. The third and final stage sees the researcher revisit her/his cumulative understanding in an attempt to codify the lessons learned. These, in turn, are shared with the researched with the intention of promoting a further round of democratic discussion and reflection designed to identify possible strategic initiatives towards a state of organisational betterment. It is not for the researcher to identify these initiatives, since it is not her/his organisational realities that are under scrutiny. Nor is the researcher to be accorded any superior capacity for understanding, despite an unavoidable technical expertise.

It is difficult to avoid making sense of this methodology in terms of a very un-critical view of research. Ironically it is very tempting to bring to mind the generic management consultancy model of practice, which would see critical accounting researchers portrayed as a radical priesthood (of quackery?). Equally, it is possible to recognise a good measure of idealism at work. Taking a less cynical view, however, Laughlin's portrayal of a critical (theoretic) methodology identifies a number of interesting attributes of any such methodology. Initially it is clear that such a methodology firmly eschews any pretensions of value neutrality. The objective of the exercise is the promotion of betterment for the majority of an organisation's members, as befits something derived from the traditions of Marxist theory of whatever stripe. Secondly, embracing such a methodology is no casual undertaking, for beyond its radical underpinnings, it should be immediately evident that researchers are required to invest a significant amount of time in their enquiries. Thirdly, critical methodology fundamentally undermines the privilege that science has traditionally accorded those who practice it. While critical researchers must possess a significant stock of highly arcane, technical knowledge, their central role is that of facilitating others coming to know what might serve their interests better. It is arguably the combination of expertise and a commitment to facilitating a progressive utilisation of a much wider range of knowledges that is crucial. Finally, the discursive process through which theory becomes translated into practice affirms that, as an instance of critical social science, critical methodology demonstrates the significance that language plays in the contemporary social development process.

5   Critical Realism

It might be argued that, strictly speaking, Laughlin's contribution is one of *a* critical methodology, i.e., a potential operationalisation of the intentions implicit within the idea of a critical theoretic (or critical social science) approach to enquiry. In comparison, critical realism (CR) can be understood as an example of critical methodology in the generic sense, and as the counterpart to positivism on the one hand and interpretivism on the other. The relative absence, to date, of much interest in what CR has to offer critical accounting research (or accounting research in general) is surprising, not least in the light of a continuing fascination with the prospectus of method or framing theories that might be embraced for research purposes.

Although many of the ideas underpinning CR had long been understood within the philosophy of science, it is generally accepted that Bhaskar's 1975 *A Realist Theory of Science* provides a crucial moment in its evolution. Initially Bhaskar advanced a general philosophy of science, termed transcendental realism, which he extended to the social and human sciences in the guise of critical naturalism in 1979. Bhaskar fashions a three-tier ontology distinguishing between the real, which is constituted by generative mechanisms, the actual, which is how these mechanisms manifest themselves in specific (actual) events, and the empirical, which is how events, and thus the existence of generative mechanisms, are experienced by individuals, including researchers. While sharing positivism's assumption that a real world exists 'out there', independent of and pre-existing our knowledge of it, for Bhaskar transcendental realism problematises positivism's failure to recognise the conditions that necessarily exist in respect of what it is possible to know about and, in turn, impact reality. In the case of the social sciences, the pre-existence of an external social reality, in the form of a social structure constituted by generative mechanisms, knowledge of which is extensively organised, again acts as a powerful constraint upon human agency. CR, a term neither coined nor initially employed by Bhaskar himself, and understood as the elision of transcendental realism and critical naturalism, has major implications for projects of human self-emancipation, including a "socialist emancipation" (Bhaskar 1989, p. vii). Since human agency is inherently endowed with the capacity for reflexivity, the possibility of transformation rather than simply and continuously accommodating to the present social order, is potentially ever present. Bhaskar (1989) is aware of the clear affinity that exists between CR, as he had developed it over the previous decade and a half, and Critical Theory, identifying Marx's Eleventh Thesis on Feuerbach as one of two quotations at the head of his "Preface" to *Reclaiming Reality.*

In terms of epistemology, CR holds that what we can know about the (external) social world can only be partial since it is not possible to fully understand the workings of the generative mechanisms that constitute it. In this regard human agency lives its life making sense of reality, to varying degrees and with differing consequences. More significantly, however, when individuals do come into contact with the external reality they bring with them an accumulated understanding of it that necessarily shapes all subsequent interactions with it and that organises or structures these interactions and thereby the accumulated experience carried forward. The default position is that normal interaction constitutes a reproduction of the status-quo, although in principle it is always conceivable that clichéd 'life changing experiences' can occur. In the case of social enquiry, the same principles apply. In the case of the researcher, an accumulated knowledge of reality pre-conditions them to think and act in particular ways, including choosing what to explore and how to do so. Once again, the default position is that of enquiries giving rise to outcomes that reinforce and reproduce the status-quo. Crucially, however, it is always possible to import alternative knowledges and insights into the research process, particularly those that are underpinned by a commitment to promote a different reality. These will necessarily shape any interaction with reality and resultant understandings, which have the consequence of reinforcing the initial way of seeing. In common with Marx' Eleventh Thesis on Feuerbach or Critical Theory (or Habermas' critical social science) CR asserts that a commitment to such engaged enquiry is to be recognised as a virtue. Objectivity or value neutrality are explicitly eschewed in the pursuit of transformational insights, while the Weberian notion of value relevance is rejected in favour of something more robust.

This brief characterisation of CR is rather different from the one that is usually found within the accounting research literature, which in large part is informed by the formulation in which it has been embraced in the organisation and management studies literature rather than Bhaskar's work. Reed (2005) provides an influential introduction to CR for such research, identifying it as a means of transcending the positivism vs post-positivism (methodologies) dichotomy within social scientific enquiry. By that time the postpositivism referred more to postmodern and post-structural thinking than to interpretivism, with a generic construction-ism providing the link between them. Modell, one of the few accounting researchers to engage at any length with CR, was initially reliant on the latter conceptualisation, identifying CR as "a potential way of bridging the polarized positions of the functionalist and interpretive paradigms" (Modell 2009, p. 209). In doing so it provides a methodological under-pinning for empirical researchers seeking to pursue triangulated, mixed methods research, a notion somewhat far removed from CR as an emancipatory methodology (see also Modell 2007, 2010). Subsequently Modell (2014) has pursued a more wide-ranging exploration of the promise of CR, which also incorporates a discussion of a number of key distinctions within the broader literature, *inter alia* the support for a less critical CR orientation, plus a review of how accounting researchers have made use of this literature to date.

6   Bourdieu

Since the mid 1990s critical accounting research has evidenced as major shift in emphasis as a result of an increasing dominance of what might be designated postcritical thinking. Echoing what was observed at the beginning of this essay, like 'critical', postcritical is a highly contestable descriptor, not least because the theoretical canon that it is applied to is clearly very diverse. At the present time, the work of three French social theorists continues to be highly influential. Foucault has been a fixture within critical accounting research almost from its inception, initially regarded by some as offering both important continuities with and insightful refinements of the traditions of Marxist theory. Over time, however, Foucault's politically radical promise has been decoupled from an increasingly rich conceptual framework that has been unpacked by his many acolytes. Latour has rarely been regarded in the former light, initially attracting interest at the beginning of the 1990s principally because of a similar, and in part shared, conceptual framework to that of Foucault. Together Foucault and Latour offer the underpinnings of a postmodern (and postcritical) sociology that takes process as its principal emphasis as means to circumvent the structure/agency opposition that shaped the various traditions of modernist sociology.

Bourdieu's entree to critical accounting research occurred a decade later. In a review of its initial impact, Malsch et al. (2011) identify early papers by Kurunmaki (1999), Neu et al. (2001) and Ramirez (2001), which, in turn, affirmed that like both Foucault and Latour, Bourdieu had an extensive corpus of work from which to draw. In an appendix to *In Other Words: Essays towards a Reflexive Sociology*, Delsaut identifies a compendium of outputs dating back to 1958 (Bourdieu 1990). Malsch et al. enthusiastically commend the increased enrolment of Bourdieu's work by critical accounting researchers, despite the very obvious difficulties that such an extensive legacy (predominantly published in a foreign language) presents. At the same time, they are worried by the emergence of a form of Bourdieu-lite, challenging their colleagues to embrace his work "holistically". More significantly, however, they are critical of the lack of political engagement evident in many of the Bourdieusian studies they review (Malsch et al. 2011, p. 220). In their view, Bourdieu should present no problems to those within the critical accounting research community who remain committed to the philosophy of praxis. This being the case, and bearing in mind a career long involvement with empirical enquiry, what insights does Bourdieu provide in respect of critical methodology?

Bourdieu's methodological approach is termed social praxeology (Bourdieu and Wacquant 1992; Everett 2002, 2016). It is firmly focused on epistemological concerns and in particular the epistemology adopted by the researcher. Initially Bourdieu requires the researcher(s) to reflect thoroughly upon her/his knowledge of any chosen research object in order to introduce a necessary distance between her/his extant working knowledge of that object. One way to characterise such practice is as an intellectual sorbet that is designed to cleanse the mind of the unfounded pre-conceptions or pre–conditions that might compromise subsequent enquiries. Grenfell (2010) identifies the second stage of Bourdieu's methodology as being constituted by three sub-stages that require the researcher to determine the topography of power resources within the chosen field (or space) for exploration, to establish the actual distribution of these resources, and thereafter the specific dispositions of the key actors within the field under scrutiny. As in the previous stage, Bourdieu challenges the researcher to continuously reflect upon how s/he understands all of these arrangements. The third and final stage, termed participant objectivation, entails the further, reflexive elucidation of the detailed insights attendant on the pursuit of the research enquiry. For Bourdieu this stage, as with the two previous stages, is best accomplished by means of a collective practice as a result of which researchers are regarded as being less likely to regress into an unreflexive state of taken for granted interpretations.

The pursuit of social betterment, understood as the promotion of the interests of the mass of society, is taken as axiomatic by Bourdieu. Throughout his life he was firmly committed to the production of knowledge for such purposes, continuously seeking to ensure that his insights were of utility to political activists and militants, regularly aligning himself with their actions and interventions. In the final decade of his life Bourdieu's radicalism became increasingly pronounced. During these years he explored the concept of the collective intellectual, arguing that radical intellectuals from different backgrounds and spaces (habitus) should recognise that their contributions were most challenging when understood as elements of a collective practice, i.e., the work of *the* collective intellectual (Cooper and Coulson 2014; see also Shenkin and Coulson 2007). In the case of academics like Bourdieu, crucial to this praxis (or praxeology) is the application of the highest standards of intellectual rigour, which provide the necessary (and credible) substitute for the traditional precept of objectivity, now to be recognised as the defining attribute of uncritical social science.

7   By Way of a Conclusion

In the process of revising and refining these pages over a period of eight months I have become conscious of a number of things. The first of these is that I don't really think that I have told many readers anything particularly new. The great majority of the content is familiar to most critical accounting researchers. The novelty, if such there is here, is how I have put these various insights together to create a depiction of what critical methodology is. A second lesson I have learned is one that is very similar to something I have sought to convey to my own students in early years cost and management classes—don't seek short cuts to understanding. I now recognise that I have long been in pursuit of a depiction of critical methodology that can readily be understood as an extension of the positivist/interpretivist couple, thereby creating a triptych. Critical methodology is different—not least because three-sided coins don't exist. The third insight is that as valuable as Marx's Eleventh Thesis on Feuerbach or any similar advocacy of the pursuit of the philosophy of praxis might be, its essentially rhetorical quality means that its purchase remains largely confined to the realm of social theory or social philosophy. As a consequence, while both critical theory (rather than Critical Theory) and critical methodology seek to promote progress towards social betterment, they do so in different, if complementary ways, each of which needs to be understood in its own terms. This observation in turn informs a final realisation, that the fundamental attribute of critical methodology is the rejection of any pretence of value freeness, value neutrality, objectivity, disinterestedness or similar prescription that a bona fide scientist is urged to embrace in the pursuit of their research activities. Such a stance has long been recognised to be difficult to justify in a blanket fashion even across the natural sciences, thereby adding weight to those within the social sciences who identify the enactment of the highest order of rigour in enquiry as providing the basis for the credibility of their own scientific practices. Seeking to change the world is not inimical to being a scientist of any type. The grounds for disqualification reside elsewhere.

The "Sustainable Development" of a Critical Accounting Project

Jesse Dillard

1 Introduction

The legacy of Tony Lowe is the broadening out and opening up of accounting and those involved and implicated therein. One means by which this legacy manifests is a decidedly critical perspective on accounting. The objective of this critical accounting is to radicalize accounting so as to facilitate formulation, implementation, and evaluation of a progressive social agenda dedicated to improving the human condition though the awakening of possibilities in those that research, teach, study, practice and use accounting.

The core premise of this perspective is social justice and the facilitative capabilities and possibilities as well as limitations and impediments of accounting and accountability systems. Distant echoes of enlightenment,

J. Dillard (✉)
School of Business Administration, Portland State University,
Portland, OR, USA

Victoria University of Wellington, Wellington, USA

University of Central Florida, USA

© The Author(s) 2016   **91**
J. Haslam, P. Sikka (eds.), *Pioneers of Critical Accounting*,
DOI 10.1057/978-1-137-54212-0_6

empowerment and emancipation still seem to rumble within the subterranean landscape, if rephrased and reframed. Central to the emerging philosophies/ideologies/proposals is the facilitation of a more democratic society predicated on the paradoxical commitment to individual and collective autonomy, this to be gained through heightened self-awareness and appreciation of the social conditions wherein we live.

Interestingly, the project has morphed from a critical accounting project to an interdisciplinary accounting project (Roslender and Dillard 2003) to an encompassing interdisciplinary and critical accounting project[1] (Broadbent and Laughlin 2013). One might ask if this represents a broadening out and opening up, or a reining in and watering down of the project. Much heat, and some light, has been generated as to how critical, Marxist, post Marxist, pragmatist, structuralist, post structuralist, postmodernist, etc., the project was, is and should be.[2] This debate among these various perspectives should be encouraged. However, it is imperative that the critical accounting project maintains its radical and political intent directed toward facilitating more democratically governed[3] social systems, be they societies, work organizations or civil society groups.

The critical/interdisciplinary accounting project is a, if not the, accounting academic opportunity to seriously and rigorously question the neoliberal mainstream generally, and the dominance of financial economics in accounting specifically. It provides a place where one can challenge the generally accepted scientific and ideological assumptions of traditional accounting. Has the project been able to maintain its critical edge, and thus, its innovative and creative energy? Does it remain true to its commitment to social justice even though its theoretical grounds may be shifting or disappearing? Is the political still recognized as the area wherein accounting resides?

My intention in this essay is to consider the "sustainable development" of a critical accounting project from a somewhat personal perspective by revisiting three different, though related, perspectives that illustrate the evolution (or transformation) in my thinking. And at some level, I think the transition also describes what is taking place within the critical accounting project. I suppose this could be described as an autobiographical longitudinal case study, some of which might be construed as ancient history, of a critical accounting project. I address these perspectives by relying on three theorizations important in motivating and crystalizing my personal broadening out and opening up. The first, reflected in Dillard (1991), considers accounting as a critical social science. The second, reflected in Dillard and Ruchala (2005) and Dillard et al. (2005), follows Laughlin's (1987) application and extension of Habermas' (e.g., 1974, 1984, 1987) critical theory. The third, reflected in Brown and Dillard (2013b), considers the interface of critical perspectives (modernist) with an agonistic perspective (post structuralist). Each of these perspectives accepts, at least to some significant degree, a constructivist ontology of social reality and recognizes the centrality of language in constructing that reality within a historical, political and economic context. One might argue that the evolution represents a broadening out and opening up of the means for understanding and facilitating the sustainable development of social justice. Alternatively, it might be argued that the evolution represents an abandonment of the fundamental political principles of social injustice resulting in a vacuous critique reinforcing the oppressive status quo. I do not present the following as a resolution of the debate but as reflections on the development of an enquiring participant in the critical accounting project who has, and continues to, struggle with these tensions. The text here does indicate alignment with the view of Noam Chomsky: *As long as the general population is passive, apathetic, diverted to consumerism or hatred of the vulnerable, then the powerful can do as they please, and those who survive will be left to contemplate the outcome.*

Given the somewhat personal nature of this discussion, a bit of autobiographical information seems to be in order. Born in the late 1940s and reared in a small textile mill town in the piedmont region of the southeastern United States, subjected to the norms, values, traditions and mythologies of the culture—a culture and intellectual climate that might be characterized in many ways, progressive not being one of them. "Professionally" educated in the institutions of the region, I dutifully entered the US Navy during the Vietnam conflict. I returned to my roots for a graduate degree anticipating a teaching career in a regional institution of higher education.

Entering my academic career as a newly minted social psychology equipped behavioral accounting researcher, empiricism was emerging as the means by which the accounting discipline could establish itself as a legitimate endeavor within the academy. The assumed functionalist, objective ontology and related epistemology underlying the "appropriate" methods and methodology were not questioned. Noting the limitations of social psychology and its methods in explaining culturally embedded complex, professional behavior, one edges over into sociology and from sociology to political theory and philosophy.

Ontological and epistemological assumptions begin to weaken, and intellectual curiosity leads to the discovery of alternative and critical perspectives. The discussion presented below reflects a process of working through these tensions, insights and ideas depicting the "sustainable development" of at least one critical academic accountant (project). In doing so, I attempt to reflect some of the tensions of the (necessary) evolution of the critical accounting project. On the one hand, it may reflect an essential broadening out and opening up of horizons that extend the relevance and reach of the project. On the other hand, it may more accurately reflect a betrayal of the critical tenets of the project in attempts to rationalize a meandering journey in search of personal and societal justification and validation for the researching, teaching and peer of accounting.

The remaining discussion is organized as follows. In the next section, I discuss accounting as a critical social science. The third section considers the Laughlin/Habermasian revisions to critical theory. The penultimate section considers Habermasian critical theory in light of agonistics and proposes that the latter provides a useful theorization for moving the critical accounting project forward. The last sections present a brief summary and reflections regarding a sustainable critical accounting project.

2   Accounting as a Critical Social Science

The first theoretical article I wrote and published in critical accounting was "Accounting as a Critical Social Science", appearing in 1991.[4] To me the work reflects the excitement of discovering, and the struggle to assimilate, the idealist promise of critical theory. In my opinion, the central ideas contained herein still represent the foundations for the critical accounting project. Enlightenment, empowerment and emancipation are the means by which autonomous subjects collectively engage democratically so as to facilitate socially progressive programs. The means by which this is undertaken requires interdisciplinary engagement providing ideological critique and the development of more democratic processes for engaging in dialogue and debate as a means for facilitating the rational evolution of social arrangements.

The technique and technology of accounting are recognized as ideologically embedded, which negates claims of objective, value free representation. The socio-political perspective re-presents a reality reflecting a particular reality that privileges some and dispossesses others. A closed self-referential system tends to reinforce and be reinforced by the dominant ideological perspectives, in the current case neoclassical economics. A response to no one "true" representation is to provide multiple representations, evoking a pluralistic perspective regarding accounting and underlying ideologies (Hines, 1989; Morgan 1989??). For accounting this calls for concern with accounting in action by studying the practice of accounting in context (Burchell et al. 1980). What is the effect of accounting and what is the effect on accounting? Early examples include Cooper and Sherer (1984), Tinker (1985), Burchell et al. (1985) and Loft (1986). To do so calls for addressing meta level context representing the causes and conditions for reproduction and transformation of society. For example, in market capitalism, according to Marxist logic, growth and wealth accumulation, translated as maximizing shareholder value, present the primary motivating and legitimizing economic and social context. As currently practiced, accounting represents and perpetuates the interests of those in power, the capitalists (Braverman 1974; Tricker 1979; Clegg and Dunkerley 1980; Lehman and Tinker 1987).

The question is whether accounting as currently practiced is interrogating the dominant socio economic system so as to expose the weaknesses of the current economic system, contributing to a critique of the current social arrangements. The conclusion reached in 1991 was no, probably not; therefore there was a need of a critical perspective for accounting that would do so.

Critical theory, based on the German Critical Theorist Marxist derivations (See Held 1980), resonated as a framework wherein accounting could be examined within the context of contemporary society. Critical social science is a decidedly modernist theory characterized as scientific, critical, practical and non-idealistic: scientific in that explanations are deduced from a few basic principles and are subjected to verification by evidence; critical in that it offers a rationally supportive negative critique of the social order; practical in that the possibility exists for some to transform their social existence through self-knowledge; non-idealistic in that change is not brought about solely by rational arguments, ideas or enlightenment.[5]

Critical social science provides a theory whereby one could begin to visualize the means by which to consider how social justice might be realized through the enticing terms of enlightenment, empowerment and emancipation. Though moving away from the more structural Marxism, this perspective is generally grounded in the modernist tenets of the traditional Marxist critique of capitalism and seemed to represent an auspicious context for critical accounting and the initial phase in my development as a part of the critical accounting project. Following the work of Brian Fay (1987), in an attempt to address the influence of both of agency and structure, critical social science operates at the intersection of social practice, institutions and self-perceptions. The framework presumes the need to theorize four dimensions or stages: a state of false consciousness; the influence of crisis; the necessity and sufficiency of education; and a plan for transformative action.

False consciousness relates to the means by which people conceive of their social status and opportunities based on false or illegitimated presumptions. From a Marxist perspective, within a capitalist society, the social order establishes and sustains self-understanding that results from reified social relations. The reified social relations reflect a false social order that is instrumental in maintaining the dominant capitalist hegemony. As individuals began to realize that how the extant social structures perpetuate a sense of false consciousness, they begin to feel alienated from the prevailing social order leading to social instability. A Marxist's interpretation states that within capitalism, decreasing profits and class polarization lead to greater impoverishment of labor and greater concentrations of wealth by the capitalist class. The cause of the impoverishment can be understood in terms of class antagonism, commodification and wealth distribution criteria. Building on the insights gained from a recognition of their social status and the inequities within the social systems, education concerns the means by which the situation might be changed. Marx suggests that individuals come to identify themselves with a particular class and in doing so recognize the irresolvable conflicts inherent in the relationships motivated by the extant social structures. Heightened class consciousness is brought about by various means as the changing social conditions are made more visible and understandable. Having recognized alienation and the possibility of overcoming it, a plan for transformative action is needed. Marx, for example, advocates the replacement of capitalist institutions such as markets and private property by more democratic, labor oriented institutions and mechanisms. Replacing repressive, capitalist-oriented social institutions by more democratic, labor oriented ones would facilitate social transformation.

Critical social science presumes that the "true" nature of existence can motivate transformative action. The power of reason can initiate change coupled with clarity of vision leading to emancipatory outcomes. However, Fay (1987) recognizes some of the limitations to a critical social science, questioning some of its assumptions. Human reason is limited in the ability to bring about change. Ideas alone are not determinants of change. Given the inherent indeterminacy of existence, rationality is not attainable. Critical social science inappropriately equates freedom and happiness and freedom and collective autonomy. Also, physical limitations constrain the ability to gain an understanding of current unsatisfactory existence. Participants are actively involved in creating history and therefore cannot overcome it in order to gain an objective view of their historically situated nature. Human beings absorb traits through their bodies, and mental consideration cannot identify or overcome them. These constraints bring into question the ability to act autonomously, exercising intentional behavior beyond the influence of extant social structures. Ultimately, Fay argues, oppression and alienation cannot be overcome through an individual's reflective observations and an evaluation of history and tradition. Also, there are, at times, external forces that cannot be overcome. At best, what can arise are approximations of reality and, thus, incomplete strategies for change.

The limitations constrain the efficacy of critical social science, but hopefully they are not totally debilitating. The radical political agenda was still a strong component that linked accounting and the socio-political environment. How could I best sustain my development as a critical accounting research/academic in light of the apparent deficiencies in the more orthodox political economy as well as the less structural derivative?

3   Habermas' Second Generation Critical Theory and an Accounting Extension

Given that Jürgen Habermas[6] was the primary second generation critical theorist, it seems reasonable to explore his response to the criticisms leveled at Marxism generally and critical theory in particular. How can this decidedly modernist philosophy reconcile with an emerging postmodern world? In critical accounting research, engaging Habermas mean engaging the work of Richard Laughlin and Jane Broadbent.[7]

Habermas seems to be trying to align radical social theory with the changing societal context faced after the dissolution and horror of the Second World War and the Holocaust. The recognition of the "linguistic turn" in philosophy motivated a reconsideration of the efficacy of grand narratives and first principles as the object of exploration and application. Theorizing social systems in terms of life world (civil society), (social) systems, steering media and steering mechanisms, Habermas describes how the social systems should reflect the norms and values of the life world, which emerge out of the deliberations within civil society. Distortions occur when the lifeworld is colonized by vested interests through the use of power and control hierarchies. Generally, this formulation maintains at least the skeletal structures of a Marxist critique. Following from Habermas' theorizing, Laughlin developed his ideas regarding middle range thinking (Laughlin 1987; Broadbent and Laughlin 2013) as a way of moving critical accounting research into the second generation of critical theory.

I encountered these ideas and found them to be a substantial part of sustaining my development as a critical accounting academic (e.g., Dillard and Ruchala 2005). Responding to the criticisms of modernists' search for defendable groundings for their theories given the recognized, constructivist nature of social systems, Habermas focused his efforts on developing the processes and procedures for reaching an understanding. Here, it appears that the Marxist critique of capitalism still (obliquely) underlies these ideas; however, such constructs as historical materialism and class stratification seem to have less purchase. Habermas (1984, 1987) proposes, in effect, first principles (validity claims) of communicative action directed toward reaching and understanding. Generally holding to the tenets of critical theory, Habermas and his colleagues attempt to broaden out and open up the traditional domain of radical politics.

Also at this time, I was becoming more aware that the post structuralists, especially the work of Michel Foucault, were being usefully engaged in the critical accounting literature. However, I was of the opinion that this approach of social critique might have moved a bit too far by apparently shedding the political in observing control and domination in social systems. There seemed to be little guidance regarding empowerment or emancipation. While there appeared that insight might be gained from viewing social systems through such a lens, I questioned the extent to which such a perspective could sustain a critical perspective and support meaningful praxis.

Habermas' theory of communicative action, and thus Laughlin's middle range thinking,[8] is predicated on an enabling deliberative democracy based on communicative rationality. Grounded in the tenets of modernity, deliberative democracy focuses on reaching consensus though rational dialogue. According to Habermas, rational dialogue is undertaken within the context of an "ideal speech situation". Rational dialogue carried out within an ideal speech situation provides a universal process whereby consensus can be reached regarding the appropriate course of action in a given situation. Coercive behaviors and differential power relationships are presumed to be suspended; all interested parties are provided an opportunity to speak and understand; and the outcome is to be determined solely on the strength of the better argument. The strength of the arguments is evaluated via the assessment of universal validity claims: truth, rightness, truthfulness and completeness. The process can be characterized as a search for one rationally agreed upon solution by members of an ongoing community deliberating together.

As with Habermas on a more general level, Laughlin's middle range thinking attempts to broaden out and open up traditional accounting and accountability systems. Laughlin and Broadbent and various colleagues' development, application and refinement of these ideas represent a central research stream of the central accounting project.[9] Enlightenment, empowerment and emancipation are roughly translated into the research domain of accounting and accountability systems. Enlightenment is theorized as critical theorem generation drawing on Habermas' conceptualization of lifeworld (civil society), steering media and systems. The empowerment relates to reaching a decision using the universal processes of Habermas' communicative action. Laughlin envisions the result being a skeletal theory to be empirically fleshed out within the unique context it is being applied. Evaluation and change (emancipation) are the result of deliberative dialogue and debate undertaken within the parameters of an ideal speech situation. Critical accounting research is seen to be an engagement between the researchers and the researched culminating in change, if deemed desirable.

The appeal, and one contribution, of Laughlin's work is the translation and application of Habermas' macro social framework to the micro level of work organizations and the specification of the effect of, and on, accounting and accountability systems. The framework provides a tangible, albeit somewhat utopian, linkage of an appealing critique of capitalism with a more nuanced and seemingly realistic approach to engagement and change. These ideas expanded my understanding and appreciation of the possibilities of critical accounting in working through some of the apparent limitations of critical theory in light of the changing (postmodern) world. The constructs of lifeworld, system and steering media depict the processes by which norms, valued and practices of civil society become distorted (colonizes) by the influence of money and power. Communicative action provides one means by which this colonization maybe be avoided or overcome through deliberative democratic dialogue and debate. The work of Jane Broadbent and others illustrated the applicability of these ideas.[10]

Reworking of critical theory addressing the limitations associated with a linguistic focus responds to criticism related to grand narratives and first principles. Middle range thinking brings Habermas' universal procedural norms into the critical accounting domain. Habermas' analysis indicates the limits of instrumental rationality in facilitating more democratic forms of engagement and accountability. The related power asymmetries result in bias and privileges accruing to those controlling the discourse. Habermas and middle range thinking presume that these differences can be suspended in pursuit of arriving at a rational consensus based on the strength of the better argument.

Having worked within the confines of communicative action and middle range thinking, one again recognizes the enabling and constraining possibilities of the ideas. For example, what if the participants are not able to suspend the asymmetrical power relationships; or what if there are irresolvable ideological or value differences that cannot be overcome? Is there a way of expanding the applicability of these modernist ideas through some type of post structuralist perspective? In other words, how can I sustain my development as a critical accounting project? That is, how can I extend my understanding so as to better address these limitations?

4   Agonistic Dialogic Accounting: Exploring Possibilities

Agonistics, as developed primary by C. Mouffe,[11] appears to have some purchase in responding to some of the limitations associated with middle range thinking and expanding my conceptualization of the critical accounting project, recognizing that the project will be ongoing and ever incomplete. This perspective was introduced into the accounting literature by Brown (2009) and continues to be developed by her and her colleagues and students with the stated goal of "taking pluralism seriously".[12] One appealing aspect of this line of thinking is that it might be construed as an attempt to theorize political critique consistent with useful insights gained from post structuralist thinking—as Mouffe (2005) states, a return to the political. Such a perspective proposes that to adequately respond to dominant hegemonic ideologies and address asymmetric power relationships arising from divergent ideological orientations, the socio-political context needs to be characterized by difference, undecidability, and antagonism, not similarity, decidability and consensus.

Instead of conceptualizing democratic practices and decision making as a process facilitating consensus, an agonistic perspective presumes a more realistic, antagonistic one that attends to contingency, difference and conflict. The formation of democratic subjects is an ongoing process of constructing political self-identities operating through processes of differentiation. Democracy is predicated on difference and legitimate democratic processes reflect dialogical processes that facilitate the exploration of these differences.

Taking pluralism seriously recognizes and enhances diversity and, in doing so, facilitates a more democratic and just society. A central question facing accounting is how to enable the meaningful involvement of all interested parties in the democratic processes by justly accounting for the appropriate phenomena in light of a wide range of differences among various dimensions? (Brown and Dillard 2013b, p. 182).

An agonistic perspective specifically considers the role of diversity, power and conflict in political deliberations and decision making so as to identify and address inequalities and injustices within the current social arrangements. This approach conceptualizes the context wherein political deliberations are taken to be characterized by asymmetric power relationships and irresolvable differences and antagonisms. Agonistic processes aim toward conceiving and implementing democratic procedures where differences are recognized and expressed. The objective is not necessarily to overcome the differences but to recognize the dominant hegemonic structures so as to provide opportunities for challenging them and imagining new conceptualizations and insights. Mouffe (2013) claims that this post structural formulation, while not overcoming all the limitations to a deliberative approach, does more explicitly and realistically theorize them. Discursive engagements are seen as interactions that potentially construct, deconstruct and/or reconstruct social and political identities, facilitating the possibilities for questioning, modifying and changing dominant narratives.

Agonistics identifies hegemonic and counter hegemonic discourses as they relate to various participants and their differing socio-political perspectives. Out of these interactions, power relationships become more evident and opposing ideas and interests more readily identified. The ongoing conflictual engagement facilitates a broader understanding of various other positions as well as an indication of heretofore unrecognized alternatives. This process does not necessarily lead to consensus because of the incommensurable ideological and value positions, power differentials, and interests present in pluralistic societies. In fact, Mouffe (2013) argues that such diversity is a necessary condition for democracy.

Within the context of western democratic capitalism, taking pluralism seriously means recognizing the fundamental differences among the various interested groups such as capital, labor, environmentalist, indigenous peoples, immigrants, ethnic and sexual/ity minorities, nonhumans, and future generations. The envisioned political process recognizes and sustains the irresolvable differences and asymmetrical power relationships in pluralistic democratic societies. Agreement or consensus is not necessarily a desirable outcome especially if it obscures the unresolved differences and unequal power relationships. Each interested party is guaranteed the right to be heard and be understood as well as to hear and understand. As with the deliberative democrats, the shared commitments are to the processes that represent forum wherein dialogue and debate take place; however, unlike deliberative democrats, here there is no expectation that this space will not be influenced by powerful self-interests and distorted communications.

Following an extensive review of the agonistics literature, Brown (2009) identifies eight principles useful when contemplating agonistic accounting and accountability systems. Four of the principles are be associated with context wherein agonistic discourse takes place and four with process that facilitate agonistic discourse. The four principles related to context suggest characteristics of an environment wherein agonistic accounting can be carried out. If one recognizes *multiple ideological orientations,* one points toward the differing assumptions, values and framings that provide the basis for positions held by the various interested groups. Highlighting *extant power relationships* identifies the unequal power relationships that have the potential to influence the range and direction of the dialogue and the debate. *Recognizing the transformative potential of dialogic accounting* instills a sense of possibilities regarding progressive change emerging from a dialogic engagement within an agonistic space. *Resisting new forms of monologism* acknowledges the necessity for immediately reopening the conversation once closure has been attained (i.e., a decision made), recognizing the presence of still unresolved issues and remaining power relationships.

Four of Brown's (2009) principles specify necessary attributes of accounting and accountability systems associate with agonistic processes. *Avoiding monetary reductionism* recognizes the need for accounting representations of an entity's activities to be expanded beyond the current quantitative monetary representations. *Being open about the subjective and contestable nature of calculations* highlights the instrumental rationality upon which calculations are based and points out their unwarranted apparent precision and incontestability. *Enabling nonexpert accessibility* asks that accounting representations not only be timely, accurate and relevant but also understandable to all participants. These three principles emphasize the need for transparency in how the accounting representations and projections are derived, their underlying assumptions and anticipated weaknesses. Given an agonistic context and the implementation of these necessary attributes, procedures are necessary to *ensure effective participatory processes* including ongoing dialogue among the interested groups where all are guaranteed the right to speak and be heard, not necessarily to agree, consistent with the requirements for agonistic dialogue and debate.

My anticipated extensions of a critical accounting project assumes that new understandings will be the outcome of agonistic engagements among the interested parties as they interact as members of an ongoing community. Spaces for imagining new accountings and accountability systems are created as the dialogue and debate progress. Such might be deemed progress or at least the best we can expect (Rorty 2006). Change occurs as political coalitions form in opposition to the dominant hegemony. Thus, change is a response to recognized impediments to individual and collective autonomy. Those on the outside become the inside, shifting power relationships, redefining political frontiers and setting new boundaries, prejudices, inclusions and exclusions. These are recognized as resulting from political processes engaged in by opposing groups having irresolvable differences and values. There is not presumption of consensus or ultimate agreement. Power differentials are implicated and presumed in the engagement.

5   Reflections

As with the formative stage of the critical accounting project, the exploration of the contributions from interdisciplinary work seems to be central to moving toward the sustainable development of a critical accounting project, taking care not to lose sight of the fundamental differences inherent in politically imbued engagements. Such a perspective seems valid whether we are referring to an individual's development or the evolution of the project. In taking pluralism seriously, I am currently investigating agonistic democracy in an attempt to relax some of the assumptions associated with deliberative democracy. The form this developmental path is currently taking is agonistic dialogic accounting, which combines the dynamics of dialogic engagement with agonistic political theory in considering the design, implementation and evaluation of accounting and accountability systems supporting progressive social programs. I currently perceive this line of intellectual endeavor to represent a broadening out and an opening up of the critical accounting project which retaining its radical intent.

In continuing to pursue this course of investigation, many issues and questions need to be addressed. For example, has the fluidity of an instantaneous and all-encompassing information fueled global market economy rendered the traditional assumptions of modernity and rationality obsolete? Can a more realistic set of assumptions facilitate a more sustainable critical accounting project? Can it extend my understanding of how accounting and accountability systems can facilitate a more democratically governed society? How can these systems assist in articulating and implementing such contested values as justice, equality and trust? How can accounting and accountability systems identify and support sustainable economic, social and natural systems? How might we engage certain groups, such as organizational management, in dialogue and debate regarding such sustainable systems? How might we identify and articulate what sustainability encompasses, whose conceptualization of sustainability is being employed and in whose interest? By what means can, and should, actions be rendered transparent? How can relevant, accurate and understandable information be identified, acquired and presented? How do each of these further the critical accounting project's goal of enhancing individual and group autonomy (emancipation) through a more complete recognition and understanding of the social reality (enlightenment) that we collectively create and the means by which it can be changed (empowerment)?

As noted above, the critical accounting project, both individually and collectively, is interdisciplinary. Considering, applying and evaluating cross disciplinary work regarding issues related to critical accounting requires a pluralistic attitude toward research and the basic ontological and epistemological assumptions that inform the related theoretical and ideological groundings thereof. For example, what are the implications for critical accounting from an analysis of the debates between the deliberative and agonistic democrats? Applying any political theory such as agonistic dialogic accounting means continually questioning the underlying assumptions and addressing the limitations. A critical perspective requires ongoing reflection on how the ideas can be implemented and how their implementation might impact other interested groups, especially minorities and those traditionally marginalized. Such reflection requires questioning how decisions are made, by whom, and how they are carried out.

Sustainable development of a critical accounting project provides a context wherein the status quo can be continually questioned, and the issues identified and exposed to interrogation through enlightened dialogue and debate. The enabling democratic processes should be designed to facilitate diversity and inclusivity (pluralism), not necessarily consensus. Unavoidable and irreconcilable status and power differences cannot be suspended or assumed away. The power of the dominant hegemonic discourse is recognized as well as the potential to replace it being inherent within pluralistic social systems. However, a sustainable critical accounting project is ever vigilant regarding the process, content and implications of change, and of replacing one hegemonic discourse with another one. With respect to accounting and accountability systems, this suggests that as critical scholars we have a serious responsibility to understand and position any action or proposal within its historical, political and economic context. To conscientiously do so requires an interdisciplinary perspective undertaken within a decidedly pluralistic ethos.

The sustainability development of a critical accounting project requires a serious questioning of the tenets of capitalism as currently implemented within the context of global market capitalism. Serious critique jointly facilitates recognition of possible alternatives and/or courses of action that could possibly lead to a more liberated state of being for the participants. Any other objective seems to be unacceptable. This means overcoming the passivity and apathy born of ignorance and a sense of helplessness. It means recognizing the unsustainability of unbridled consumerism. It means providing the vulnerable with an unaccustomed and understandable voice. It means pointing to those in power and illuminating their abuse of it. It means contemplating the outcomes though the rationality of all effected parties. It means acting as the conscience and critic of society. It means acting as if the world depended on it. Nothing less is a serious abdication of our responsibility as critical accounting academics to sustainably develop and those who must live with the consequences thereof.

Notes

1. The term critical accounting project is used as a collective to include this genre for accounting research.
2. For example, see *Critical Perspective on Accounting* 1994, 5(1), Grey 1994; Hoskin 1994; Neimark 1990, 1994; Tinker et al. 1991; Broadbent and Laughlin 2013.
3. Variants of democracy can take many forms (e.g., see Held 2006). The terms as used here in a rather generic sense to refer to participatory governing processes and institutions.
4. I often contemplate what would have transpired had this work not been published. Would the promise and passion have been pursued? I'm indebted to the benevolence of Lee Parker and the guidance and perseverance of Richard Laughlin.
5. See Fay (1987), especially p. 26.
6. Habermas' work is extensive, covering many issues over many years. The works of primary interest here are Habermas (1973, 1984, 1987).

7. Broadbent and Laughlin have contributed substantially to the critical accounting literature. A review of their work is beyond the scope of this discussion. See Broadbent and Laughlin (2013) for a summary of some of their work.

8. For a more extensive discussion and explanations see Habermas (1984, 1987), Laughlin (1987), and Broadbent and Laughlin (2013; esp chapter 3).

9. See for example Laughlin (1987, 1995, 2004, 2007), Broadbent (2002), Broadbent and Laughlin (1997, 1998, 2013) Broadbent et al. (1991), Dillard (2002), Lowe (2004), Power and Laughlin (1996).

10. See for example the extensive work by Broadbent and others, especially regarding "new" public management. See Broadbent and Laughlin (2013) for an introduction and discussion.

11. Mouffe (1997, 1999, 2000a, b, 2005, 2013), Laclau and Mouffe (1985/2001).

12. See Blackburn et al. 2014; Brown 2009; Brown and Dillard 2013a, b, 2014, 2015; Brown et al. 2015; Dillard and Brown 2012; Dillard and Roslender 2011; Dillard and Yuthas 2013; Söderbaum and Brown 2010; for a review see Dillard and Brown 2015.

A Brief Historical Appreciation of Accounting Theory? But Who Cares?

Michael J.R. Gaffikin

Although I had met him earlier, I really got to know Tony Lowe in his post-Sheffield period. Many others had worked with him at Sheffield and elsewhere for many years and already knew him well. My association arose when he spent time with us at Wollongong and we had many long hours of discussion over matters of mutual concern about and around our "chosen discipline". I do not think that at that time we could have been characterised as "old men" (well, he was quite a bit older then me!)—the sort of whom Yeats asked why should they not be mad (Yeats 1965, p. 388)—but, of course, we soon became them.

One of our concerns was the narrow intellectual vision of many of those regarded by many to be the leading scholars in the discipline. As is now well accepted, Tony had earlier set out to create a new community of scholars who would seek recourse to a wide range of disciplines to assist in developing an understanding and explanation

M.J.R. Gaffikin (✉)
Department of Accounting and Finance, University of Wollongong, Wollongong, New South Wales, Australia

© The Author(s) 2016   **109**
J. Haslam, P. Sikka (eds.), *Pioneers of Critical Accounting*,
DOI 10.1057/978-1-137-54212-0_7

of and for improving accounting in order that it contribute more use-fully to benefit societies generally and business practices specifically. Up to that time mainstream accounting research relied too heavily on dominant—fashionable and ideologically driven—economic theory. Thus, his contribution to new styles of accounting scholarship was extremely significant (cf Cooper 2014): it could develop as a broader (than just economics) social science.

1   Social Science[1]

A few hundred years ago, there were disciplines referred to as natural philosophy and moral philosophy. The former evolved into the natural sciences, the latter into the social sciences. However, like so many of the terms we use regularly, the term social science is difficult to define pre-cisely and has been the subject of much debate. Wikipedia states that "social science is a major category of academic disciplines, concerned with society and the relationships among individuals within a society". Thus, social science is the study of aspects of human society. It has, over the last 200 years, been heavily influenced by positivism with the under-lying assumption that the study of societies can be undertaken scientifi-cally. Closely associated with this, then, is the intention that it will apply the methods of the "natural sciences" to study human society. Sometimes the term has been taken to mean the discipline sociology but in a broader sense, the term includes a variety of specific disciplines that have evolved very differently and remain so. Thus, while collectively the term may be used to imply the use of scientific methodology, several other methodolo-gies have been promoted.

Accounting can be included with those disciplines concerned with aspects of human society because, clearly, it is a "system of thought" designed by humans to assist human decision making and influence (human) behaviour. Therefore, a social constructionist ontology, rather than a realist ontology, would seem to be a more appropriate basis for conceptualising accounting. Consequently, rather than attempting to recreate the methods of the natural sciences, it is more appropriate that accounting turn to the methods that recognise the human aspects of the discipline rather than claim an intellectual status akin to the natural sciences. Unfortunately, accounting theorists and researchers have been very slow to recognise this as is evident in the heavy involvement in the neo-empirical research programs over the last 50 years. There is some truth in the view that accounting is a fairly "young" intellectual discipline and has yet to demonstrate the maturity of self reflection and understanding. To date it has been happy to accept the position of being a sub-discipline of (and consequently inferior to) economics. As a result, it has relied heavily on economic theories and methodologies in which, until recently, positivist (neo-empirical) methodologies have dominated. This is not to suggest for one minute that accounting is not closely associated with economics because it largely deals with economic phenomena. But it deals with such phenomena from a very different point of view (otherwise it *would* simply be part of the discipline of economics). While the more sceptical would argue that accounting is the "handmaiden of capitalist economics" this merely reflects a conservative and overly deferential viewpoint because there are several aspects of accounting which are very separate from simple economic analysis, for example control systems, information processing and behavioural considerations. Nevertheless, in terms of theoretical or conceptual development a great deal of accounting research has followed the practices in economics perhaps because many economist have argued that their discipline is the social science *par excellence* and that its methods more than other social sciences are the closest to the natural sciences.

However, in the last 60 years there were been major intellectual upheavals in all the social sciences. In 1958 the very influential book by Peter Winch, *The Idea of a Social Science,* was published. In the book, Winch challenged the dominant form of social inquiry (including economics) which was positivist and functionalist. In so doing, he denied that inquiry in the social sciences could proceed on the same basis as the natural sciences. The social sciences, more specifically, to him, the discipline of sociology, were more akin to philosophy than (natural) science; more the unfolding of discourse than chains of causation. However, given that research in accounting from that time has persisted with the mistaken belief that establishing a science of accounting was dependent on showing that research in this discipline proceeded along the lines of a scientific method, Winch's book seems to have not had much impact on accounting researchers. Fortunately, whether it be directly attributed to Winch or not, there have been many accounting scholars, largely due to or at least consistent with Tony Lowe's influence, who recognised the thrust of his message and a variety of alternative approaches to developing accounting theory appeared.

2   The Development of Alternative Accounting Theories

By 1970 there had been several different approaches to developing an accounting theory. Amongst the many were included the works of very well intentioned individual theorists such as Chambers and Mattessich. Their works, and that of others, emerged from the desire to employ rigorous research methods and logical analysis to stated assumptions and propositions as to the purpose of accounting, especially the production of general purpose financial statements. These works were classical modernist (positivist) works in that they advocated the appropriateness of an essentially hypothetico-deductive scientific method to achieve intellectual rigour in accounting. Many of the major works of these theorists were published in the 1960s, but there were several similar major works on accounting published prior to this decade, for example William Paton's *Accounting Theory* (1922), John Canning's *The Economics of Accountancy* (1929) and Stephen Gilman's *Accounting Concepts of Profit* (1939).

There were also attempts by various professional bodies to develop a theoretical basis for accounting: initially the search for generally accepted accounting principles, then accounting standards and a conceptual framework on which the standards can be based. At first these attempts were represented by commissions to individual (or groups of) accounting theorists, the best example of which is Paton and Littleton's, *An Introduction to Corporate Accounting Standards* first published in 1940 but reprinted very many times until the 1980s. Later, these attempts developed into commissions to committees and then officially designated research divisions of the professional bodies to develop "guidelines for theory development" and later to independent organisations specifically charged to develop these "theoretical statements". As these attempts changed there was a change in the function of the published pronouncements; there was a change in their authoritative scope. That is, the pronouncements became parts of a system of regulation which has expanded from recommended statements of best practice for members of professional bodies to a complex international system of mandatory practices. Regulation has been substituted for theory—it has become the "required theory" underlying accounting practices.

In the latter years of the 1960s, there were several factors that coalesced to change the face of accounting research and theorising. These included the development of doctoral programmes in accounting where students were given rigorous training in quantitative research methods, neoclassical economic and finance theory and the use of new information processing technologies (especially the use of computers). Coincident with this was the growing availability of large scale stock market data bases initially funded by the business community with a demand for business research to be directly related to extant business practices. Out of this background emerged the seminal articles by Ball, R. and P. Brown "An Empirical Evaluation of Accounting Numbers" (1968) and Beaver, W.H. (1968), "The Information Content of Annual Earnings Announcements" which were discussed in Gaffikin 2005. From here the "floodgates opened" and neo-empirical research in accounting, including positive accounting theory, was born and became the dominant form of research publications in the accounting literature. As indicated above, this research was embedded in a neo-liberal ideology and unshakeable belief in the power of the market to solve almost all of society's problems.

At the same time, there were major changes in attitudes to research in the social sciences. There was a growing acceptance of the belief that positivistic scientific epistemology was inappropriate for the social and human sciences. Because these disciplines involved human and social aspects, a belief in the possibility of objective, value neutral research methodologies was held to be impossible. Thus, there was a rejection of the long held modernist belief that methods described as those employed in the natural sciences, and held to be the highest standards of intellectual rigour, could be universally applied to all disciplines. Alternative methods were sought which had underlying ontological and epistemological positions different to the positivist programme that had dominated Western thinking for so long. There was a greater awareness that understanding the processes of knowledge required, in turn, an understanding of language and cultural and societal factors which had previously been disregarded in the process of theory development.

Neo-empirical accounting research emerged from a conservative business school environment typically found in the USA. It is steeped in the neo-liberal ideology in which the rights of individuals and the market mechanism are fundamental beliefs. That is, neoclassical economics, which is central to this ideology, seeks to explain the actions of independently minded individuals interacting with one another only by means of market competition; the rights of individuals are supreme and their interaction is achieved through the operations of the market mechanism. The only constraints are provided by nature. Therefore, there is no need of social institutions or government intervention—no form of externally imposed regulation. This implies the individual or decision-making unit has full knowledge of what is best for her, him or it (see Klein 2007). Neoclassical economics is a cornerstone of the monetarism espoused by Friedman which came to dominate what is referred to as Chicago School (The University of Chicago) economics in which almost all of the early neo-empiricist accounting researchers were trained. These acolytes spread this belief to other institutions as they took up academic positions in them. So effective were they in doing this that it has become a dominant style of research in accounting which has been enforced by business schools (on their students and new colleagues) and many journal editors (despite being contrary to the underlying tenets of the movement—individual choice!). This dominance has led to it often being described as *mainstream accounting research*.

3   Accounting as Social Science

As indicated above, accounting can be regarded as a social science. Lowe and Tinker, some time ago, clearly agreed with this:

> Accounting as a discipline and accountancy practice should…be regarded as integral parts of social science and social behaviour. (1989, p. 47)

So did Hopwood:

Accounting is coming to be regarded as an interested endeavour. Rather than being seen as merely residing in the technical domain, serving the role of neutral facilitator of effective decision-making, accounting is slowly starting to be related to the pursuit of quite particular economic, social and political interests (1989, p. 141)

The social nature of accounting had been recognised much earlier. For example, in the 1930s the unusually named DR Scott had published a book (1931) which stressed the historical and social character of accounting. Scott argued that society and its institutions (including the economic) constantly change and if accounting is to be a useful in providing an understanding of "economic realities" then accounting should be considered from a much broader (than a merely technical) perspective. Scott developed his argument on the basis of an economic theory different to most others of the time—the institutional economics espoused by people such as his colleague, economist Thorstein Veblen.[2]

Since that time there have been many others who expressed similar views. In an article published in *The Accounting Review* one of the co-authors of one of the most significant auditing monographs,[3] Mautz (1963), argued that accounting met the accepted defining criteria of a social science. Therefore, educators and researchers needed to re-evaluate their approach to the discipline to recognise the rigorous demands of social science and practitioners could then make more use of research results.

Accounting has understandably been predominantly concerned with the financial reporting of corporations as they are the primary form of business organisation in most societies. There have been many who have demonstrated the significant changing nature of the corporation over the last two hundred years. Perhaps one of the most well known early works to address this issue was *The Modern Corporation and Private Property* by Berle and Means.[4] Ladd argued that these changes had resulted in a "new orientation of business responsibilities and new concepts of appropriate business activities and objectives" (1963, p. 2). This re-orientation meant that the responsibility of corporate management went beyond the satisfaction of stockholders' interests to include a much greater social responsibility yet "accounting concepts and procedures are firmly based on the premise of the paramountcy of the ownership interest" (p. 2). To Ladd, accounting had clearly not kept pace with business developments partly as a result of "inertia—from and unwillingness to change procedures which have worked in the past" (p. 31). He cogently argued for a change in accounting method to reflect that very great changes in the nature of the corporation and its activities. This included the added dimension of corporations as "good citizens" (in societies).

Another person to argue for the need for a fundamental change in accounting was the English accounting theorist, Trevor Gambling, described on the dust jacket of one of his books as someone who had "earned the reputation as an awkward and original thinker in a field where original ideas are not much expected". In his *Societal Accounting*, he attempts to reconcile traditional accounting theory and practice with broader economic accounting such that accounting could be used to signal wider social issues and concerns (based on accepted social indicators). Gambling's major contribution to accounting thought has been to draw attention to the limitations of traditional narrow accounting thought. In many respect, like some of the others discussed above, he was ahead of his times as it is only recently that many of his ideas have been seriously taken up by other accounting researchers and theorists. There are many others than those mentioned above who have recognised the need for a change in the way accounting is perceived if it is to properly serve the needs of a more broadly defined set of users.

One thing that becomes clear is that accounting, as a social science, has to reflect the changed ontological, epistemological and methodological assumptions that occurred in the other social sciences. As reflected in the Hopwood quotation, there has been a growing realisation that accounting is not merely a neutral, technical endeavour but reflects the economic, social and political viewpoints of those who are engaged in its practice. Morgan was even more explicit:

> …accounting researchers are obliged to face the dilemma that they are really social scientists…and to keep abreast of new developments and be competent at their craft, they will need to devote serious consideration to the nature and practice of what counts as good social research (1983, p. 385).

In recognising the social nature of accounting it becomes clear that the positivist, natural science approach to accounting research is not appropriate—it had been rejected in most of the social sciences. The naïve assumptions (such as value free propositions and efficient markets) in the neo-empirical approach are insufficient to reflect the "real" role of accounting in society and in fact, suggest Lowe and Tinker (1989, p. 48), "may be disastrous for the practical usefulness of financial accounting statements". And Tomkins and Groves (1983) argue that adopting an approach other than that claimed to be used in the natural sciences may bring accounting theory and practice much closer together.

From Table 1 it can be observed that neo-empirical research (as employed in—and dominating—mainstream economic and accounting research) is based on a realist ontology. Neo-empirical researchers believe there is an objective reality that exists independent of any human agency (human involvement). Following on from this then, human beings are viewed as interacting with this reality passively—that is, they do not create the reality but have to live around it. Therefore, human behaviour can also be objectively observed—its response to "a real world". Accordingly, how humans respond to external stimuli (their surroundings and their attempts to exist therein) can be predicted. Consequently, social order is controllable; societies can be managed. The means by which knowledge of such an idealised world is obtained follow from this ontological position.

In respect of knowledge claims, empiricism and testability become paramount. However, as Christenson (1983) has demonstrated, in accounting research, there is considerable confusion as to the process of empirical testability. Causality is a problematic notion and complex causal modelling and extensive multivariate analysis, designed to demonstrate causality, have had not proved otherwise. It remains a highly disputed concept.

Table 1 (Some) assumptions of neo-empiricism

Ontological
That there is an objective external reality
That human behaviour is purposive
That social order controllable
Epistemological
Observation is separate from theory and is for either verification or falsification causality

Thus, there are many problems with attempting to employ the methodology of the natural sciences in *any* discipline let alone one so obviously a social phenomenon as is accounting. This led Mautz to argue that the discipline must "accept more responsibility for value judgements" because while the accountant may attempt to adopt an impersonal disinterested viewpoint "the truth is that his (sic) data include value judgements and for him to ignore such considerations is to ignore important aspects of his data" (1963, p. 319).

4   Alternative Research Methodologies

Accounting researchers have drawn on a number of theoretical frameworks that have been used in the social sciences. There is a logical difficulty in attempting to describe or classify some of these because "by definition" they defy classification.[5] However, for pedagogical (instructive) purposes a description of what they involve can be undertaken. They mostly employ **qualitative** rather than **quantitative** research methodologies and this is sometime taken as a defining characteristic. To varying degrees, they are concerned with notions such as language, culture, interpretation, reflexivity, discourse, text, power and history.

A simple difference between quantitative and qualitative research is presented in Table 2. One of the major steps in quantitative research is the identification of variables. The variable is central to quantitative research—it is a concept that varies—quantitative research uses the language of variables and is primarily concerned with the relationships between them: the aim is to establish the casual structure of the variables. This is possible because of the realist ontology adopted. Therefore, variables are representations of the real world. They can be objectively determined so the aim is to observe them and establish a causal relationship the outcome of which can then be generalized to other (similar) situations (sets of variables). The researcher remains separate—outside from—the data in order to maintain objectivity. In qualitative research the interest is in the processes and the behaviour of individuals in response to an ever changing—a dynamic—world. The researcher tends to be intimately involved with the subject under investigation and acknowledges the

Table 2 Research differences

Quantitative research	Qualitative research
Seeks facts and causes of phenomena	Concerned with understanding actors' behaviour
Uses controlled measurements	Naturalistic and uncontrolled observation
Claims objectivity	Subjective
Seeks verification/confirmation through reduction	Seeks to discover and explore
Is outcome oriented	Process oriented
Claims to use hard and replicable data	Claims data is valid and rich
Produces generalisable outcomes	Is nongeneralisable
Assumes stable reality	Assumes a dynamic reality
Assumes an outside perspective	Assumes an insider perspective

Adapted from Blaxter et al. (2002), *How to Research*, Oxford University Press

subjectivity of the results, which are presented as of potential interest to others but which are not generalisable because each situation will differ.

For example, a capital markets study will be a quantitative research study. Stock market data are collected and summarised (reductionism) to indicate evidence or confirmation of an hypothesis and the claim will be that this—stock price reaction—will always occur in similar situations. The researcher will be committed to a realist ontology where the reality is represented by the stock market prices. The same study can be replicated in another stock market with the same results which will (again) confirm the results of the original study as a representation of the hard reality. On the other hand, a behavioural study could examine stock market prices that result from the actions of a group of investors in certain situations. The results would not be generalisable as these circumstances and the behaviour of individuals would never be identical. The qualitative study may well involve quantitative data (stock prices) but the significance of them would not be the same as in a quantitative study where they are considered to be hard, objective facts.

This example is a simplified one and the differences between the research methods are likely to be much more significant. Whereas there is one methodology that is privileged in quantitative research this is not so in qualitative research. The methodology in quantitative research will be positivist scientific method (probably some form of hypothetico-deductivism). In qualitative research, many forms of research (research methodologies) exist each regarded as the most appropriate in differing situations. Some of these will be as equally positivist as neo-empirical research, some will retain the essential characteristics of modernism, some will totally reject modernist precepts and some will be based on very radical philosophies. In the accounting literature there is a plethora of adjectives describing some so called theory adopted in a particular research study. Many of these are epistemologically extremely dubious!

5   Subjectivity Versus Objectivity

A key underlying assumption in whether quantitative or qualitative research approaches are adopted is a belief in the neutrality of the resulting knowledge; in other words, is it possible to be objective when researching? As indicated above, quantitative researchers believe objectivity is not only desirable but possible (and even essential!). On the other hand, qualitative researchers believe objectivity is not possible, therefore, the researcher should acknowledge her or his subjectivity. These positions can be contrasted in terms of the classification of assumptions described (and terminology employed) in earlier discussion as indicated in Table 3.

In accounting the neo-empirical research adopts the objectivist position and this research is sometimes referred to as *nomothetic* which means that it sets out to establish law-like generalisations. For example, research examining the effects on share prices of an accounting method choice will claim the result as something that will always occur in similar situations. Such research will tend to use large numerical data bases from which

Table 3 Underlying theoretical assumptions

Objectivist view		Subjectivist view
Realist	Ontology	Constructionist
Positivist	Epistemology	Anti-positivist
Intended to create law-like Generalisations	Methodology	Intended to provide specific non-generalisable descriptions
Mainly quantitative	Appropriate methods	Qualitative

conclusions will be drawn out. The original research will be replicated using different data bases and after the conclusions have been confirmed sufficiently they will form a scientific law. On the other hand, a subjectivist approach is sometimes referred to as *ideographic* which simply means that the focus will be on cultural and historical particulars and a description will be made on the basis of the researcher's interpretation (for example, a case study). As indicated, in subjectivist, qualitative research no method is privileged over others so there are many variations some of which will now be discussed.

6   Accounting Theory as Critique

In the accounting literature there has been a tendency to refer to any non-positivist accounting research as critical theory research. Unfortunately, this has also been true in much of the social science research literature and it can refer to a range of theories that take a critical view of society and social processes. Thus, the term has been used quite loosely and can have a very broad meaning. This is sometimes unfortunate because, strictly speaking, **critical theory** refers to the work of a group of social theorists and philosophers called the Frankfurt School working in Germany early in the twentieth century. Their work was continued in the rest of the twentieth century by one their students, Jurgens Habermas, and, in turn, some of his "students" have carried on (and developed and extended) his work to the present day.

(Frankfurt School) Critical theory has hugely influenced social theory, largely as a result of the work of Habermas. It is complex, so any summary here is highly simplified. Some essential characteristics of critical theory are its rejection of positivism as the sole arbiter and generator of knowledge largely because of its lack of self-reflection which leads it to reduce epistemology to a crudely mechanical methodology. Self-reflection requires the acceptance of the importance of human agency in the creation of knowledge. This is necessary because, without it, oppressive power relations are hidden. Crudely speaking, if you do not think about what and how you know things, your actions may be simply reflecting what others want you to do, so you would be reinforcing the dominant and powerful views that exist in society. For example, accountants believe they are acting in a value natural and objective manner and reporting on economic reality. However, it is important to know what "reality" is being represented—what attributes are being measured and how they are presented in a financial report. Through self-reflection one is freed from past constraints (such as dominant ideology and traditional disciplinary boundaries) and thus critical theory is emancipatory.

Critical theory was initially strongly influenced by Marxism but "developed in contrast to the crude materialist, determinist and allegedly scientific Marxism that had become orthodox in the Soviet Union" (Simons 2004, p. 2); rather, it developed what is often referred to as Western Marxism. Despite Habermas' rejection of the scientism of the positivist program (which he believed was only one of many forms of knowledge) he continued to remain attached to the idea of modernity and viewed the Enlightenment as a worthy but unfinished project.

There have been several accounting studies advocating critical theory. Perhaps the strongest advocate has been Richard Laughlin who was later joined by Jane Broadbent as well as other co-authors. A more general case for accounting as a critical social science was made by Dillard (1991) who uses the work of two prominent accounting authors to demonstrate the benefits of a more critically oriented approach. To this extent, Dillard's work is a good summary of some of the key considerations in adopting a critical theory approach. On the other hand, Laughlin's work is more directed to employing critical theory to solve "real life" accounting problems and issues. His work examines accounting systems in organisations and he makes a case for a critical theoretical understanding. Previous, technical positivist attempts to understanding the operation of accounting systems, he argues, have not contributed to our understanding of accounting in practice (Laughlin 1987). Many of the advantages of using critical theory were seen by its advocates as most suited to accounting in organisational contexts and can, therefore, be said to have improved our understanding of management accounting.

In his later work Laughlin, especially that written with Broadbent (and in her own work), turned attention to accounting and accountability in the public sector (under the New Public Management). Their work extended their use of critical theory to include the later work of

Habermas which examined issues of law (juridification) (for example, Laughlin and Broadbent 1993) and communicative action (how understanding is communicated).

In a later paper Laughlin (1999) argues that there are at least four important characteristics of critical accounting. First, it is always contextual. That is, it recognises that accounting has social, political and economic consequences. Secondly, it seeks engagement, which means that it is always undertaken to change (improve) the practice or profession of accounting. Thirdly, it is concerned at both micro (individuals and organisations) and macro (societal and professional) levels. And, fourth, it is interdisciplinary in that it engages with and borrows from other disciplines. Thus, critical accounting is much more broadly concerned with the practice, profession and discipline of accounting than traditional studies.

The work of Prem Sikka clearly illustrates Laughlin's characteristics. He is somewhat of a political activist in accounting and has taken issue with the profession for not having more forcefully aided the fight against issues such as money laundering, fraud and transnational crime and professional body insouciance (indifference to many of these issues) (see, for example, Sikka and Wilmott 1997).

Critical accounting has influenced research in many countries and in 2002 a special issue of the journal *Critical Perspectives in Accounting* was devoted to "Critical Accounting in Different National Contexts". In this issue Broadbent asks why we need critical accounting. Her response argues that in a world pondering over the allocation of scarce resources "We need to ensure the use of accounting does not represent certain interests at the expense of others". And, she continues, "Constructions and interpretations of accounting information must pay attention to the cultural imperatives of those it seeks to control as well as those who are using it as a tool of control" (p. 444). Thus, critical accounting seeks to unmask the often hidden interests of those who would seek an unjust allocation of a society's scarce resources so that all interests in society can benefit. The spectacular corporate collapses and fraud seen early in this century—and before—clearly indicate that such maladjusted interests exist.

7   Accounting Theory as Interpretation

It should be remembered that classifying the alternative methodologies is antithetical to the essence of many of these alternatives. Classification usually presumes a fixed basis for categorisation—a fixed "reality"—which is the very thing many of these alternative methodologies reject. Therefore, it is restated that such grouping is done for instruction to those unfamiliar with the philosophical complexities involved with these alternative views of how knowledge is created. While the Frankfurt School critical theorists adhered to a belief that there are foundations to knowledge, those who strongly hold a social constructionist ontology deny that it is possible to determine such foundations (or, in fact, their existence at all). This has important implications for how knowledge is perceived. Foundational beliefs are taken as certain and beyond doubt—they exist independent of any human agency. Constructionists believe that knowledge is produced by human societies: we do not discover knowledge so much as make or construct it. We create concepts, models and systems to make sense of our experiences. Accounting, of course, is a good example of a constructed knowledge. However, our experiences are constantly changing so our constructions have also to change. Accounting in the nineteenth century is different from accounting today. Our understanding is dependent on how we interpret our changed experiences. Such interpretation does not exist in isolation but depends on societal norms, social demands, language and other considerations. There is a range of research and theory approaches that concentrate on interpretation. These approaches, like critical theory, are necessarily interdisciplinary. For example, it is important to understand the political, social, legal, economic, linguistic, cultural and historical context of interpretation. There are many variations of these interpretive approaches to knowledge some dating back to the just before and after the turn of the twentieth century as in the work of Max Weber (a major classical sociologist) and Edmund Husserl (founder of the movement known as modern phenomenology). Other approaches include those known as philosophical hermeneutics, ethnomethodology and symbolic interactionism. While these are rather complex sounding titles, they all share the aim of attempting to enrich peoples' understanding of the meaning of their actions in order that they can change their worlds through such self-understanding.

One of the earliest works to draw attention to the potential of improving accounting practice by using interpretive theories in accounting is that by Tompkins and Groves (1983). Their central intention was to argue that accounting research had traditionally uncritically borrowed models and methods from the natural sciences which were very often inappropriate for studying accounting practice. "Naturalistic" rather positivist approaches would result in a better understanding of accounting practice. This is a strange use of the term "naturalistic", but others have used it and it is intended to relate to non-positivist methods including some interpretive approaches, namely ethnomethodology, symbolic interactionism and transcendental phenomenology.

Ethnomethodolgy seeks to determine how people go about their daily practices (hence the title of the Tompkins and Groves paper!) and what "rules" lead them to derive meaning from their actions: how do they make sense of their world. Therefore, Tompkins and Groves suggest that it might be applied to determine how accounting influences the actions of others or understanding of events. Accounting "rules" are determined from accounting practice; that is, the significance and meaning of the rules emerges from how accountants (and others) interpret and act on them.

Symbolic interactionism was developed at the University of Chicago and is similar to ethnomethodology except it is more concerned with the actions and interpretation of individuals. Meanings do not reside in objects but emerge from social processes. Individuals act on the basis of the meaning they attach to things and this becomes evident as they interact in society. Tompkins and Groves suggest this research approach could be used to study financial control. By examining how various individuals respond to financial decision information it will be possible to identify "key people" who are aware of "the larger macroeconomic determinants of behaviour" (Willmot 1983, pp. 394–5).

Interpretive approaches have been used more in management accounting than financial accounting. Chua (1986, pp. 615–617) provides an excellent example of the significance of an interpretive approach by comparing two pieces of research related to budgetary processes: one a traditional approach, the other an interpretive study. She demonstrates that whereas in the former the "budgetary control system" is seen to exist as "a facet of reality that is external to the world of the researchers" in the latter the budget is "symbolic not literal, vague not precise, value loaded not value free"—in fact, the budget shapes reality through the meanings people place on it and how it influences their actions within the organisation. In another article Chua (1988) shows that management accounting research has used the interpretive approach and points out some difficulties with its use in accounting. In the paper Chua explains the difference between symbolic interactionism and ethnomethodology and suggests some new insights over the traditional approaches to management accounting research that the interpretive perspective brings and how it can continue to be used to advantage.

8   Accounting Theory as Structure

Early in the twentieth century a French linguist, Ferdinand Saussure, developed an approach to the study of language which concentrated on underlying structures which he argued underpinned all language. Later, his approach was adopted to apply to a form of social analysis in which the structures of social organisation took priority over the human aspects. The name **structuralism** refers to the methodological and theoretical approaches to culture and social analysis which assumes societies can be studied in a manner similar to a Saussurian structural analysis of language.[6] Therefore, the theoretical study of accounting would concentrate on the "structures" on which accounting is built. The emphasis would be on the unobservable but structural relations between conceptual elements to expose the essential logic that binds the "structures" together. The object of investigation is studied as a system.

The accounting profession's search for GAAP and then a conceptual framework can be viewed as a "structuralist" approach—however, this has never been consciously considered. Nevertheless, the search for the essential logical elements that bind accounting systems and result in financial reports being prepared is very similar to the structuralist approaches taken in other disciplines (notably anthropology).

However, economic theory has been greatly shaped by structural thinking. In fact Saussure "took economic theory as *the* model for his highly influential semiotic theory of language" (Macintosh 2002. p. 9); and one commentator has said that "Economics, be it noted, is the structural study par excellence" (Sturrock quoted in Macintosh 2002, p. 9). Because accounting has relied so heavily on economic theory, Macintosh goes on to demonstrate that it too has been heavily structuralist and he illustrates this with agency theory: "Agency theory is prototypically structuralist" (2002, p. 10). However, few accounting researchers have consciously seen their research as being directly shaped by structuralist theory.

9   Accounting Theory as Language

The cliché—accounting is the language of business—has been around for many years. Knowledge can only exist through communication and language is the most common media of communication. Therefore, to understand how knowledge of accounting is established it is useful to study language. And if accounting is the language of business, this becomes even more important. However, the study of language is highly complex and there are several ways by which this may be undertaken. The ancient Greeks saw language as comprised of signs and a common word for the study of language, **semiotics** (or semiology in Europe), has Greek origins (interpreter of signs). Other terms used in the study of language include linguistics, rhetoric, hermeneutics and discourse analysis (and many others).

About the same time that Saussure, in Europe, was developing his semiotics, his theory of language (which was to become the basis of structuralism as mentioned above), one of America's most important philosophers, Charles S. Peirce, was creating his semeiotic, his theory of signs which he believed extended to a whole system of philosophy. Peirce was also the founder of **pragmatism**, the theory that holds that a proposition is true if holding it to be so is practically successful or advantageous. He also greatly influenced the development of logic.[7]

Saussure was primarily concerned with the development of a theory of language central to which is the notion of the **sign** which is, in turn, a combination of the paired elements of *signifier* and *signified*. The signified is the concept (for example of "catness") and the signifier is the sound image (the sound—spoken—or sound image, "cat"). One thing to note is that the sign is arbitrary; that is, they can differ from one language to another. It is also important to realise that not only are different signs used in different languages this leads to users of those signs thinking differently: the influence of culture which shapes the way people think. In "accounting language" the word asset is a signifier and the concept of asset ("assetness") is the signified but just what is the concept of asset has been the subject of debates for many years. It can be future economic benefit but on what basis is this measured?

As indicated in the previous section, Saussure's work was primarily intended as a theory of language. However, it was taken up by other disciplines such as anthropology by Levi-Strauss, psychology by, for example, Lacan and in many other disciplines including economics. The ultimate aim was to determine the underlying structures. Two other features become evident. First, if underlying structure are sought then the individual (human) is no longer relevant because she or he exists independent of the underlying structure. Secondly, such analysis is *synchronic*, it is ahistorical—structures are independent of time. The opposite of synchronic is *diachronic*—changing over time. Structuralist analysis, therefore, ignores history and development. To some scholars who originally subscribed to structuralism, this was a naïve understanding of how language actually works. Therefore, they rejected structuralism (as it stood) and sought ways of extending or changing it to make it more reflect the fact that language changes over time depending on how individuals and societies interpret the signs contextually. These scholars came to be known as **poststructuralists** (because they came "after" structuralism), but they developed their ideas in very different directions and all rejected the label. The common features of their work are first, a recognition that language is viewed as the medium for defining and contesting social organisation and subjectivity. Secondly, they hold that individuals are knowing and rational subjects and are necessary for the creation of knowledge.

These views can be compared to the mainstream positivist notion of knowledge. To the positivists knowledge was comprised of uncovering the elements of a real world and formulating the knowledge in a neutral theoretical language. The individual therefore is only a "device" for uncovering this knowledge. The poststructuralist view is quite the opposite—it is through language that knowledge comes into existence and this language is comprised of a socially derived and accepted set of signs which every individual interprets in their own way. Two of the most well known of the so-called poststructuralists are Michel Foucault and Jacques Derrida. Foucault turned to history, Derrida took language and meaning to the extremes, breaking it down, deconstructing it into its barest elements. There are several studies in accounting which have adopted a Foucauldian approach but very few who have employed Derrida's analysis.

Foucault was one of the most influential thinkers in the second half of the twentieth century and still exerts a strong influence on theory in the social sciences and philosophy, so it is little wonder that some accounting researchers have been attracted to his ideas. Foucault is a notoriously difficult person to categorise, but there are three phases of his work. In the first, he referred to the method as archaeology and it displays his structuralist roots although it has moved well beyond Saussurean structuralism. The method in his second phase he called genealogy and, in the third phase it is described as being concerned with discourse ethics. Themes found in his work include history, language, discourse, subjectivity and power.

Although he is often seen as a historian, Foucault's history is not that of the traditional historian. Rather than seeing continuous progress and development he looks for disruptions. He does not seek out simple causality but rather seeks to determine the factors that made social institutions and beliefs possible throughout history. Comprehending these helps understand where we are now. Therefore, in accounting, those that have employed his approach have mostly resorted to historical study. Stewart says that Foucault has:

> ...provided a theoretical schema within which to problematize and question accounting, and break away from a unidimensional picture of its development. Accounting has not been created just by capitalism or industrialization

or ownership or organizational structures. Rather, the emergence and functioning of accounting in its various contexts is a complex phenomenon, due to the interplay of many different influences (1992, p. 61).

Stewart cites several works in accounting that have employed a Foucauldian perspective—they have examined such topics as the professionalisation of accounting, the emergence of administrative power, the development of cost accounting in the UK and the role of the state in developing accounting. The aim in Foucauldian studies is to see "accounting as transcending time and space considerations and developing into a set of supra-historical accounting techniques that will be better able to meet the needs of the organization" (p. 58). Hoskins and Macve (1986) have argued that double entry bookkeeping emerged from the context of disciplinary techniques developed by medieval monastic orders. Furthermore accountability and control received an impetus from the development when universities developed a system of monitoring student performance through examinations—"a power-knowledge framework" (p. 123). Loft (1986) demonstrated that the professionalisation of British accounting was influenced by the need for cost accounting during the First World War. There are numerous other studies in accounting that employ a Foucauldian perspective.

10   Accounting Theory as Rhetoric

Rhetoric is an old discipline dating back to the fourth century BC. Its contemporary meaning is the art of persuasive communications and eloquence. Some time ago Arrington and Francis pointed out that every author attempts to persuade (or perhaps seduce) readers into accepting his or her text as believable (1989, p. 4). It is important to note here the terms author, persuade and text. The author will subjectively select the rhetorical devices she or he feels will be most useful in persuading others of a particular position. The word text is widely used and means more than a written document—it now refers to many other things in which meanings are being conveyed such as films, speeches, advertisements, instruction manuals, conversation and, of course, financial reports.

Mouck (1992) demonstrated how positive accounting theorists employed several rhetorical devices to persuade others that positive accounting theory is the only way to truth. Rhetoric is most commonly encountered in literary studies. However, in 1980 McCloskey published a paper in the *Journal of Economic Literature* entitled "The Rhetoric of Economics" which spawned a new movement in economics, consistent with similar movements in other social sciences, which has seen rhetoric as an alternative to positivist epistemology.[8] Whereas epistemology is based on a set of established abstract criteria, rhetoricians hold that truth emerges from within specific practices of persuasion.

One of McCloskey's primary aims was to draw the attention of economists to how they use language and how language shapes their theories. Similarly, Arrington and Francis seek to show how "the prescriptions of positive theory function linguistically rather than foundationally and cannot purge themselves of the rhetorical and ideological commitments" (1989, p. 5). Arrington and Francis move beyond a simplistic analysis of language and draw on the work of Derrida to make their case. Derrida's work is highly complex and extends the discussion of signs and language to extremes. His concern is with deconstructing the text. That is, unpacking the text "to reveal, first, how any such central meaning was constructed, and, second, to show how that meaning cannot be sustained" (Macintosh 2002, p. 41).

Largely due to its complexity and its controversial reception by some quarters of the academic community there have been very few studies in accounting drawing on Derrida's work. However, his central message that language cannot be the unambiguous carrier of truth that is assumed in many methodological positions should never be forgotten or overlooked. As with other poststructuralists, Derrida saw all knowledge as textual—comprised of texts. Derrida believed that all Western thought is based on centres. In this sense, a centre was a "belief" from which all meanings are derived; that which was privileged over other "beliefs". For example, most Western societies are based (centred) on Christian principles. Perhaps it could be stated that accounting is centred on capitalist ideology. Deconstruction usually involves decentering in order to reveal the problematic nature of centres. So, it could be argued that many accounting problems arise from problems with capitalism—it has changed so much over the years that it is hard to be precise. Another example could be the way so much accounting thought has been centred on historical cost measurement. In many discussions over the years, until recently, it has been "assumed" that historical cost is the basis for measuring accounting transactions. Therefore, advocates of alternative measurement bases were viewed as if they were heretics.

11   Accounting Theory as Hermeneutics

Hermeneutics is the study of interpretation and meaning and, as a formal discipline, was initially used several hundred years ago by biblical scholars interpreting biblical texts. In the mid nineteenth century it became a discipline for the critique of the attempted application of (natural) scientific method to the human sciences. Hermeneutics, as the interpretation of meaning of texts and other works (for example art works) was the recommended methodology. In the twentieth century hermeneutics was extended from an epistemology to an ontological position, that is, extended from focussing on knowledge to being (existence) thus making it a valuable approach to understanding social organisation such as accounting. This extended view of hermeneutics usually results in it being referred to as philosophical hermeneutics. However, the focus is still on language, meaning and interpretation. It is also common to find reference to the hermeneutic circle. This is because interpretation inevitably requires understanding through language and the interpreter comes to the matter under consideration with an historical understanding—language is developing over time. Thus, it is inevitably circular— "new" understanding is based on previous (historical) understanding: meaning is grasped from past interpretations because that is all there is. Consequently any value-free inquiry is not possible and truth only exists as shared interpretations—knowledge can only be regarded as knowledge when it is accepted by an audience.

There was, in the social sciences, a growing interest in interpretation and this has been referred to as the hermeneutic turn. Boland (1989) has argued that this hermeneutic turn was also reflected in accounting research. To him, this was manifest in the work of those researchers wishing to break from the subjectivist-objectivist dichotomy and who saw the renewed interest in subjectivist approaches to theory as having considerably more potential for a fruitful understanding of accounting.

12   Different Accounting Theory

The discussion above has provided a brief view of some of the many different approaches to accounting theory that have developed over the years.[9] While they are very different in specific orientation they do share some characteristics. Collectively they are often referred to as critical studies. While the term critical theory has a specific meaning it is also used to refer to a heterogeneous set of theories that generally can trace their roots to the European rather than the Anglo-American philosophical tradition. Embracing an alternative philosophical framework has served as an antidote to the sterile positive prescription of the mainstream methodological hegemony. Critical accounting studies take a wide range of stances from highly conservative to (a few) extremely radical but they all have the intention of trying to improve accounting practice by making accountants more aware of the wider social, political and economic consequences of their practice. And, as Morgan has indicated "the more one recognizes that accounting is a social practice that impacts on a social world, the less appropriate natural science approaches become (1983, p. 385). Critical studies, then, are united in opposing the use of positivist scientific methodology in pursuing accounting research because it specifically excludes any human or social considerations under the misguided apprehension of producing objective knowledge. One consequence of accepting accounting as a social practice is that it imposes greater responsibilities on accountants to be more aware of the social implications of their practice, In order to do this many researchers have turned to research undertaken in the social sciences as exemplars for appropriate methodologies.

A dominant theme in critical studies is an awareness of the role of language in producing knowledge. It is through language that accounting is constructed and constructs a reality Thus, many of the alternative methodologies have been dependent on the many and varied approaches to the philosophical study of language such semiotics, linguistic analysis, rhetoric, hermeneutics and deconstruction. Language has always been a central concern of philosophers but there was, according to American philosopher, Richard Rorty (1992), a "linguistic turn" in many disciplines in the later half of the twentieth century. There has been a far greater awareness of the importance of language to the creation and understanding of knowledge. Thus, language plays an important role in most of the methodologies developed in the social sciences and, consequently, in most critical accounting studies.

Other important elements commonly encountered in critical accounting studies are cultural consciousness and awareness of the importance of history. Languages are created in societies and the impact of culture is crucial to any understanding of a language. Languages change over time despite the position adopted by Saussure and positivists; there are no universals. Associated with this realisation is that societies are regulated by rules and conventions so it is important to determine how individuals interpret the rules and conventions. Critical accounting researchers have taken up many of these issues in their work. Interpretation is a very individual exercise so subjectivity and reflexivity are important considerations of human behaviour.

All of these epistemological considerations are reflected in the fact that most critical accounting researchers practice and advocate qualitative research methods. Therefore, the research undertaken by critical accounting researchers is going to be very different to that practised by neo-empirical researchers. Both critical and neo-empirical researchers are attempting to determine a "truth". In order to make some evaluation of these truth claims, it is important to appreciate from where the researcher is coming.

13   Accounting Theory: Who Cares?

As I assume my status of old man, I find I am quite disillusioned with accounting—the practitioners, the professional bodies and even the academic world. I have observed and have, in the words of Yeats, got to "know what old books tell". A working life seeking a form for accounting theory now seems to have been one of "chasing rainbows" as "the gold" at their end is a myth. However, I am certainly not alone as the community questions the practitioners and profession as the following examples indicate:

> The most-cited concern was the worry that the [accounting] profession is dropping behind not just its clients, but the world as a whole, seeing its core services rendered obsolete by technology, their value to clients plummeting. (Hood 2015)

And:

> Technology thought leader and educator Doug Sleeter described it very simply: "The [accounting] profession is struggling to maintain its relevance in the eyes of clients. As a whole, the focus is still too much on compliance services and not enough on going deeper with client engagements". (Hood 2015)

And:

> And not everyone was as confident in the strength of the profession's reputation. Two leaders with a broad international perspective were worried about very specific concerns. "In the wake of sporadic corporate failures over the past decade or so, the most important issue has been demonstrating the value of accountants to society," said International Federation of Accountants CEO Fayezul Choudhury. "There has been a crisis of confidence in the profession itself". (Schneider 2015)

This is, of course, not surprising given the practicing accounting communities' insouciance (and even, at times antagonism) to long-term considerations which, in turn, is not surprising given their close association with the dominant mainstream, neo-liberal, economic thought. However, what is more disturbing is the similar position adopted by the academic accounting community (NB this is a generalisation). This community has provided little or no resistance to the "darker" developments that have taken place in academe such as the rating and rankings games being foist on what was once an independent community on which much societal progress had depended (cf. Singh 2008). To me, this has shaped the development (??) of contemporary accounting research activity. For example, journals which were once at the forefront of innovative and socially conscious research have degenerated (perhaps we can say had "a conservative turn"?) into even publishing a "special issue" on causality, a cornerstone of the positivism favoured by the neo-liberal economics community. What is more, Nietzsche argued against its existence (Nietzsche 1968, pp. 293–297). I also note a preponderance of so-called management accounting research which *to me* has always indicated an alignment with the economic/business hegemony: disappointing for a journal that once was at the cutting edge of innovative and philosophically and socially aware accounting thought.

Does it matter? Of course it does. Plato held the position that theory and politics were always intertwined and Zizek echoes this with his claim for the "mobius strip of politics and economy" (2006, pp. 246–252). The interaction of politics and theory is dramatically illustrated in the anti-theory movement in US literary studies in the 1980s and 1990s (and probable still). The 1980s started with a growing interest in theory as manifest in the work of several philosophers from France (e.g. Foucault, Derrida, Krisheva) but also other places, and there resulted many changes to curricula, pedagogy and research. However, these positive developments were abruptly restrained at the end of the decade by "the institutional cultural equivalents of Reaganism" the agents of which "were and still are often the same as the 'anti-theory' agents within the universities and the media" (Bove 1992, p. x). This is the same Reagan who is reputed to have claimed that his favourite and most influential authors were Hayek and Milton Friedman. I often wonder whether the anti-theory movement in US literary studies circles is echoed in the near absolute domination in accounting of positive research.

There are probably many other reasons. The "theory wars" in literary studies in the USA, but also in the UK, as they are commonly referred to, are quite difficult for outsiders to understand. The difficulty revolves around the meaning of theory. The meaning that one has is almost certainly preconceived—it is based on one's epistemological proclivities. This is often unfortunate as many new (or not so new) would-be authors would attest. One of the most used reasons by editors or reviewers of a paper submitted to a journal for its rejection is that there is a lack of (a) theory! This has resulted in the "invention" of a plethora of so-called theories. They are used as justifications of observations and claims made. Despite this, however, there are several policy positions which do not seem to rely on "theoretical" justifications. For example, theoretical justifications for accounting regulation are rare. This implies that "theory" has been replaced by "regulation", a political process. Needless to say, the implications of this are enormous as it reinforces again the link between economics and politics. In an economically globalised world where we are told international financial reporting standards are necessary to facilitate the free flow of capital, it raises questions as to whose interests are privileged? This echoes the problems with the euro crisis and Greece in terms of policies being promoted by those "in power" (cf Douzanis 2013). The "solutions" proposed by the EU reflect neo-liberal ideology.

Unfortunately, a long-held notion in accounting is that we operate free from bias—value free, neutrality and therefore objectively. This is straight positivism; that the knower can stand outside the world and see it for what it is. The non-positivist approaches to knowledge creation have shown this to be total myth. This rejection has implications often overlooked. From Table 3 above it can be noted that this would entail adopting (social) constructionist ontology. Researchers have to be aware that in studying subjects who then become the objects of the study they are studying in part themselves (e.g. where researchers study a social entity, e.g. accountants, they are studying a group that could include themselves as part of the entity). Thus, they are "saying something" about themselves. This is known as the need for reflexivity in research (see Steier 1991). With the expansion of technology this has become a little more complex. People are largely now virtual selves—a virtual self being a "person who spends a good deal of time online and working with computers and who acquires her identity from this activity" (Agger 2004, p. 179). The consequences are obvious as reflected in the quotations from Hood above. It has changed the world with which accounting and accountants have to deal. Mickhail has studied an example of this phenomena, which was called metacapitalism. He states:

> MetaCapitalism change strategy has exacerbated the intensity and frequency of structural resource allocation changes within the largest global

corporations and this has amplified their market volatility. The Big 4 audit firms, who monopolise 85 per cent of the global audit market, have failed their agency role within the financial markets. The findings from the analysis of nearly 70,000 corporations reveal that they have failed to recognise the complexity of the new technological structural changes to resource allocation, even after analysing their conventional analytical methods, which should have signalled the problems.

Charitably, this suggests a failure to comprehend how technology has changed our world; more sceptically, it suggests deliberate manipulate of the circumstances for self-interest!

Some have argued that the advent of the computer has changed the meaning of research and theory. The speed and capacity, they suggest, has meant less need for theory as data (the quantity of) replaces information. I am not sure about this as the receivers of the data would still need some means of processing the data to make it "useful". Nevertheless, from the quotations, it seems that accountants are having difficulties with this change.

Another matter to consider is that accountants have expanded their sphere of interest to encompass social and environmental considerations. Admirable as this is, there does not appear to be many situations in which accountants are assisting in easing the issues and problems that have arisen but rather have placed an emphasis on analysing what corporations are reporting rather than doing. The problems persist. Some have suggested this, like the impact of new information technologies, has changed the nature of that which accountants deal and requires a re-think by accountants. For example reconsider the definition of capital as suggested by Gleeson-White (2014).

Of course, the source of many the world's economic woes stem from the unrestrained power now yielded by transnational corporations. Despite the substantial evidence mounting as to how these corporations abuse their positions, governments seem impotent (see, for example Bakan 2004; Corporate Reform Collective 2014).

There are many economic ills facing the world not all of which are attributable to accounting or accountants or solely the responsibility of them. However, accounting and/or accountants are seen to be implicated in many. Much of the work of the critical accounting movement over the years has made visible what was previously invisible. That is, it has highlighted the importance of accounting to the operation in so many aspects of modern economies. Thus, accountants are no longer able to claim to be innocent presenters of value neutral, objective information: in choosing which information to present, they have had to make conscious choices. As such they are likely to align themselves to certain interests. In almost all situations this has been business interests, including large corporations. As much of the critical accounting movement has demonstrated, this alignment has been with the dominant economic power holders in societies—the economic hegemony. This power has been created by politically supported economic interests within an accepted system. This system is, of course, capitalism which has, over time adopted various poses and names, for example late capitalism, financial capitalism, consumer capitalism, fast capitalism etc. Whatever name is used, by definition, capitalism is about capital; its accumulation and preservation. In recent times there has been an increase in how the word capital can be used. Gleeson-White (2014) has argued that there are six capitals—financial, manufactured, intellectual, human, social and relationship and natural, the first two being the traditional. It is difficult to see how intellectual (as the term has been used) is much different from the traditional. It is the same notion of ownership of property but rather than tangible property, as is "manufactured", it generally refers to what was once called the "intangible" property (assets) of organisations. The other three seem to be examples of the "neo-liberal project" in which "Everything is subjected to a particular economic logic" and what is "At stake is not 'the market economy' but the 'market society' " (Douzanis 2013, p. 29). Gleeson-White is first to admit that it is "part of the conceptual basis for 'value creation' " quoting Druckman who says "For too long businesses have expressed themselves only in the narrow form of financial transactions" (2014, pp. 190–191).

Gleeson-White is arguing for an expansion of the role of accountants which in itself is admirable. This is that to which I was alluding at the start of the paper—what Tony Lowe and I believed was wrong with accountants—the narrow intellectual vision. In looking at the emergence of the critical accounting movement I sought to determine the "origins" of that sort of reasoning. This brought me to look at the works of Heidegger and Neitzsche. The latter believed that the knowledge of the world was best expressed in literature, the former that it existed in poetry.

In order to make a fairer society our knowledge must go well beyond that demanded by the "neo-liberal" project. Its central element, the capitalist system, has not worked well. The troubled world lurches from crisis to crisis with solutions generated by the system itself—such is the power of the rhetoric of its adherents. For example, the recent global financial crisis was generated by the abuses of the system by sectors of it who were then "rewarded" by the system (through its power over governments). This was not the first time this had occurred as any historical investigation would surely show. A survey of free market capitalism around the globe found an average of only 11% across 27 countries "feel that capitalism works well. An average of 23% feel that capitalism is not sustainable and that an entirely new economic system is needed" (Gilman-Opalsky 2011, p. 20; for those who believe in statistical significance!). One does not have to be a "raving radical" to believe that capitalism has failed. Nobel prize winning economist and one time Chief Economist of the World Bank, Joseph Stiglitz says that "Markets have clearly not been working in the way that their boosters claim" (2012, p. xi). To him, "A more efficient economy and fairer society will come from making markets work like markets—more competitive, less exploitive—and tempering their excesses. The rules of the game matter not just for the efficiency of the economic system but also for distribution. The wrong rules lead to a less efficient economy and a more divided society" (2012, p. 267). Stiglitz was not the first to arrive at these conclusions. Over a century ago the novels of Charles Dickens, Zola and many others writers had brought it to the world's attention in their works.

Can accountants cope with all this? Can we produce knowledge—theories—that lead to a more efficient and fairer society? Do we care? Will we continue to seem to be only interested in self gain and seek alliances with those with economic power that have resulted in gross wealth inequality? Despite the advice of Hill and Newa (2004), I think I will side with Nietzche and resort to literature—perhaps continue reading Proust—De Botton (1997) says it will change my life.

Notes

1. The following sections builds on and updates material that was published previously as Chap. 7 of Gaffikin (2008).
2. Institutional economics concentrates on the social systems that constrain the exchange and use of scarce resources. In doing so it explains the emergence of alternative institutional arrangements and their influence on economic performance through controlling access of economic actors to resources by various means. Over the years it has been championed and debated by many very important economic theorists who have continued to try and develop a theory of economic institutions.
3. Mautz, R.K. and H.A. Sharaf, 1961, *The Philosophy of Auditing*, Florida: American Accounting Association.
4. Berle, A.A. and G.C. Means, 1932, *The modern corporation and private property*, New York: Macmillan Co. Both authors have also written several other subsequent works individually and with other co-authors.
5. This is because some of them rely on a (social) constructionist rather than a realist ontology. That is, by definition they do not exist as independent objective entities.
6. Although most usually associated with Saussure, structuralism most likely originated in (the then) Czechoslovakia and Russia.
7. Pragmatism is the archetypical American philosophy and has been dominant in American thinking. While it has probably influenced many accounting theorists one who admits to being an adherent is Barbara Merino. Most of her research has been in history of accounting, see, for example Merino (1989).
8. McCloskey later expanded the argument and published a book by the same name: *The Rhetoric of Economics*, University of Wisconsin Press, 1998. Other economic rhetoricians have criticized that work as being too conservative and deferential to neoclassical economics and have greatly extended the arguments of the rhetoric of economics movement; for example, James Arnt Aune's *Selling the Free Market: The Rhetoric of Economic Correctness*, New York: The Guilford Press,

2001. Arnt Aune's argues, like Mouck (1992) that neoclassical have resorted to various rhetorical devices to sell the idea of the free market but he goes further by demonstrating that politicians and commentators (including novelists) have also rhetorically contributed to the selling of liberalisation, privatisation, globalisation and transnationalisation (ie the free market and minimum political intervention) economic (and social) policies (see Stiglitz 2012).

9. There have been many other proposed approaches drawing on the work of philosophers or social theorists. For example, labour process studies initially drew on Marxian ideas; actor network theories draws on the work of French techno-science Latour, Callon and others; post colonial theoretical studies point out the legacy of colonisation; and there have been historical sociological studies—the new history. See Lodh and Gaffikin (1997).

Informings for Control and Emancipatory Interests in Accounting: New Reflections on the Intellectual Emancipation of Accounting and the Possibilities of Emancipatory Accountings

Jim Haslam

We are all tainted by the society or the world of which we are part. That is, we are all (variously) lacking in ethics and all too much of what we do collectively and (variously) individually helps only reproduce and even helps to build the problematic complex of which we are part. Given that, how can we hope to do much to put in order—making a positive difference in terms of global well-being and social and individual fulfilment— a world shot through with problems? Ashby (1956) in his *Introduction to Cybernetics* and Laclau and Mouffe (2001, the first edition being 1984) in their *Hegemony and Socialist Strategy* share in common, beyond all the differences, a concern to grapple with this question. This observation in one sense highlights something that (today) appears rather mundane— who does not now (in *some* sense) see the world (and themselves situated in it) as problematic, would want it changed for the better and would like

J. Haslam (✉)
School of Management, University of Sheffield, Sheffield, South Yorkshire, UK

© The Author(s) 2016   **143**
J. Haslam, P. Sikka (eds.), *Pioneers of Critical Accounting*,
DOI 10.1057/978-1-137-54212-0_8

to find a way how? One might ask: Are not the differences between these writers more important? Yet there is here also an indication of a continuity that invites more reflective consideration on the differences (and similarities). Such an invitation is rather strengthened than it is negated in the logics of theoretical developments of recent decades.

For a critical perspective, these theoretical developments, notably as labelled post-structuralism, postmodern theory and post-Marxist theory, have opened up new possible significances in the past, including through new, more considered and in a sense more sympathetic interpretations of past thought. The retrospective thus takes on added significance. Here I reflect on Tony Lowe's contribution in relation to a substantive aspect of organizations and society that interested him hugely: communicative systems of informing for control. In offering these new reflections, I seek to suggest an appreciation of Lowe's contribution that sees it in relation to a critical commitment to a radical progressiveness aimed at countering our problems, 'putting things in order'. In this respect, I make connections to the perspective on and articulation of the construct emancipatory accounting that I have worked on with my collaborator Sonja Gallhofer over several decades. If control (and accounting) and emancipation may appear to many to stand uneasily in juxtaposition (Gallhofer and Haslam 2003; Gallhofer et al. 2015), my concern is to offer new reflections that bring out a continuity of radical and engaged commitment in Lowe's work that remains inspiring today, while, related to this, promoting in particular senses the relevance and usage, perhaps implicitly, of the construct emancipatory accounting.

Taking up this task is potentially overwhelming, given the subject matter that is integral to it, and something like an outline argumentation is presented here, and to some extent in a style beyond academic orthodoxy—with an emphasis on the concern to inspire further work in terms of thought and praxis. Aside from references included in the list at the end of the book, I include here a bibliography to encourage further reading. And I develop some of the argumentation not so much by reference to Lowe's published works but especially by reference to various interactions I had with him during his life over several decades (variously as a student, collaborator and more generally). I believe that Lowe had a more significant impact on the appreciation of accounting, and its interface with management/control conceived broadly, more precisely through such interactions—inspirational and challenging—and what they engendered than he did through his own actual authored works (notwithstanding the significant contribution of these). I begin below by reflecting on Lowe in relation to what in Gallhofer et al. (2015) is termed the delineation of accounting, before then adopting a more chronological framing that discusses Lowe's interest in systems and cybernetics, the sense in which his work develops in alignment with Habermas and then Lowe's reflections on postmodern thought. I go on to elaborate on the Gallhofer and Haslam collaborative work on emancipatory accounting before returning to the appreciation of Lowe's work and concluding.

1 The Delineation of Accounting in the Context of Control

Tinker (1985, p. 206) notes that 'subjects like accounting must be invented or created'. We can ask, what is the general concept of which the accounting of accountancy practice is but one possible manifestation? Lowe was concerned to address this question, which later, in work with colleagues, I have articulated in terms of the issue of accounting delineation (see Gallhofer and Haslam 1997; Gallhofer et al. 2015). In addressing it (not directly—in keeping with what was often Lowe's style), it is not that Lowe regarded the accounting of accountancy practice, including the accounting of the accountancy profession that many of his students aspired to join, as of limited interest as a focus itself. Far from it—he sought to promote the better understanding of (and engagement with) the functioning of this accounting through in-depth critical interpretive research and reflection; and in his own definitions of 'accounting' for purposes of empirical study he often tended towards what many would see as conventional or mainstream definitions (I remember a discussion Sonja Gallhofer and I got engaged in with Lowe about this in the context of drafting the only publication, beyond conference proceedings, in which Lowe and I are together amongst the co-authors, Lowe et al. 1991). Yet he was also concerned to go beyond established and conventional views in respect of accounting's delineation (especially given his critical way of viewing the accountancy profession), most evidently in his more normative or prescriptive theorising.

In the 1970s, his theorising here reflects an interest in two aligned areas: systems and cybernetics. His theorising reflects an appreciation of systems thinking. This was informed by a reading of systems theory and also an appreciation of sociological reflection on systems of communication and control—sociological reflection evident, for instance, in the works of Talcott Parsons and Niklas Luhmann (albeit that these latter works stand in an antagonistic relation). Parsons' work on social systems theory was a key reading for his more junior colleagues back in the 1970s and I can remember Lowe enjoying a meeting he had with Richard Münch, a scholar of Parsons, during a research trip to what was then the Federal Republic of (West) Germany. And his theorising here reflects an interest in the aligned discipline of cybernetics, which Norbert Wiener (1948) had defined as the science of communication and control in animal (more especially the human) and machine. I first engaged with Tony Lowe in 1978 when a student at the University of Sheffield. The main text Lowe recommended on the theoretical component of the first year accounting course at Sheffield in 1978 (along with some key articles and book chapters on systems thinking and general systems theory) was W. Ross Ashby's (1956) *An Introduction to Cybernetics*. Lowe described it as a book for life—and in doing so reflected an interest in the individual and communicative systems of informing within the context of organizations and society. It was here deemed important to appreciate that every good regulator of a system must be a model of the system to be controlled (see Conant and Ashby 1970) and Ashby's law of requisite variety and its relevance to control—its relevance to what Stafford Beer termed the viable system (see Beer 1959, 1966, 1972, 1979). Beer (several of whose books were promoted for reading by Lowe on the Sheffield course) and Lowe were both at Manchester Business School (along with Tony Tinker, whom Lowe advised as a doctoral student and who joined the staff at Sheffield in the 1970s). It appears clear that Beer, who did much to translate cybernetics and biological analogy to the case of the management of organizations, including State-led organizations, influenced Lowe's thinking, while from the wider field of systems and cybernetics Klir and Ashby were especially influential.

Thus, Lowe addressed a general idea of information-for-control. Information was an important resource of a system and its usage supported the control of the system in its environment. Information could also be communicated to the environment to help create a more favourable environment for this control project. Regarding the dimension of accounting delineation here, one can appreciate the abstraction involved. There is no clear boundary to information-for-control, which clearly goes beyond, while including, what is typically understood as conventional accounting. In my own work reflecting on accounting delineation (notably in Gallhofer et al. 2015, but see also Gallhofer and Haslam 1997), the difficulties of articulating the most general delineation of the accounting concept are elaborated. These difficulties are well illustrated in the efforts of Gray et al. (1996) in relation to the articulation of social accounting as a broad form of accounting delineation (see Gallhofer et al. 2015). How do you deal with the issue that accounting in its most generic form, encompassing all its possibilities and actualities, would tend, for instance, towards including all recording, all informing, all communication? The Gallhofer et al. (2015) study articulates the generic notion but then points to its very limited usefulness in itself, beyond its role in broadening vision—although that in itself is significant. The important point to appreciate here, emphasised in Gallhofer et al. (2015), is that there are many *accountings* (the plural that was popularised in the academic literature by Anthony Hopwood but can be found also in Samuel Johnson's dictionary, where reference is made to its usage in South's sermons of the early eighteenth century—the reference is also taken to the Oxford English Dictionary) that can be geared to many purposes of control (such as the control of a particular organization). And here I would stress the need to appreciate, as critical writers, the variety of particular accounting delineations—one should be concerned to promote, for instance, the study of what some call counter accounting as well as conventional accounting as dimensions of the accounting focus. Following the logic of this, one should also stress here the importance of attempting to clarify or appreciate the particular meaning of accounting as used in particular argumentation on or implicating accounting—reflective analysis indicates that so diverse are the possible meanings that it may be that those engaged in a debate on accounting may come to talk past each other without realising that a key source of their disagreement is their differing in their very conception of accounting. The key point here is that a broad delineation of accounting was implicit in Lowe's appreciation of the notion information-for-control—and this reflected a questioning approach and a broad vision of the accounting focus.

2   Control

Let us begin this section by quoting a number of texts from the literature on cybernetics and systems control. These quotes give a flavour of the influences upon Lowe from his reading of this literature:

> 'The social system tends to be dominated by images...especially of the future, which act cybernetically, constantly guided by perceived divergences between the real and the ideal' (Boulding 1974, p. vii)
>
> '...possibly the model of the world as a great organization can help to reinforce the sense of reverence for the living which we have almost lost' (von Bertalanffy 1955, p. 83)
>
> '...for an understanding not only the elements but their interrelations as well are required' (von Bertalanffy 1968, p. xix)
>
> 'No classification is complete and perfect for all purposes' (Klir 1967, p. 69)
>
> 'These two spectactular transitions, of human agony and societary collapse, are connected—not only at the phenomenal level, but in their etiology...In the most extraordinary way, we are blind to this' (Beer 2004, p. 774)
>
> 'The systems approach begins when first one sees the world through the eyes of another' (Churchman 1968)

The artist A.R. Penck's *Ein Mögliches System* would appear to portray notions of control through cybernetic systems with at the very least a touch of irony. To the extent that Lowe conceived of communicative systems of informing as informings for control in normative or prescriptive terms, does Lowe undermine a radical progressive commitment? How can a critical researcher advocate 'control'? Does Lowe's earlier systems orientated work at least reflect an overly conservative position?

In reflecting on the idea of a Management Control System, Lowe (1971) delineates a prescriptive framework or model of organizational control. He clearly sees something positive, then, in the notion of control. Is that very seeing already problematic? In relation to control considered as a generic idea and in terms of its possibilities, it is not difficult to legitimize at least in part the notion of control. If we were to see control as absolutely negative then the idea of looking after younger members of society, implicating in some way their control in the name of their protection and development, would be seen as abhorrent, let alone the (related) caring for adults (a category that in relation to children is readily deconstructed—child/adult is not the equivalent of debit/credit in double-entry book-keeping but a much fuzzier and overlapping delineation with important aspects of continuity, see Gallhofer and Haslam 1995). All forms of planning along with all notions of 'self-control' would here be thrown out. While one may be concerned to see negative dimensions of a particular phenomenon of or particular kinds of control, and impugn crudely positive and overly simplistic appreciations of control processes linked to problematic goals or problematic outcomes, it would seem particularly eccentric to banish control as a prescriptive notion altogether.

In the realm of theorising prescriptively control systems and communicative systems of informing for control, Lowe (who, incidentally, found art works, music and poetry, as well as academic thoughts, very inspirational) was concerned to highlight features of control in a quite generic sense, reflecting a tendency in systems theory. The same may be argued of Beer. Beer, moreover, was not only an inspiration for Lowe but explicitly sought, as evident in his work in Allende's Chile in the early 1970s, to promote in practice what he saw as more *emancipated* forms of work. Beer put enormous effort into developing a cybernetic system of governance of the state sector in Allende's Chile at the behest of the socialistic government. And in this context he promoted the autonomy of workers in terms of decision-making and control at all levels of the organization, taking issue with the dominant models for organizational functioning of the 'real world socialism' of the time. Beer was devastated at the coup in 1973 that led to the overthrow of Allende and the manifestation of Pinochet's more authoritarian regime (see Beer 1974, 1975, 2004). It would not be unreasonable to conclude that Lowe's vision of control—even in the more naïve and conservative aspects that one can indicate in Lowe's earlier systems orientated work, more especially with the benefit of hindsight (*subter*)—is close to Beer in being aligned to a radical progressive commitment (see Checkland's 1999, reflections on criticism of systems thinking in management—systems is here seen in terms of a method that in its 'soft systems' form is more interpretive than positivist and can be aligned to critical work). In any case, Lowe was hardly an unquestioning ally of the establishment.

Lowe's critical perspective is not as evident on the face of it in his own published works as it is in published works of those he influenced. For instance, in respect of some of his colleagues at Sheffield in the 1970s: Tony Tinker's work developed from an interest in systems and cybernetics in a more Marxist direction, while Tony Puxty and Richard Laughlin developed their interest in systems and cybernetics into an Habermasian perspective on accounting. Lowe did not try to dissuade these developments among his close collaborators and in the case of the Habermasian work he saw the strong linkages to systems theory: Parsons' action theory can be and is widely seen as a social systems theory and as having substantive influence on both Habermas and Luhmann (who in turn influenced each other) (see Giddens 1984). In conversations with the author in the 1980s, Lowe gave a further, more substantive indication of an alignment to Habermas' intervention in the German Critical Theoretical tradition by expressing strong sympathy for the position of Bernstein (1976). This is one of the closer and more substantive indications we have of Lowe's emancipatory interest in a German Critical Theoretical sense: Habermas' own writings and the (Habermasian) Critical Theory of society as articulated by Bernstein (1976) had considerable appeal. His collaborative publications reflecting this appeal (and involving Puxty and Laughlin—and Wai Fong Chua who graduated the year before myself at Sheffield and went on to do a PhD there) substantively reflected (consistent with Bernstein 1976) the Habermasian commitment to a critical and interpretive theoretical and methodological perspective and approach, including the Habermasian critique of positivism. On the same research trip to German cities referred to earlier, I recall Lowe making great efforts to contact Habermas by phone to request an interview about modes of regulation (I can remember hearing a very busy Habermas decline the request).

The influence of Parsons and then the alignment with Habermas is consistent with Lowe here holding on to a quite optimistic and arguably problematic view of the possibilities for society of openness, communication, democracy and organization. His earlier work had tended to imply that organizational survival (at a particular operational level) entailed societal satisfaction (echoing what some have termed 'structural functionalism' in Parsons)—this view is clearly problematic, implicating especially excessive optimism (cf. Sikka et al. 1995). He subsequently seems to be at least aligned to a Habermasian vision of the possibilities of communication in society. Again, some critical commentators would see an excessive optimism in this context too (even if its emphasis on communicative possibilities is already a pragmatist development).

Yet one should here note that any commitment today to the idea that society or the world can be practically made a better place may be reasonably argued to be optimistic and to some extent would rest on a less than sure scientific foundation. Granted, there are differences between the (even) more pragmatist post-Marxist positions, which are today coming to influence the formulation of critical perspectives, with their emphasis on an imperfect agonistic democracy and departure from Habermasian deliberative democracy, and the Habermasian perspective that Lowe's developing systems orientation was ostensibly more aligned to (taking on board here aspects of Habermas' critique of systems theory). Yet, as Gallhofer et al. (2015) point out, there are substantive similarities between these positions more especially *in their practical operationalisation* and they share an affinity to the extent of their explicit attachment to the view that the world can, through the intervening act, be made a better place.

Aspects of the postmodern and post-structuralist theoretical developments in the social sciences and humanities, perhaps especially as received in the literatures of accounting and management, must partly have depressed Lowe. His was an acute sense of how society's relatively rich and powerful, if they are not beyond being persuaded of nobler paths, seek to make use of anything—including theory—to place obstacles in the way of socially progressive change where it is perceived to undermine their position. More generally, he was acutely aware of how suffering and problems might go unnoticed through a failure of perspective (he thought the reproduction of the human species was at risk in a way that was not being taken seriously).[1] He would have seen these phenomena at work in dimensions and applications of the developments. At the same time, in conversations I remember with him in New Zealand, Lowe appeared to appreciate something of how social constructivism, more modest epistemological claims (and the further alignment to going beyond positivism) and an emphasis on at least going beyond a crude universalism to appreciate other cultures could also serve to open up new vistas of possibility. It is difficult to substantiate this further, but this is my sense of a number of conversations I had with him. This latter position has congruence with the position reflected in the work I have been developing with Sonja Gallhofer and other collaborators, a position which especially is informed by a reading of the post-Marxist theorising of Ernesto Laclau and Chantal Mouffe. I turn to articulating this below.

3   On the Construct of Emancipatory Accounting

In pursuing the interrelated tenets of critical theoretical work, I have sought—in relation to accounting as a differentiated universal that thus encompasses a variety of actual and potential information-for-control practices—to understand the actual, envision a state of betterment and otherwise engage to change things (see Held and McGrew 2000; Gallhofer and Haslam 2003, 2008). Expressing the tenets in this way helps to indicate a continuity with the contribution of Lowe delineated above. There are three key aspects of the nature of the theoretical intervention I have sought to help mobilise. One, the concern to elaborate accounting delineation, I have already given some attention to and the only point I would perhaps usefully add here is to note my view that accounting delineation itself has an emancipatory dimension in expanding the boundary around what might be mobilised as and studied as accounting (the reader might here recall Lowe and Tinker's, 1977, not unrelated concern to promote the intellectual emancipation of accounting). A second key aspect is the particular developing of a mode of social analysis of accounting through a critical interpretive theoretical lens.

This second aspect is best articulated by reference to the third that is highlighted here, the mobilising of a construct emancipatory accounting, which is done in each of the three dimensions of critical theoretical praxis (*supra*), including in the developing of a mode of social analysis of accounting. In work with Sonja Gallhofer, my interpretation of the construct emancipatory accounting has shifted over time as we have come in our theorising to reflect developments in the social sciences and humanities that have been elaborated as postmodern, post-structuralist and post-Marxist. Let us then turn to how I have interacted over emancipatory accounting over time.

Leaving aside for the moment the question of accounting delineation, the meaning linked to the construct emancipatory accounting is clearly dependent upon how emancipation is understood. While emancipation is typically understood in terms of liberation from some variety of repressive set of chains, and is a common idea in Marxist and critical theoretical discourse, it has a possible broader connotation. If we understand the concept of emancipation in very broad and loose terms, something like the improving of society, or, to put it slightly more boldly, the transforming of a community, society or the world to a better place—which we shall see is the kind of understanding we have been approaching recently in discourses of emancipation—then emancipatory accounting would be a similarly broad and loose construct. And in that case, while there would be disagreement over the agenda or agendas which an emancipatory accounting or emancipatory accountings is or are to serve, there would be quite general agreement over the very idea of emancipatory accounting, quite general agreement over notions such as accounting being a practice to engender social betterment. Indeed, beyond the explicit construct emancipatory accounting, broad and loose articulation of accounting as being meant to contribute to 'social welfare' or to serve the 'public interest' is common in texts on accounting policy, academic and professional. While the existence of different views on what constitutes betterment, welfare and the public interest problematises the efficacy of the mere expression of such commitment, as does the manifest difference between expressing a commitment and how and to what extent it is followed through in real world operations, emancipatory accounting in this broad sense may at least in terms of its possibilities be generally acceptable. Yet, as we shall see, the construct has a contemporary significance.

Today the construct emancipatory accounting needs to be seen in terms of the mobilising of accounting in relation to a range of legitimate identities, interests and projects and in terms of the aligning of these in a progressive movement. Emancipatory accounting here becomes significant including as instances of (albeit imperfect) accountability and communication in agonistic democratic processes. Further, accounting in this respect needs to be seen as a process that functions on a continuum—it is more or less emancipatory or socially progressive in its impact; conversely more or less oppressive—its impact reflecting its shifting elemental dimensions in relation to contextual dynamics. And consistent with that logic, at any moment in time any accounting practice may be theorized as a mix of emancipatory and oppressive forces. This appreciation of emancipatory accounting, which goes beyond the monochromatic mobilizing of the construct by Tinker (1984, 1985) (whose appreciation is a particular interpretation of Marx based on Ollman, 1976), is built up in the critical theoretical perspective of Gallhofer and Haslam (e.g. Gallhofer and Haslam, 1991, 2003; Gallhofer et al., 2015), which becomes a new pragmatist and post-Marxist articulation. This is elaborated below.

Gallhofer and Haslam (1991) draws upon Frankfurt School theorising and Walter Benjamin to theorise accounting as a multi-dimensional and mutable phenomenon operating in a dynamic context. Accounting is theorised in terms of dynamic and interacting dimensions or elements: not just in terms of its content but also in terms of its users and usages—and also its form and aura (how it is perceived in society). The study indicates how the same basic accounting content can change in its effects, becoming conflict-enhancing (and emancipatory) rather than conflict-resolving for the socio-political order, with a change in the other elements (and/or the wider context of which accounting is part)—in Gallhofer and Haslam (1991) there is considerable emphasis on the aura dimension, with some attention given to users/usages and form. The conclusion that conventional accountings can be emancipatory is here an important development. Gallhofer and Haslam (1995) later problematises the view of conventional accounting as negative (a common treatment in critical and social accounting discourses) by referring to establishment concerns about the promotion of accounting publicity (making things visible to the public) for banks in the 1830s—what today we typically consider as a conventional accounting was then seen by some as ushering in a radical democratic revolution threatening established authority. Gallhofer and Haslam (2003) goes on to embrace a continuum thinking that theorises accounting as more (or less) emancipatory on a continuum (see Prokhovnik 1999) in a contextual dynamic.

Gallhofer and Haslam (2003) and Gallhofer et al. (2015) reflect an appreciation of developments in post-structuralist, postmodern and post-Marxist thought that is especially influenced by the thought of Laclau and Mouffe. Here, the situated position of the political act renders the act less than pure, encouraging caution and (new) pragmatism (there is advocacy of a particular reflexivity here—see Connolly 1987—and also a reflexivity involving deconstruction, see Andersen 2003). At the same time, this situation is linked to or is suggestive of the potential of a variety of emancipatory projects—a focus on labour is not abandoned (cf. Žižek 2000) but it is added to in terms of a variety of (progressive) projects. According to Laclau and Mouffe (1987, p. 80): 'We are living...one of the most exhilarating moments...a moment in which new generations, without the prejudices of the past, without theories presenting themselves as "absolute truths" of History, are constructing new emancipatory discourses, more human, diversified and democratic. The eschatological and epistemological ambitions are more modest, but the liberating aspirations are wider and deeper...'. Taking this form of plurality seriously (Gallhofer et al. 2015) means a challenging attempt to align the various projects, interests and identities (see also Brown 2009; Brown and Dillard 2012). This challenge and the variety of pursuits implicate emancipatory accountings, none of which are 'pure' forms. In Gallhofer et al. (2015), it is noted explicitly that the logic of this thinking is that an accounting at a given moment in time is a mix of (unstable and dynamic) emancipatory and repressive forces. What this thinking also implies is new vistas of possibility for pragmatic emancipatory projects implicating accounting that are of more general appeal. Emancipatory accounting's continuing relevance is here emphasised, while its tendency to mundaneness ought not to counter its role to secure social betterment (see ŽiŽek 2014). In these ways, then, the refinements in social and political theory point to an affinity with earlier discourses seeking 'control' for betterment and the overcoming of problems.

Through the lens of these developments, is it reasonable then to consider Lowe's conceiving of informings-for-control as phenomena positioned for the achieving of individual, organizational and social goods as in line or readily aligned with the emancipatory interests of a new pragmatism? As noted, the above is only an outline argumentation in this regard.

4   Concluding Comments

I recall Tony Lowe in the early 1980s once opining that so little research had been done on accounting. Of course, since then there has been a dramatic explosion in accounting research (albeit that Lowe would have found much of it as problematic—in, for instance, its over-simplifications and conservatism). But against the vision of communicative accountings functioning together (in communities and societies, in our world) and in interaction with the context in which they are embedded—a context that would here include also silent, confidential spaces—so as to contribute (in relation to wider socio-political dynamics and praxis) to emancipatory and progressive developments for the individual and (global) society, Lowe's words continue to resonate.

(With thanks to Sonja Gallhofer, Richard Laughlin and Prem Sikka).

5   Further Reading

Ackoff, R. (1974). *Redesigning the future: A systems approach to societal problems.* New York: John Wiley.

Ackoff, R., & Rovin, S. (2003). *Redesigning society.* Stanford: Stanford University Press.

Adler, P. (Ed.). (2009). *The Oxford handbook of sociology and organizational studies: Classical foundations.* Oxford: Oxford University Press. Oxford Handbooks Online.

Adriaansens, H. (1980). *Talcott Parsons and the conceptual dilemma.* London: Routledge Kegan Paul.

Alvesson, M., & Willmott, H. (1992). On the idea of emancipation in management and organization studies. *Academy of Management Review, 17*(3), 432–464.

Alway, J. (1995). *Critical theory and political possibilities: Conceptions of emancipatory politics in the works of Horkheimer, Adorno, Marcuse and Habermas.* Westport: Greenwood Press.

Arrington, C., & Watkins, A. (2002). Maintaining 'critical intent' within a postmodern theoretical perspective on accounting research. *Critical Perspectives on Accounting, 13*(2), 139–157.

Benhabib, S. (1986). *Critique, norm and utopia: A study of the foundations of critical theory.* New York: Columbia University Press.

Benhabib, S. (1992). *Situating the self: Gender, community and postmodernism in contemporary ethics.* Cambridge: Polity Press, in association with Oxford, Blackwell.

Bernstein, R. (1976). *The re-structuring of social and political theory.* Oxford: Blackwell.

Bogdanov, A. (1913–17). *Bogdanov's Tektology,* (Collection of Bogdanov's work, edited in 1996 by P. Dudley). Hull: Centre for Systems Studies.

Boulding, K. (1956). General systems theory: The skeleton of science. *Management Science, 2*(3), 197–208.

Boulding, K. (1966). The economics of knowledge and the knowledge of economics. *American Economic Review, 1*(6), 1–13.

Boulding, K. (1985a). *Human Betterment.* London: Sage.

Boulding, K. (1985b). *The world as a total system.* London: Sage.

Boyd, A., Brown, M., & Midgley, G. (1999). *Home and away: Developing services with young people missing from home or care.* Hull: Centre for Systems Studies.

Bronner, S. (1994). *Of critical theory and its theorists.* Oxford: Blackwell.

Butler, J., Laclau, E., & Žižek, S. (Eds.). (2000). *Contingency, hegemony, universality: Contemporary dialogues on the left.* London: Verso.

Calhoun, C. (1995). *Critical social theory: Culture, history and the challenge of theory.* Oxford: Blackwell.

Cooper, D., & Hopper, T. (Eds.). (1990). *Critical accounts.* London: Macmillan.

Crowe, M. (1996). Heraclitus and information systems. *Systemist, 18,* 157–176.

Derrida, J. (1994). *Specters of Marx: State of the debt, the work of mourning and the new international.* New York: Routledge.

Eagleton, T. (2001). Ideology, discourse and the problems of 'post-Marxism'. In S. Malpas (Ed.), *Postmodern debates* (pp. 79–92). Palgrave: Basingstoke.

Flood, R. (1990). *Liberating systems theory.* New York: Plenum Press.

Fuchs, P., & Luhmann, N. (1994). Speaking and silence. *New German Critique, 61,* 25–37.

Gabardi, W. (2001). *Negotiating postmodernism.* Minneapolis: University of Minnesota Press.

Gallhofer, S., & Haslam, J. (1993). Approaching corporate accountability: Fragments from the past. *Accounting and Business Research, 23*(91a), 320–330.

Garnham, N. (2000). *Emancipation, the media and modernity: Arguments about the media and social theory.* Oxford: Oxford University Press.

Gilliers, P. (1998). *Complexity and post-modernism: Understanding complex systems.* London: Routledge.

Gregory, W. (1996). Discordant pluralism: A new strategy for critical systems thinking? *Systems Practice, 9,* 605–625.

Habermas, J. (1978). *Knowledge and human interests.* Cambridge, MA: Polity Press.

Habermas, J. (1987a). *Theory of communicative action.* Cambridge, MA: Polity Press.

Habermas, J. (1987b). *The philosophical discourse of modernity: Twelve lectures.* Cambridge, MA: MIT Press.

Habermas, J., & Luhmann, N. (1971). *Theorie der Gesellschaft oder Socialtechnologie.* Frankfurt: Suhrkamp.

Harnden, R., & Leonard, A. (Eds.). (1994). *How many grapes went into the wine? Stafford beer on the art and science of holistic management.* Chichester: John Wiley.

Holub, R. (1991). *Jürgen Habermas: Critic in the public sphere.* London: Routledge.

Jackson, M. (2000). *Systems approaches to management.* New York: Klüwer/ Plenum.

Jay, M. (1993). *Downcast eyes: The denigration of vision in twentieth-century french thought.* Berkeley: University of California Press.

Klir, G. (1969). *An approach to general systems theory*. New York: Van Nostrand Reinhold.

Klir, G. (2005). *Uncertainty and information: Foundations of generalized information theory*. Hoboken: John Wiley.

Kolb, D. (1986). *The critique of pure modernity: Hegel, Heidegger and after*. Chicago: University of Chicago Press.

Laclau, E. (1990). *New reflections on the revolution of our time*. London: Verso.

Laclau, E. (1992). Beyond emancipation. *Development and Change, 23*(3), 121–137.

Laclau, E. (1996). *Emancipation(s)*. London: Verso.

Latimer, D. (Ed.). (1989). *Contemporary critical theory*. New York: Harcourt Brace Jovanovich.

Laughlin, R., & Lowe, E. (1990). A critical analysis of accounting thought: Prognosis and prospects for understanding and changing accounting systems design. In D. Cooper & T. Hopper (Eds.), *Critical accounts* (pp. 15–43). London: Macmillan.

Lehman, C. (1992). *Accounting's changing role in social conflict*. New York: Markus Wiener.

Lehman, C., & Tinker, T. (1987). The 'real' cultural significance of accounts. *Accounting, Organizations and Society, 12*(5), 503–522.

Lowe, E., & McInnes, J. (1971). Control in socio-economic organisations: A rationale for the design of management control systems. *Journal of Management Studies, 8*(2), 217–227.

Lowe, E., Puxty, A., & Chua, W. F. (1989). *Critical perspectives in management control*. London: Macmillan.

Mingers, J. (1980). Towards an appropriate social theory for applying systems thinking: Critical theory and soft systems methodology. *Journal of Applied Systems Analysis, 7*, 41–50.

Mingers, J. (1995). *Self-producing systems: Implications and applications of autopoiesis*. New York: Plenum.

Moeller, H. -G. (2012). *The radical Luhmann*. New York: Columbia University Press.

Mouffe, C. (1993). *The return of the political*. London: Verso.

Mouffe, C. (1998). Radical democracy: Modern or postmodern? In A. Ross (Ed.), *Universal abandon?* (pp. 31–45). Minneapolis: University of Minnesota Press.

Münch, R. (1987). *Theory of action: Towards a new synthesis going beyond parsons*. London: Routledge Kegan Paul.

Nederveen Pieterse, J. (1992). Emancipations, modern and postmodern. *Development and Change, 23*(3), 5–41.

Parsons, T. (1937). *The structure of social action*. Glencoe: The Free Press.

Parsons, T. (1951). *The social system*. London: Routledge Kegan Paul.

Richardson, A. (1987). Accounting as a legitimating institution. *Accounting, Organizations and Society, 22*(4), 345–355.

Robertson, R., & Turner, B. (Eds.). (1991). *Talcott Parsons: Theorist of modernity*. London: Sage.

Ross, A. (Ed.). (1988). *Universal abandon? The politics of postmodernism*. Edinburgh: Edinburgh University Press.

Sikka, P. (2000). From the politics of fear to the politics of emancipation. *Critical Perspectives on Accounting, 11*(3), 369–380.

Spivak, G. (1987). Speculations: On reading Marx after Derrida. In L. Attridge, G. Bennington, & R. Young (Eds.), *Post-structuralism and the question of history*. Cambridge: Cambridge University of Press.

Stamp, E., Mumford, M., & Peasnell, K. (Eds.). (1993). *Philosophical perspectives on accounting: Essays in honour of Edward stamp*. London: Taylor and Francis.

Thorns, A., & Locket, M. (1979). Marxism and systems research: Values in practical action. In R. Ericson (Ed.), *Improving the human condition*. Louisville: Society for General Systems Research.

Tinker, T., & Lowe, E. (1982). The management science of the management sciences. *Human Relations, 35*(4), 331–347.

Tinker, T., & Lowe, E. (1984). One-dimensional management science: The making of a technocratic consciousness. *Interfaces, 14*(2), 40–56.

Tinker, T., & Neimark, M. (1987). The role of annual reports in gender and class contradictions at general motors, 1917–1976. *Accounting, Organizations and Society, 12*(1), 71–88.

Ullrich, W. (1988). Churchman's 'process of unfolding'—Its significance for policy analysis and evaluation. *Systems Practice, 6*, 583–611.

Von Bertalanffy, L. (1955). An essay on the relativity of categories. *Philosophy of Science, 22*(4), 243–263.

Whittaker, D. (2003). *Stafford beer: A personal memoir (including an interview with Brian Eno)*. Overbury: Waverstone Press.

Wright, R. (1989). *Three scientists and their gods: Looking for meaning in an age of information*. New York: HarperCollins.

Note

1. Lowe made reference to this by reference to the painting depicting the fall of Icarus, which is prominent in a W.H. Auden poem that contains the following lines: About suffering they were never wrong/ The Old Masters: how well they understood/Its human position: how it takes place/While someone else is eating or opening a window/or just walking dully along (From W.H. Auden, *Musée des Beaux Arts*, first published in *Another Time*).

Think Different: Accounting as a Systems Theorist—Gender, Race and Class

Cheryl R. Lehman

1 Introduction

Knowledge is knowledge is knowledge. (Lowe and Puxty 1990, p. 55)

Transformation is where the action is for feminists: promoting innovation, challenging the status-quo and interested in how societies change. Similarly intrigued by the process of paradigm shifts, Lowe suggested it is an issue 'more important as time goes by, the problem of *change*' (Lowe and Puxty 1990, p. 60, emphasis in the original). To be actively participating in change Lowe observed, 'people interact with one another [and] they define reality...real people with intentions and consciousness, rather than prisoners inside socially-conditioned roles' (Lowe and Puxty 1990, p. 67). Thus we begin with the premise that human beings are meaning-making and although particular meanings may dominate in historical junctures, cultures and economic regimes, this knowledge is a

C.R. Lehman (✉)
School of Business Administration, Hofstra University, New York, NY, USA

© The Author(s) 2016   **163**
J. Haslam, P. Sikka (eds.), *Pioneers of Critical Accounting*,
DOI 10.1057/978-1-137-54212-0_9

contested terrain. By influencing reality we can abolish hierarchies and dislocate power. Changing reality holds potential and suits contemplation for researchers.

Lowe's view complements that of feminist-intersectionality research, aimed at eradicating prejudice and re-configuring meanings. Although issues related to gender are prevalent in this paper, we will interchangeably use multiracial, feminist, gender, and intersectionality to denote research fostering the simultaneity of race, gender, and class in altering social relations (see Holvino 2010).[1] Gender is a form of power relations enmeshed within societal hierarchies. Integral for transforming inequalities in gender and other relationships are the intersections of gender, class, ethnicity, race, colonial history, sexual orientation and religious beliefs (Tanima 2015).

Adopting and confirming Lowe's stance of a knowledge-creating aspect of the accounting profession, multiracial-gender research recognizes there is no one history or truth. As envisioned by Lowe, our discourse contributes to the creation of knowledge. Because our research becomes part of the reality by which we live our lives we seek to understand its impacts and to encourage reflection. The main aspiration of this paper is providing ideas for expanding research possibilities in the genre, agreeing that 'The accounting system exists within a contextual framework … only of value so long as it affects human behaviour' (Lowe and Puxty 1990, p. 68).

We begin in Sect. 2 by reviewing research on the division of labor, historical hierarchies and nature versus nurture discussions given the importance of these issues in gender controversies. We also illustrate that these inquiries parallel Lowe's outlook regarding the creation of power differences as a social phenomena not inevitability. Section 3 addresses the predicaments that although advances have taken place in intersectionality-gender research in accounting, there are significant limitations and we examine critiques. Section 4 provides a context for moving forward. Examining valuation, exposing discrimination, recasting possibilities, and reflecting on contradictions that emerge are among the recommendations. Challenging deeply embedded beliefs was a noteworthy vision of Lowe for improving the discipline and its impact. We also consider the influence of neoliberalism in its pervasive use of market techniques for erasing social aspects in all policies. Addressing the continuing deceptive appeals that accounting is an objective discipline, we urge intersectionality research to directly oppose such claims. Section 5 presents brief conclusions.

2   Re-thinking Meaning on Difference

2.1   Labor Divisions and Hierarchies

Biology is not destiny in creating inevitable divisions of labor for males and females. Flexibility befitted daily life in early human existence (3.5 million years ago to 800 BC) with activities likely pursued similarly by members of both sexes (Coontz and Henderson 1986; Lerner 1986; French 1986). More importantly, status and roles regarding work and life were equally shared and there was neither prestige nor hierarchies between male labor and female labor. Clearly, in contemporary life divisions of labor along sex lines do exist, with a myriad of separations depending on cultures and economies. Contemporary evidence also reveals distinct differences regarding status and expectations. It is a division of labor with constraining social positions for women and groups considered 'outsiders', persisting for centuries, and they are, in the language of Lowe, a social construct (Bennett 2008; Kelan 2010; Kessler-Harris 1981; Lehman 1992a; Loft 1992; Maupin and Lehman 1994; Oakes and Young 2008; Penn and Massino 2009; Shearer and Arrington 1993).

Refuting the inevitability of a status-laden sexual division of labor, theorists view these hierarchies as generated through cultural, institutional and economic configurations by which social relations and separations are sustained. That prospects are limitless, roles variable, and that the sexes are neither divinely nor biologically ordained for privilege has been a significant advance for intersectionality research. Recognizing that there can be equal valuing for males and females in social and economic life renders policies restricting activities as suspect and unnecessary. In disputing biological reductionism researchers note: gender is a socially constructed role we are taught. Women's biology determines that they are child bearers (increasingly being altered with new technologies), but a gender system assigns women to be child rearers.

2.2   Re-thinking Nature Versus Nurture

Relatedly, research in gender has nuanced views for understanding manifestations of difference and the nature-nurture divide. It is here, once again, that Lowe's perspective is mirrored in recognizing expectations are created; they are social practices and intrinsically variable. As such, in the important nature versus nurture controversies, gender literature concludes roles are socially designed and are not destiny (Angier 1999, 2007; Collins 2009; Eisler 1987; Hartmann 1979; Kirkham and Loft 1993; Lehman 1992b, 2012; Lerner 1986; Loft 1992; Nussbaum 2000). While transgender and other significant literature suggest biology matters, our discussion focuses on the social interventions and resultant hierarchies at the core of literature problematizing discrimination.

One illustration disputing 'difference' claims is to look at human brains, where there is ample scientific evidence that they are shaped by experience and culture (not male or female biology). Wellknown examples include: the portion of the brain associated with navigation is enlarged in London taxi drivers; and in the brain region linked to left-hand finger movement, right-handed violinists have differentiated brains. 'You can't pick up a brain and say "that's a girl's brain" or "that's a boy's brain," [said] Gina Rippon, a neuroscientist at Britain's Aston University …The differences between male and female brains are caused by the "drip, drip, drip" of the gendered environment' (Burkett 2015).

Evaluating conventional views of 'nature' is Haraway's path-breaking book, *Primate Visions: Gender, Race, and Nature in the World of Modern Science* (1989). Challenging a claim often heralded in accounting and the business community—that merciless competition is natural and necessary for survival—she describes scientific studies in which nurturing sick primates is typical and more natural. Thus cooperation and caring, not competition and fighting, is the prevailing and predominant behavior within species, contesting repeated orthodox beliefs (see also Angier 1999, 2007; Coontz and Henderson 1986; Eisler 1987; Lerner 1986; Runyan 1999).

Another insight came with feminists rallying to the phrase "the personal is political" in the 1960s, similarly embraced by intersectionality research in the 1970s and paralleling Lowe's dismissal of the artificial construction of separate worlds (for example separating social, economic, class, gender and ethnicity). In education, business rhetoric, and accounting research Lowe rejected the bizarre concept that economic issues could be separated from social issues. Similarly denying dichotomies of private versus public, legal versus moral, and theory versus activism, Lowe and intersectionality research understood such dualisms as fictitious and undermining the rights of those most vulnerable. Feminists provide ample illustrations of how the personal is political, such as domestic violence, educational opportunities and access to birth control. Similarly, the science community has long recognized that research creates meanings (Angier 1999, 2007; Rose and Rose 1970; Zukav 1989).

Re-imagining accepted beliefs of 'difference' between females and males is articulated by Katha Pollitt (2005). Both tongue in cheek and quite seriously, Pollitt contemplates her dilemma when asked to sign a 'women's peace' petition.

> It made the points such documents usually make: that women, as mothers, caregivers and nurturers, have a special awareness of the precariousness of human life...At present it permeates discussions of just about every field ...business writers wonder if women's nurturing intuitive qualities will make them better executives...Haven't we been here before? Although it is couched in the language of praise, difference feminism is demeaning to women. It asks that women be admitted into public life and public discourse not because they have a right to be there but because they will improve them...why should the task of moral and social transformation be laid on women's doorstep and not on everyone's ... no other oppressed group thinks it must make such a claim in order to be accommodated fully and across the board by society...to want to earn a living, exercise one's talents, get a fair hearing in the public forum...Why isn't being human enough?

Also reflecting problems of fairness and illustrating the personal is political is a US Supreme Court ruling contested by Justice Ruth Bader Ginsburg in 2007. She was enraged when the court rejected a discrimination suit of Lilly Ledbetter against Goodyear Tire plant—Ledbetter was being paid 71% of men's wage in her category of seniority. After the 5 to 4 vote, Judge Ginsburg took the unusual step of reading her dissent from the Bench. Exemplifying how social conditioning underlies knowledge she wrote, 'In our view, the Court does not comprehend, or is indifferent to, the insidious way in which women can be victims of pay discrimination' (Collins 2009, p. 357).

Discrimination is by no means unique to the above case; a pervasive gender pay gap (GPG) exists across the globe (see Hausmann et al. 2010; Nussbaum 2000; Strier 2010). OECD (Organization for Economic Co-operation and Development) data for 2005 reveals countries median wages for men at 15% higher than women, exceeding a 20% gap for the United States, Canada, Germany, Japan, Korea, and Switzerland. More recent 2010 OECD data indicate that women (irrespective of family obligations) earn on average 16% less than men, and as women climb up the ladder female top-earners make 21% less than their male counterparts (OECD 2012). In their Global Wage Report 2014/15, the International Labor Organization (ILO) reported that globally women's average wages are between 4% and 36% less than men's, with the gap widening in absolute terms for higher-earning women (ILO 2014). For 2013, the US 'ethnic' wage gap is significant: the ratio for males: white to black to Hispanic is reported as 100%, 75%, 67%; to white women, black women and Hispanic women as: 78%, 64% and 54% (National Committee on Pay Equity 2015).

3   Gender-Intersectionality Research in Accounting: Beginnings

In 1992 a watershed of gender-intersectionality research exemplified Lowe's assertion that nothing could be examined in absentia and that the ubiquitous separation of social and economic spheres in accounting was erroneous and extreme. Cooper (1992) contributed to dislocating meanings by questioning what accounting 'accounted for' when environmental degradation is named an externality, or ignored, or considered an exchange needing a 'price'. Accounting for whose understanding and vision? Gallhofer's (1992) concern with the erasure of class mirrors Tony Lowe's foresight to tackle issues of political praxis in accounting research. Lowe was conscious that first-world abundance generated academic work often separate from problems across the globe. Like Lowe, Gallhofer's curiosity led to assessing where power and knowledge reside in analysis of class and challenging global capitalism. Similarly Hammond and Oakes (1992) supported the needs of the already underrepresented, providing inspiration for gender, race, and ethnicity research. Ciancanelli (1992) contributed that gender is a process, not fixed, and it is rooted in asymmetric power distribution, not biology. Capturing a social-systems view Ciancanelli wrote, "the basis of class, race, sex or business function, are social constructions. They are not in any sense biological or natural" (Ciancanelli 1992, p. 136).

Coinciding with Lowe's appreciation of changing societal interrelationships, critical accounting theorists examined economic rights and global discrimination, and a diverse discourse developed. Yet in evaluating gender research in 2008, Broadbent and Kirkham questioned the lack of greater advancement. 'Why had we not moved on?...Why had the ground-breaking work that had appeared ...in 1992 not been built on and replicated?' (Broadbent and Kirkham 2008, p. 465; see also Dambrin and Lambert 2008; Dillard and Reynolds 2008; Haynes 2008; Komori 2008; Parker 2008; Walker 2008). Such questioning encourages retrospection.

3.1   Making Meaning Count: Accounting Critiques

Discrimination based on ethnicity and gender is pervasive in contemporary society, with wage gaps one manifestation. It is thus understandable that in the accounting discipline researchers questioned and compared wages, status and roles between males, females and ethnicities. Research exploring the gender pay gap proliferated as well as studies of the low proportion of female and 'ethnic' partners, and on the relationship between advancement and personality types and characteristics. This research, while important on some level, became increasingly over-determined and less relevant to deeper, more meaningful research and change. As such, the critique of this work is well founded and well documented (see, for example Annisette 2003; Annisette and Trivedi 2013; Ciancanelli et al. 1990; Gallhofer 1998; Jeacle 2006; Kim 2004, 2008: Kirkham 1992; Kirkham and Loft 2001; Komori 2008; Lehman 2012; Shearer and Arrington 1993).

Dambrin and Lambert (2012), examining the discourses in 'rarity at the top' publications, observed one should not presume 'choice' of partnership is a goal for all auditors—male or female. Cooper (2001) suggests, 'Although there have undoubtedly been major advances for women in the past decades these have nearly all been advances in "bourgeois feminism"…and *fewer* real gains for working women' (emphasis in the original, Cooper 2001, p. 218). Incorporating a broader view of what gender-in-accounting research might be, Cooper quotes Broadbent, '"I would wish to see the issue of equal rights for those of color or those who are socially disadvantaged raised and brought to account…what it feels like to operate at the economic bottom margins of society"' (Cooper 2001, p. 240). Issues of class and marginalization remained underdeveloped, with Cooper encouraging research "to disrupt the liberal humanist desire for women to progress on the same terms as men asking why women would want to be like the type of men who reach the top hierarchy in the accounting profession anyway" (Cooper 2001, p. 241).

Questioning markets-are-best mentalities is fundamental to deepening gender-ethnicity-accounting research and is in the spirit of Lowe's aversion to merely quantification, as is any accounting research devoid of the social aspects of the discipline (Lowe and Tinker 1977). Lowe rejected the idea that shareholder wealth maximization, efficiency, or objectivity were acceptable criteria by which to judge research and the discipline's choices. Lowe would certainly agree with the statement, 'For the last thirty years, when asking ourselves whether we support a policy, a proposal or an initiative, we have restricted ourselves to issues of profit and loss—economic questions in the narrowest sense. But this is not an instinctive human condition: it is an acquired taste' (Judt 2010, p. 34). This means consciously noting the constitutive nature of accounting and assessing it as neither a technical activity nor asocial. As such we are influenced by many critical accounting researchers, including Lowe, in advocating that accounting be viewed broadly.

Lowe recognized that 'accounting is only of importance in a given context [and advocated] opening up accounting to the real-world-of-affairs' (Lowe and Puxty 1990, p. 54). We thus propose that research narrowly focusing on 'success' and 'achievement' is unfortunate. Sometimes manifested as a 'Romance of Micro Entrepreneurship', or 'Romance of Financial Empowerment' form of research we agree that financially unburdening any marginalized group is a necessary and often empowering transformation. However it is insufficient and it is an incomplete emancipation. Our greater concern is the enduring neglect of basic rights for underrepresented groups and violence against them, and thus the necessity to break accounting's silences and appreciate accounting's role in economic and social spheres (Lehman 2012).

Positive discourses regarding microfinance include claims that it initiates a 'virtuous spiral' of economic, social, and political empowerment. However, an increasing body of literature suggests otherwise (Tanima 2015). Not only are there questions regarding economic achievements, but also serious questions regarding the models being promoted and their underlying assumptions of development, social relationships, political processes, power, and empowerment. True transformation wrestles with discrimination and subordination as complex, multi-dimensional, all-pervasive processes, embedded in different and mutually reinforcing levels (Tanima 2015).

4   Expanding the Field: What Might Be Done?

Once we allow ourselves to be disobedient to the test of an accountant's profit, we have begun to change our civilization. (John Maynard Keynes)

We suggest that moving beyond 'achievement' as previously measured can enhance gender-intersectionality research groups. Choices of how we measure and privilege certain forms of work have been addressed in

Waring's seminal work, *If Women Counted* (1988), disputing the UN's exclusion of what had been deemed 'women's work': the unpaid majority of women's labor participation: childcare, parental care, household work, farm labor, etc., in national accounts. This negating of women's productivity represents a negation of political and economic power. Thus fundamentally changing how we think, valorize, and discuss the value of work advances inquiry. 'Women do two-thirds of the world's work and produce nearly 60 percent of its food; however, they own less than one percent of the world's farmland and earn only 10 percent of the world's income… three quarters [are] without access to education' (Gayle in Bisoux 2010, p. 20). Our literature can contribute to assessing accountability, exposing the inequities, and as Lowe promotes, contextualizing these effects.

Why accounting? Accounting numbers have the capacity to 'produce certain forms of visibility and transparency…[to] configure persons, domains and actions as objective and comparable' (Mennicken and Miller 2014, p. 25). But accounting and numbers are inevitably infused with our predilections and beliefs. This does not render accounts irrelevant; it renders them powerful and consequential on vulnerable populations, confirming that our reflections are important. Calculability and accounting are potent valuing activities that 'increasingly leave "ordinary people" outside of the processes of knowledge generation and use' (Boyce and Greer 2013, p. 110). By counting particular characteristics 'they appear to be set apart from political interests and disputes…yet they are deeply involved in these worlds, shaping subjects [and] social relations' (Hansen and Muhlen-Schulte 2012, p. 3). We seek to engage in detailing and reflecting social dimensions such as class, discrimination, power and violence.

One dilemma is that the act of measuring is restrictive and does not significantly change underlying structural repressions. Indeed, we may unwittingly erase that which we haven't seen or yet identified. Spivak (2010) notes that while UN, EU, and other reports may lead to the passing of important laws protecting vulnerable groups these limited gestures are often 'missionary impulses' with imperfect interventions. They may even be considered 'tremendously well-organized and broad repressive ideological apparatuses' (Spivak 1996, p. 2). Using data as sacrosanct, as if exemplifying objectivity reduces social phenomenon to simplistic representations. A number is 'always invested with meaning, potentially disguising as much as it reveals' (Hansen and Muhlen-Schulte 2012, p. 1). The quandary of quantification is why some researchers recommend, 'staying on the margins'. How can one quantify abuse or inequality? If economic and social systems are suspect, what can quantification achieve? We have great sympathy with these insights yet look at the issue of needing to start broadly and reflectively.

As a systems theorist, Lowe would perceive social change as a process deliberated by individuals and shaped by social and historical forces. People are active participants, they have agency and they are creators of their worlds when opportunities and possibilities exist. Vulnerable groups know that social justice is not captured in the logic of calculative rhetoric. Following a long tradition in critical accounting research we support research that gives voice to their narratives, aimed at revealing the emancipatory potential of alternative, or counter-accounts, seen as tools of resistance and change (Gallhofer et al. 2006; Paisey and Paisey 2006; Sikka 2006). In order to 'challenge, problematize and deligitimate those currently in a dominant position of power ... shadow accounts...[create] alternative representations, new visibilities and knowledge [to] represent the views of oppressed social groups' (Dey et al. 2010, p. 1). Participants seek a voice in these discourses, and counter accounts and thus visibilities are complex, contradictory, and sites of emancipatory struggle. Visibilities are fluid and as many have observed the task of binding societies together is always incomplete, resisted, and the social cannot be eradicated. There are no simple answers or easily recommended paths but there are multiple possibilities for thinking differently.

4.1   If You Don't Start Somewhere, You Go Nowhere

Accounting is about this: it is concerned with how certain technical matters (accounting principles and reports) affect people and the relations between them. The inputs to accounting are human actions, and the output of accounting information is likewise a human action. At every turn, in the contextual nature of accounting, one comes across human nature. (Lowe and Puxty 1990, p. 55)

It is this essence; our inputs matter, motivating us to make things visible; accounting numbers have the potential of providing a voice. Accounting's silence regarding environmental degradation has been lamented and so too is accounting's evasion regarding violence against women and ethnic groups. Creating visibilities are powerful legacies of critical accounting research. For this reason, some accounts are provided below:

> 'The number of women who die because of gender-related violence, deprivation and discrimination is larger than the casualty toll in all the wars of the 20th century combined…Globally, women aged between 15 and 44 are more likely to be injured or die as a result of male violence than through cancer, traffic accidents, malaria and war combined…The causes are multiple, but…the simple fact [is] that…a woman's life and dignity are worth less than a man's.' (Winkler in Lederer 2005)

> The World Health Organization estimates that globally one woman in five will be the subject of rape or attempted rape. (UNIFEM 2006)

> 'The global statistics on the abuse of girls are numbing … The reason for the gap is not that we don't know how to save lives of women in poor countries. It's simply that poor, uneducated women … have never been a priority either in their own countries or to donor nations.' (Kristoff and WuDunn 2009, pp. 33–34)

Developing new concepts and methods and exploring the consequences of power are plausible innovations. These include reconfiguring what we mean by causality and advocating for greater transparency, as well as calculating and exposing the numbers. Challenging the 'inevitability' of violence, refuting 'natural causations', and advocating for accountability all provide opportunities for transformation. As Gayatri Spivak affirms, these can only be partial transformations until the economic and social structures perpetuating violence are revealed and no longer under the radar (Spivak 2010), but they are beginnings.

Given the limits of conventional accounting, intervention includes greater explorations with the use of dialogic accounting, introducing ideas of re-examination, new understandings, problematizing existing situations, re-narrating existing situations and identifying solutions (Bebbington et al. 2007; Brown 2009, 2010; Dillard and Roselender 2011). Dialogic accounting rejects universal economic-oriented narratives, promoting views of societies instead as contested narratives and thus accounting as a discipline is regarded as a potential medium fostering democratic interaction, de-centering power, re-shaping knowledge, and providing a mechanism for engagement (Tanima 2015).

4.2   Making Change Under Neoliberalism

> There is an *essentially dynamic* aspect of the use of accounting information which has not yet been articulated by researchers: in effect, the way in which the "social" accounting set defines the reality of the organization through human action. (Lowe and Puxty 1990, p. 69, italics in the original)

Increasingly in neoliberal societies life is characterized by extending market logic to all arenas of social life and accounting is a vital technology in neoliberal governance and rule. Accounting makes things governable and knowable and through accounting techniques, in the guise of objectivity, there is an ever-ruthless result, as it is generally acknowledged that neoliberalism has increased the bifurcation of the world's rich and poor (Judt 2010; Klein 2007; Rosenberg 2002; Sikka 2000; Piketty 2014). Challenging and defying sterile techniques that have been inserted into arenas 'which are properly the domain of human judgment' (Power 2004, p. 772) intersectionality research seeks to create new visibilities and accounts.

Global neoliberal policies could not be enacted without support of economic theories, accounting numbers, and a claim that pure markets go hand in hand with democracy. Accounting literature acknowledges the symbiotic relationship between accounting and neoliberal rule (Burchell 1993; Miller et al. 2008), and the expansion of economic form to all social fields. 'As Stuart Hall puts it, "the very idea of the "social" and the "public" has been liquidated"' (in Sikka 2006, p. 761). Accounting techniques contribute to the façade such that 'our reliance on accounting measures to "speak the truth" in policy debates has provided additional legitimacy to market oriented policy outcomes' (Andrew 2011, pp. 194–195). Calculating does not erase morality, and accounting researchers have recognized neoliberalism's affront: a process by which "a relative handful of private interests is permitted to control as much as possible of social life" (McChesney 1999, quoted in Merino et. al. 2010).

Under neoliberalism, marketization dominates and thus microfinance and microcredit are endorsed as enhancing empowerment. By belying the social, cultural, class, and other constraints under which oppression takes place these financial solutions are detrimental. Structural power imbalances remain and become invisible under neoliberal calculative practices and rule. Because women are represented disproportionately among the world's poor, neoliberal globalization has been especially harmful to women (although not to all or only women) (Jaggar 2002; Runyan 1999; Sen 2003). Laws banning sex discrimination are unenforced, women are over-represented among low-paid 'sweatshop' workers, and cutbacks in social programs related to families are among the more gendered features of global neoliberalism. The deteriorating health of women in the South is linked to neoliberal economic policies. It is an alarming illustration of Lowe's systems theory in process: a drastic decline in health is inseparable from politics and economics (Jaggar 2002).

Accounting research can problematize policies and in the spirit of Lowe's sensibilities aspire for transformation. Dialogic accounting and shadow accounts seek emancipatory change by exposing and reflecting on hitherto invisible or silenced dynamics contributing to further harm of those most vulnerable (Agyemang and Lehman 2013; Chwastiak 2013). As with Freire (1970) the aim is to embrace the genesis of different viewpoints, while also denying that one worldview should dominate. In this manner, critical research is emancipatory.

5   Conclusions

Lowe was concerned with evaluating the adequacy of accounting practice as a step toward improving it. The effect of traditional accounting market based research, particularly in a neoliberal regime, has continued the deterioration of socially enhancing practice. Lowe's interest in change and paradigm shifts encourages examination in times of social change. It is a process by which individuals, institutions, perceptions and actions are shaped by social forces and a complex understanding of how ethnicity, gender, class and privilege are socially constructed guides an expansive research program. Knowledge and meaning are the products of our agency and choice; accounting researchers are neither passive participants nor victims or prisoners. As active participants, Lowe's legacy suggests reflective dialogues, creativity, counter-accounting and new narratives for examining the world when opportunities and possibilities exist. As possibilities for change are always manifesting, this is how change happens.

This paper sought to recognize Lowe's enormous contribution to the discipline and intersectionality research in thinking differently and expansively. This includes Lowe's embrace of the socio-economic-political aspects of the discipline, his understanding of power, and his work highlighting that human beings are dynamic agents, capable of reflexivity. Examining issues of inequality are fundamental to deepening intersectionality-accounting research and we seek, in the spirit of Lowe, to dialogue how such social justice might be furthered.

Note

1. Ethnicity is being used in a broad manner, regarding background, culture, and language; names and categories for identities, ethnicities and race are complex. As an example, in the USA, the Census Bureau collects 'racial' data based on self-identification "in the eyes of the community ...[not an] attempt to define race biologically, anthropologically, or genetically" (US Census Bureau 2013).

Acknowledgement   With appreciation for the support of Hofstra University.

Dedication   In memory of my beloved mother, Lillian H. Shoulson.

A Critical Look at the IASB

Geoff Whittington

1   Introduction

Tony Lowe and I were contemporaries as professors of accounting in the UK, and our educational backgrounds also overlapped: we both trained as English chartered accountants and took undergraduate degrees in accounting at the LSE. However, our subsequent experience and intellectual preoccupations diverged. I followed the conventional (for an LSE graduate) path of regarding economics as the conceptual basis of accounting, whereas Tony was concerned with its wider organisational and social context. Of course, these are not mutually exclusive approaches, and anyone involved in policy making (as I have been) comes to understand the relevance of the broad perspective offered by critical thinkers such as Tony.

The author is grateful to Geoff Meeks, Steve Zeff and the Editors for constructive suggestions on an earlier draft. The author bears responsibility for any remaining deficiencies.

G. Whittington (✉)
Judge Business School, University of Cambridge, Cambridge, UK

© The Author(s) 2016   **179**
J. Haslam, P. Sikka (eds.), *Pioneers of Critical Accounting*,
DOI 10.1057/978-1-137-54212-0_10

This paper is a tribute to Tony, and his colleagues in the "Sheffield School"which he founded, because it considers the development of the International Accounting Standards Board (IASB) as an adaptive institution, responding to social and economic pressures and changing its policies accordingly. It does not attempt analysis in terms of critical theory, which would be beyond my competence, but it does hopefully demonstrate the importance of political and social influences, which I experienced at first hand, as member of the IASB from 2001 to 2006.

2   Origins: The IASC

The IASB had its origins in the International Accounting Standards Committee (IASC), which was founded in 1973 and superseded by the IASB in 2001. The IASC was a private sector body, created by members of the accounting profession and supported by professional bodies and securities regulators in many countries. Its history has been recorded authoritatively by Camfferman and Zeff (2006).

The IASC was a response to the increasing globalisation of capital markets, which created a need for comparability between financial reports prepared in different countries but addressed to the same capital markets, and the parallel expansion in the number of global companies, each of which might be listed on several national stock exchanges and have subsidiaries registered in a variety of countries. Thus, there was a demand for a common language of accounting, which would ease the problems of cross-border communication. The beneficiaries of such a development would be participants in the capital markets (improved comparability reducing information processing costs) and preparers of accounts (comparability reducing the costs and risks of preparing group accounts of transnational holding companies), so that it is not surprising that the supporters of the IASC were professional accountants and security market regulators.

In its early years, the IASC attempted to narrow the variety of international practice by issuing standards that, in its view, represented the best of available current practice but allowed alternative treatments where these were well-established. Later, particularly after 1987, it adopted a more pro-active policy, attempting to lead rather than follow existing practice and to narrow the range of permitted methods. It was aided in this by its conceptual framework, issued in 1989. In the early years, the IASC standards drew on national standards, and these were most strongly developed in the English-speaking ('Anglo-Saxon') world, where the importance of stock markets and the consequent need for transparent financial reporting were the greatest. Moreover, the conceptual framework of the IASC drew heavily on that of the USA's Financial Accounting Standards Board (FASB) and the technical experts who developed the IASC standards tended to be from the Anglo-Saxon countries, which were the best resourced. This was demonstrated by the emergence of the 'G4+1' group, which produced an impressive volume of technical research to support the IASC's work in the 1990's. The G4 were the UK, the USA, Canada, Australia and New Zealand (a late addition, which confused the title) and the 1 was the IASC itself: all of the national members were from English-speaking countries. As the twentieth century came to a close, the IASC, with its large committee and thin technical resources, faced increasing difficulties in attempting to lead, rather than follow, the world in setting standards for such complex areas as financial instruments. It became obvious that a new structure was needed, and the IASB replaced the IASC in 2001.

3   The IASB in 2001

The IASB had a Board of twelve full-time and two half- time members, chosen primarily for technical competence, although there was also a concern to have a world-wide geographical balance and a balance between preparers and users of accounts. It was supported by a much larger technical staff than the IASC and had a much higher income than its predecessor, derived mainly from preparers and users of accounts. Fund-raising, appointments and overall supervision of the process were in the hands of the trustees of the IASC Foundation. Thus, the structure resembled that of the USA's FASB.[1] The organisation, like the IASC, was based in London, perhaps confirming the Anglo-Saxon image.

Table 1 IASB Members, 2001, by country of residence

USA	5
UK	2
Australia, Canada, South Africa	3
'Anglo-Saxon' sub-total	10
France, Germany, Switzerland	3
Japan	1
'The Rest'	4
Total	14

The initial membership (Table 1) also confirmed an apparent Anglo-Saxon dominance. Ten of the 14 members were from Anglo-Saxon countries. However, it should be emphasised that the members (unlike those of the IASC) were not regarded as delegates for their home countries. Rather, they were appointed as technical experts whose task was to derive standards that were in accordance with the IASB's objectives and consistent with its conceptual framework. Seven members were assigned as liaison members for specific countries (Australia, Canada, France, Germany, Japan, the UK and the USA), but the purpose of that relationship was to promote dialogue between the IASB and other particularly active standard setters rather than to provide those standard setters with an advocate on the Board. Nevertheless, the background of the members would necessarily influence their views on accounting standards, and the thinking of the Board was likely to be dominated by the perspective of advanced capitalist countries, if not 'Anglo-Saxons'.[2] Three initial tasks were identified by the IASB: the 'improvements project', the creation of a 'stable platform' for European Union (EU) adoption of international standards, and convergence with FASB standards to enable the USA Securities and Exchange Commission to consider the recognition of international standards on USA capital markets. Each of these tasks made heavy demands on the IASB's time, sometimes in conflicting ways.

4   Pressures and Alliances, 2001–2006

The *improvements* project was concerned with considering, and where appropriate implementing, an extensive list of proposed improvements to the existing IASC standards,[3] which had been suggested by IOSCO, national standard setters and other regulators and constituents. It focused on details, such as the restriction of optional treatments, which could be dealt with by amending existing standards rather than developing entirely new ones.[4] The IASB's worthy intention was to respond to its constituents, but the process of 'patching' existing standards rather than developing new ones proved to be arduous and time consuming. The project was completed later than originally intended, in December 2003, but still in time to allow EU adopters to have a 'stable platform' in 2005.

The *EU adoption of IASB standards* had seemed to be an unexpected benefit to the IASB when, in 2000, the European Commission announced its policy to adopt the standards from 2005 for EU listed companies. However, the benefit also carried costs. One cost was the need to provide a 'stable platform' of standards for EU companies that were new adopters of IFRS. This constrained the ability of the IASB to introduce new standards around this time. A greater cost was that when the EU published its regulation to enforce IFRS adoption, it introduced an elaborate endorsement process. Adoption of IFRS was not to be automatic, and each standard had to be endorsed as being suitable for the needs of the EU, the final decision being at the political, rather than technical, level. This proved in practice to be a real obstacle to the adoption of IFRS in the case of IAS 39 (Financial Instruments) whose hedge accounting provisions were unpopular with banks, particularly French banks. As a result, there was political lobbying (even involving the President of France) against certain provisions that disallowed 'macro hedging',[5] and these provisions were 'carved out' (i.e. omitted) from the version of IAS 39 that was approved in 2004 for application in the EU. An IASB amendment to IAS 39, the 'fair value option', was also controversial in Europe. It sought to extend the use of fair value measurement by permitting (but not requiring) its use for certain financial instruments. This was opposed by the European Central Bank (ECB), as a regulator of the EU banking system, on prudential grounds. In this case, the IASB tightened the requirements for the use of the option and this satisfied the ECB, thus avoiding another long-term 'carve-out' of the standard.[6] These controversies provided the IASB, and its trustees, with a clear message that the trust and co-operation of constituents had to be earned rather than demanded.

The IAS 39 issues were symptomatic of a wider unease in the EU over the transition to IFRS. Many businesses, in particular, were uneasy about the way their traditional methods of reporting to investors were being changed. For example, there was a strong current of opposition to the IASB's tentative proposals to focus the income statement on comprehensive income (including all gains and losses of the period) rather than some more limited concept such as operating profit. This discontent was probably increased by the perception that the IASB was dominated by an 'Anglo-Saxon' culture that was alien to continental European traditions. Such perceptions were encouraged by the IASB's *convergence programme* with the USA's FASB.

The USA had the largest capital market in the world, and access to it was attractive to many of the IASB's constituents, including those in Europe. Overseas companies listing on US stock exchanges were required by the SEC to reconcile their accounts to US GAAP (the standards required by FASB). The attractiveness and convenience of using international accounting standards would obviously be increased if those standards were accepted in the USA without the need for reconciliation to US GAAP. A report by the SEC issued before the creation of the IASB (SEC 2000) had contemplated this possibility, but had also made clear that this would require convergence of FASB and international standards. The IASB initiated such a process in 2002, in the Norwalk Agreement with FASB. This pledged the two boards to work together on future projects, including regular joint meetings of the two boards and joint staffing of the technical work. This proved to be a burdensome commitment in terms of board and staff time, although it did eventually (in 2007) lead to the SEC withdrawing the reconciliation requirement for overseas companies using IFRS. Moreover, it constrained the IASB's scope for choice over agenda and solutions, reinforcing the views of critics, particularly in Europe, that the IASB was dominated by Anglo-Saxon thinking, as exemplified by the FASB.

The apparent privileged status given to the FASB was reinforced in 2005 by the abandonment of the special liaison relationship for the six other leading standard setters. This was accompanied by an extended programme of looser but more inclusive liaison worldwide with standard setters and their constituents. This weakened the impression that there was a privileged 'inner circle' with special access to the IASB's processes, but it left the USA, as represented by the FASB, in a uniquely privileged position.

The rest of the world, other than the USA, the EU and the former 'liaison' countries, was, of course, extremely important because it represented the IASB's future recruiting ground for the use of its standards. Such countries had a voice in the IASB's deliberations, through submission of comments as part of the 'due process' for developing standards, and also through the IASB Advisory Council, but these were passive rather than active roles in standard-setting. Amongst these were developing countries which were particularly supportive of developing a simplified international standard for smaller entities (the SME standard). It is a reflection of their growing influence and the support that they received from the IASC Foundation Trustees, that, despite the IASB's initial resistance to the idea, the SME project was eventually put on the agenda and a standard appeared in 2009.

5   Standards Development and the Emergence of the Fair Value View: 2001–2006

As we have seen, the IASB was constrained in its early work by a number of factors. The strongest influence on its output was the agreement to work closely with the FASB, which had a greater number of support staff than the IASB and also had considerable momentum from its work in progress. This was perhaps most obvious in the Business Combinations project, in which the FASB had progressed much further than the IASB at the time of the Norwalk Agreement, so that the IASB became a follower rather than a leader. The result was a standard (IFRS3, 2004) which appeared to follow many prior decisions of the FASB. Notable examples were the banning of merger ('pooling of interests') accounting and the amortisation of goodwill (replaced by impairment testing). These were seen as controversial changes in many countries, notably in the EU and Japan. Another area in which the IASB drew heavily on prior technical work by the FASB was Share Based Payment (IFRS2, 2004). This was a triumph for the IASB in the sense that it was the first standard in the world to require the expensing of stock options, which had been vehemently opposed by business leaders. However, it drew heavily on the prior work of FASB in developing a draft standard for the USA.

The work in progress of the IASB during this period also reflected the influence of FASB thinking. This was particularly apparent in the work towards creating a new joint conceptual framework for the FASB and the IASB. The new version of the framework proposed to elevate decision usefulness to investors as the sole objective of financial statements, removing the traditional stewardship objective and it was proposed to substitute representational faithfulness for reliability as a fundamental property of good accounting information. As a consequence of these changes, prudence was deleted from the framework: formerly, this had been in the IASB's framework as a reasonable exercise of caution in measurement, arising from the stewardship relationship.[7] These proposals appeared to align better with the US approach to financial reports as being directed primarily to the investor in the market (decision usefulness) rather than the more traditional approach (favoured widely in Europe and Japan) that they were addressed primarily to existing shareholders (stewardship) as part of the accountability of management.[8]

Within contemporary proposals for new standards, there were specific issues that seemed to arise from the market orientation of the IASB/FASB approach. 'Day 1' profits, for example, were an issue in the revenue recognition, insurance and provisions projects. 'Day 1' profits are recognised at the inception of a project when the obligations under it are valued at fair value and are offset against revenue arising from the contract. This contrasts with the traditional approach to profit recognition, which records the initial obligation under a contract as being equal to the consideration received, recognising profit only when the obligation is discharged either by the passage of time or by the fulfilment of specific obligations (Lennard 2002). Fair value was also an issue in relation to assets, notably financial instruments, where certain categories (instruments available for sale and held for trading, and all derivatives) were required by IAS39 to be recorded at fair value. This was later extended by the controversial fair value option.

Because fair value was a pervasive theme in the more controversial aspects of the IASB's work (supported by the FASB) at this time, the broad stance of the IASB/FASB has been characterised as the *Fair Value View* (FVV). The FVV is elaborated and illustrated by reference to various IASB standards and proposals, as of 2006, in Whittington (2008). Essentially, the FVV is based upon the assumption that reporting to financial markets for the purposes of investor decisions (basically, valuation of the firm's securities) is the guiding purpose of financial reports. It is assumed that this process is carried out ideally in the context of perfect and complete markets, so that market prices can be observed directly for all assets and obligations, or readily inferred from the prices of similar assets and obligations. Thus, *fair* value, defined as a current market selling price, offers a faithful representation of the present value of the benefits (or obligations) associated with any item in the accounts. This is the world of 'deep and liquid markets' which featured in many of the discussions of FASB and the IASB. It is also closer to the world of the USA, or to the self-image of the USA's financial regulators, as exemplified, for example, in the SEC's apparent belief that US markets were the most efficient[9] and best regulated in the world; hence, IFRS accounts had to be reconciled with US GAAP, rather than the reverse, in order to achieve the highest quality. Elsewhere in the world, in many countries there was less reliance on the stock markets for finance and for corporate governance, a greater concern for stewardship (with its focus on past transactions and events) and less belief in the completeness and efficiency of markets. Such countries did not therefore accept the FVV as their overall framework for financial reporting, or US GAAP as the most appropriate system of accounting for their purposes, and this was the basic source of their discontent with IASB/FASB views on many issues.

The FVV was attractive to 'technical' standard setters, such as the majority of the IASB and the FASB because it offered a clear logical framework from which solutions to particular accounting problems could be deduced: the answer being invariably to measure all items at fair value. Hence, it was important to revise the conceptual framework in such a way that it was compatible with the FVV, for example, by replacing the criterion of reliability (which fair value might fail to meet, in the absence of deep and liquid markets) with that of faithful representation (which might be expected to be met by fair values, representing the current state of affairs, rather than historical cost, representing a past state of affairs). The *alternative* to the FVV was much less clear in its detailed implications (Whittington 2008) but essentially it recognised that accounting data are part of a wider information set (including, for example, macro-economic data and forecasts) that are used for a variety of purposes (including share valuation and stewardship but also a wider range of economic and social evaluations). Thus, accounting data are inputs into the models of individual users (which will differ from one another) and provide useful *information* for this purpose, rather than precise *measurement* of decision variables such as the value of a firm's equity. The measurement of such variables is the prerogative of the user rather than the preparer of accounts: hence, for example, financial analysts are responsible for the valuation of shares and use accounts as one source of information in the process. Hence, the standard-setter's role is to identify the information needs of different users and to make the difficult choice of prioritising those needs, having regard to cost constraints. This approach also requires a conceptual framework to guide the standard setter in making this difficult judgment, but the framework is unlikely to offer unique deductive solutions to accounting problems.

6   Retreat from the Fair Value View, 2007–2015

The Fair Value View appears to have reached its zenith around 2006, the year in which the present author retired from the IASB, so that subsequent events are discussed from the perspective of an external observer with no privileged access to the IASB's deliberations.

The retreat from the FVV was gradual and, at first, almost imperceptible. Neither was it complete, and the changes were not all in the same direction. As late as 2011, the standard on fair value measurement (IFRS 13) was issued. This mimicked an earlier (2006) FASB standard, which had defined fair value for the first time as the *price* for which an asset could be *sold* (or a liability extinguished), whereas it had previously been defined as the *amount* for which an asset could be *exchanged*. Hence, the new definition made clear for the first time in IASB standards that fair value referred to *exit* rather than *entry* values (such as replacement cost) and that *transaction costs* (such as the costs of the sale transaction) should be ignored. This is, of course, consistent with the FVV that fair value should reflect the market's informed view of the present value of the economic benefits attached to an asset (or the economic obligations attached to a liability). However, the IASB emphasised, in issuing the standard, that this was not intended to extend the use of fair value but rather to clarify its meaning when it was used. Moreover, it reviewed the use of fair value in existing standards to ensure that the new definition was consistent with the intention of those standards: something which it had been reluctant to do when the adoption of the new definition was first discussed, in 2006.

Despite deviations from the general pattern, such as IFRS 13, the period from 2007 to the present (2015) saw significant retreats from the FVV, which in 2006 had seemed likely to become more pervasive. In the conceptual framework project, the IASB has retreated from its previous ambition to identify a single ideal measurement objective such as fair value. Its current position (as in the 2015 exposure draft) is that the measurement method should reflect how a specific item is used by the reporting entity, and that the measures used should include cost measures (including historic cost) as well as fair values.[10] The conceptual framework review has also reinstated *stewardship* as an objective of financial reports with equal status to that of decision usefulness. With regard to particular standards, the IASB has abandoned its plan to replace IAS 37 (on provisions and contingent liabilities) with a universal standard on liabilities which would apply fair value measurement. Consistent with this, its new revenue recognition standard (IFRS 15, 2014) does not advocate the measurement of contractual obligations at fair value. Rather, it avoids recording 'day 1' profits, which would be recognised under fair value, by recording the initial obligation as equal to the contractual obligation, reducing this subsequently by reference to the delivery of specific contractual obligations rather than the declining fair value of the obligations. A similar approach, avoiding 'day 1' profits, is being adopted in the insurance accounting project, which has not yet led to the issue of a new standard. The financial instruments standard, IAS 39, is in the process of being replaced by a revised standard, IFRS 9. The new standard retains the use of fair value for measuring certain specific financial instruments but does not significantly extend the use of fair value to all or most financial instruments, as was once feared. Moreover, the use of a mixed measurement model for financial instruments is consistent with the latest view of measurement adopted in the conceptual framework project: fair value is used for financial instruments in appropriate circumstances, notably when they are held for disposal so that their selling price is highly relevant.

7   Causes of the Retreat

The IASB's change in direction since 2006, away from the FVV, shows that it has adapted to its environment. The principal factors that drove and enabled this adaptation were as follows:

- *External pressures* on the IASB.
- *Changes in the membership* of the IASB.
- *Changes in the structure of the Foundation* which oversees the IASB.
- *The need to retain and recruit new countries* as users of IFRS.

The last of these is the most fundamental: IFRS are adopted voluntarily by national regulators, so the success of the IASB enterprise depends ultimately in gaining their approval. The changes in the structure of the Foundation and the membership of the Board represent the Trustees' response to this challenge. The first factor, the IASB's own response to external pressures, reflects the constitution of the IASB, notably its 'due process' for developing new standards, which require it to be transparent about its deliberations and expose them for comment by constituents. We shall consider the contribution of each factor in turn.

8   External Pressures on the IASB, 2007–2014

The IASB received inputs from its constituents in a variety of ways, including comment letters on 'due process' documents, discussions with advisory bodies and working groups, and direct contact with regulatory bodies that approved its standards for national adoption.

The closest of the latter type of arrangement was the collaboration with the FASB, mentioned earlier, which was directed towards gaining SEC approval for IFRS accounts to be accepted for listing on US exchanges. This was reinforced later (2006) by the Memorandum of Understanding with the FASB, which committed both parties to accelerating the convergence programme, and in 2007 the SEC duly approved IFRS for overseas registrants. The SEC also consulted on allowing IFRS to be used by US companies, but it became apparent that this was unlikely to happen. Moreover, it became apparent to both boards that working together was time consuming and that the work of convergence became more difficult when it addressed issues such as deferred tax which were deeply embedded in national institutions and established practices. Joint work on convergence continued and new standards appeared as part of the convergence process, but by late 2014, the IASB Deputy Chair (Mackintosh 2014) was anticipating that the programme would end with the issue of the new standard on leasing (expected in 2015). The declining importance of the FASB collaboration enabled the IASB to work independently on the revision of the conceptual framework, including the retreat from some aspects of the FVV.

Another strong influence was that of the EU. This was important throughout the IASB's history but grew stronger as the EU increased the severity of its approval process for endorsing individual IFRS by adding submission to a committee of the European Parliament (November 2006). This followed the controversies over IAS 39, discussed earlier, and subsequently it allowed the European Parliament, in response to the financial crisis, to force further changes to IAS 39 that relaxed the conditions for switching from fair value to historical cost (2008, discussed in Andre et al. 2009). Whatever the merits of such interventions, they provided a strong incentive for the IASB to accommodate views that were acceptable in the EU, and these were generally different from the FVV.

The Financial Crisis, which started late in 2007, posed a more general challenge to the FVV. The illiquidity of financial markets which precipitated the failures in the banks seemed to contradict the idea of 'deep and liquid markets' that underlay the FVV, so that the use of fair value was questioned even in the USA. Some even suggested that the crisis was caused by fair value accounting (Plantin et. al. 2008), although the empirical evidence for this is unconvincing (Barth and Landsman 2010; Amel- Zadeh and Meeks 2013). However, extreme illiquidity suggested that fair value (defined as a selling price) did not reflect value when assets could not be sold, and the IASB set up a Financial Crisis Advisory Group (2008–2014) which advised it particularly on the treatment of financial instruments. This helped to shape the new IFRS 9, which is currently replacing IAS 39. This maintains the use of mixed measurement methods and limits the use of fair value to particularly appropriate circumstances, whereas the pioneers who developed IAS 39 as 'an interim standard' most likely hoped that its replacement would be based on full fair value.

Apart from these high profile pressures from powerful bodies, the effect of the IASB's due process should not be under-rated. Constituents often complained that the IASB did not listen to them, but that was really a complaint that their own particular views were not adopted. Given the variety of views on most subjects, it would have been impossible to accept them all, so disappointment by some was inevitable. There is evidence that comment letters and other forms of consultation did affect the IASB's decisions,[11] and as the constituency became progressively more diverse, through wider geographical adoption of IFRS, the voices that were heard by the IASB became less dominated by the 'Anglo-Saxon' world. At the same time, the members of the IASB were becoming more diverse and therefore more likely to have a natural understanding of the representations of diverse constituencies.

9   Changes in IASB Board Membership

The appointments of the original IASB Board members were for different time periods, in order to generate a steady replacement process, rather than a potentially disruptive situation in which most of the Board

Table 2 Members in January 2015, by IASB geographical classification

North America	3
Europe	4
Asia-Oceania	5
South America, Africa	2
Total	14

Notes
Europe includes one UK
Asia Oceania includes two Australasians
Africa is South Africa (one member)
Source: Pacter 2015, p. 21

members left together, with a consequent loss of experience. As of January 2006, the membership of the Board was virtually unchanged from that at inception (Table 1). Two casual vacancies had arisen due to individual circumstances and the replacements were 'like for like' in terms of geographical origin and professional background. Later, the planned retirement process started to have effect, and by July 2011 none of the original board members remained in office. During this period (2006–2011), the Trustees adopted a policy of wider geographical spread and less emphasis on technical expertise in selecting members. New members provided a stronger representation of the user perspective, starting with the appointment of a former securities market regulator, Philippe Danjou, in 2006, and a leading equity analyst, Stephen Cooper, in 2007. This policy culminated in 2011 with the appointment of a new Chairman who was an economist by professional background, a former finance minister, and a non native English speaker.

The composition of the Board in 2014 appears in Table 2.

This shows that the number of 'Anglo-Saxon' members reduced from 10 out of 14 in 2001 (and 2006) to 7[12] out of 14 in 2015. Although the numbers involved may not seem large, this constituted a significant shift in the balance from the 'Anglo-Saxons' to the rest of the world, the latter having lost a majority position. Moreover, the 'Anglo-Saxons were in fact a diverse group, the UK, for example, being a member of the EU, so that classifying them as a bloc is an over-simplification. However, the numbers do indicate a broadening of the background of board members and offer a partial explanation of the Board's increased willingness to depart from the FVV during the period between 2006 and 2015.

10   Changes in the IASC Foundation Constitution

The changing membership of the IASB reflected a more general change in the organisation of which the IASB was a part. The original constitution of the IASC Foundation had anticipated the need for adaptive change by incorporating a requirement for quinquennial reviews. The first of these, which concluded in 2005, gave the Trustees the right to comment on the IASB agenda, increased the number of trustees (broadening the geographical coverage in the process) and added accounting for emerging economies and small and medium enterprises to the IASB's objectives, thus potentially requiring the IASB to adopt projects that were of relatively greater interest to economies and constituents who tended to be ignored by a 'technical' standard-setting board focused on the needs of stock market investors. The requirements for a balance in the technical experience of board members were relaxed, and the liaison standard setter role was abolished, thus potentially relaxing the influence of the most advanced economies, particularly the Anglo-Saxons. The IASB's voting majority for issuing standards was increased from a simple majority (8/14) to 9/14. Combined with the changes in membership, this meant that the total Anglo-Saxon vote was no longer sufficient to pass a standard, even if the 'Anglo-Saxons' could be persuaded to vote unanimously in the same direction. The overall effect of these changes was to widen the accountability of the IASB, reducing the 'technical expert' orientation of Board members, strengthening oversight of the Board's work, including agenda development, and reducing the apparent domination of the 'Anglo-Saxon' countries, or, more generally, the advanced economies.

A further review of the IASC Foundation constitution took place in 2008–2010, as a result of which the name of the organisation was changed to the IFRS Foundation. A more substantive outcome of the review was extension of the process of improving consultation and monitoring of the IASB and the Foundation, in order to assure its ever-widening constituency that it was operating in a transparent and responsive manner, in accordance with its stated objectives. Specific changes resulting from this review included the establishment of the IFRS Foundation Monitoring Board (2009) to monitor the work of the Trustees, including the power to appoint Trustees. The members of the Monitoring Board were, in turn, to be appointed by public market regulators, which provided legitimacy for the organisation. A triennial public consultation on the IASB agenda was introduced, and an Accounting Standards Advisory Forum was established in order to provide a vehicle for communication between the IASB and national standard setters. The Trustees subsequently made major revisions to the Due Process Handbook (2013). Thus, the consultation process became more formal and transparent, and the IASB's members more accountable to the constituency of participants in the various consultation processes.

11   Recruitment and Retention of Countries Recognising IFRS

The IASB has no legal or legislative powers to require adoption or enforcement of its standards. For that it relies on voluntary adoption by national and international legislators and regulators, whose support is essential for IFRS to succeed. This is why the Monitoring Board, nominated by market regulators, is so important, as a means of establishing communication and trust between the creators of IFRS and those who adopt and enforce them.

In terms of adoption of IFRS, the IASB (including the full range of institutions within the Foundation) has been remarkably successful. By 2015, of 138 jurisdictions surveyed by Pacter (2015), 114 required IFRS for domestic publicly accountable entities reporting to capital markets. This included the countries of the EU, which, despite the controversies surrounding IAS 39, had successfully adopted and implemented IFRS with the exception of the 'carve-out' on hedge accounting, which affected less than two dozen banks, out of a total of more than 8,000 entities. The notable exception is the USA, where US GAAP is still required, but even there IFRS has been accepted for foreign registrants on US exchanges, and the SEC has contemplated the possibility of allowing domestic entities to choose IFRS, although there has been little sign that it is yet ready for such a change. Elsewhere in the world, more countries continue to adopt or recognise IFRS, including many developing countries seeking financing from bodies such as the World Bank, which prefer accountability to be in an accounting language, such as IFRS, that has international credibility. This explains why the IASB and its Foundation have broadened their geographical outreach.

In order to cope with this expanding and changing constituency, the IASB has, as we have seen, adapted incrementally but significantly, because its standards need to be compatible with the cultures and environments of the jurisdictions that use them. However, the IASB would not have been successful in widening the adoption of its standards if the demand for international standards had not existed and perhaps increased. This arises from the increasing globalisation of capital markets and the need of national jurisdictions to develop credibility to gain access to those markets. It is notable, for example, that one of the outcomes of the second triennial review was the creation of an Emerging Economies Group (2011). It is also notable that, during the period 2001–2015, the 'Anglo-Saxon' economies have declined in relative importance, due to the rapid growth of emerging economies, notably China, which has provided an IASB board member since 2007. Thus, developments in the IASB have mirrored developments in the world economy.

12   The Price and the Dangers

The process of reaching out to a wider constituency creates difficulties. Institutionally, it is possible to have wider consultation and representation, but in setting standards, a wider constituency means that a wider range of views has to be considered, whilst at the same time maintaining the consistency and coherence of the standards. Thus the price of widening the constituency might be to dilute the quality of the standards. At worst, the standards might be changed for the specific purpose of placating a particular interest group rather than because it was perceived as an improvement in the standard. The power of lobbying by interest groups is well documented at the level of national sta ndard-setting, and these forces are multiplied in the case of an international standard-setter (Zeff 2002).

Such pressures are at their greatest when a particular jurisdiction is being persuaded to join or to remain in the IFRS community. There have been seven obvious cases where the IASB has responded to these situations. The first was the threatened EU carve-out of the fair value option in a proposed amendment to IAS 39, at the behest of the ECB, to which the IASB responded successfully, as described earlier. A second was the modification of the treatment of redeemable equity instruments, which was done to accommodate co-operative entities, particularly in New Zealand (IASB, 2008). A third was the exemption of government entities from the definition of related parties (IAS 24, revised 2009), which was designed to accommodate the needs of China, where government participation in business is pervasive. A fourth, also designed to meet the specific needs of China, was the revision of the application of 'deemed cost' in IFRS1 (Camfferman and Zeff 2015, p. 530). The fifth was the concession on transferring financial instruments from fair value to amortised cost, which, as described earlier, was made under pressure from the European Parliament (amendment to IAS 39, 2008). The sixth was a transitional exemption (IFRS 14, 2014) and new project on accounting for regulatory deferral accounts (a concept previously unknown to IFRS) which was undertaken to ease the difficulties of certain regulated Canadian firms at the time of Canadian first-time adoption of IFRS. The seventh was the separation of 'bearer' plants from produce in the revision of IAS 41 (June 2014), which was a concession to Malaysia.

Each of these amendments had a practical rationale, but it is disputable whether some of them could be regarded as consistent with existing standards and whether any inconsistency indicated that the existing standards should be changed. This draws attention to the danger that standard-setting could become dominated by narrow self-interest rather than principle, whereas the IASB hopes to develop principles-based accounting which will serve the greater good of the broad constituency.

This in turn raises the question of how these principles are to be determined. The IASB's approach, which it is currently pursuing, is to develop a *conceptual framework*, defining the objectives, properties and other fundamental assumptions that it will make in setting standards. The framework is developed through due process and therefore represents an accepted and transparent set of principles. Under the FVV, the framework would lead directly to a specific method of measurement (FV) and recognition criteria consistent with that ('recognise anything that has a fair value to the entity'). Under the alternative view, the framework will set out the desirable properties and objectives of financial reports but its principles will be less prescriptive, leaving more room for the judgement of the IASB in setting specific standards. For this reason, it is important that IASB members are supported by a due process that ensures both transparency in the decision-making process and acceptance by the constituency.

13   Conclusion

The historical record shows that the IASB has, in its first fifteen years, successfully pursued its mission and progressively adapted to its changing environment. As its international constituency has broadened, so has international participation in the IASB organisation and its consultative processes. From being potentially dominated by 'Anglo-Saxon' influences at its inception, the IASB is now (2015) more representative of and accountable to the world which it serves.

The danger of the change from a 'technical' body to a body that interacts at all stages with its constituency is that it may become more 'political' in the worst sense, i.e. yielding to the influence of powerful interest groups rather than achieving a consensus by transparent and rational debate. We have identified two safeguards against this: First, for the IASB in setting standards, an effective conceptual framework; Second, for the IASB organisation as a whole, a transparent system of oversight and due process. Work on these two projects is an ongoing concern of the IASB and the IFRS Foundation respectively.

Notes

1. This was no accident. The structure had been advocated strongly by Lynn Turner, Chief Accountant of the influential SEC, on the ground that it would enhance the credibility of the IASB in international capital markets (Camfferman and Zeff 2007, pp. 480–1).

2. The IASB's early resistance to developing a standard for Small and Medium Entities (SME's) was an instance of apparent indifference to the particuar needs of developing economies, but, consistent with the theme of this paper, the IASB did change its views in the light of representations from its constituency, and its 'SME' standard was issued in 2009.

3. The existing IASC standards were adopted by the IASB at its first meeting, in 2001. These continued to be referred to as International Accounting Standards (IAS), whereas new standards issued by the IASB are referred to as International Financial Reporting Standards (IFRS).

4. Thus, the concept of an 'improvement' was a limited one, confined to amending existing standards by increasing their clarity and removing unnecessary alternative treatments, with the overall objective of achieving greater transparency and comparability in accounts. The introduction of new accounting treatments would have required a completely new standard, passing through full due process, rather than the 'improvement' process.

5. That is, hedging of a whole portfolio in aggregate. IAS 39 was based on hedging individual securities rather than portfolios.

6. Whittington (2005) provides an account of these events from the perspective of an IASB member, written at the time when they occurred.

7. Both prudence and stewardship have been revived as concepts in the current conceptual framework proposals (IASB, 2015). This illustrates the increased responsiveness of the IASB to its constituencies, which is discussed later in this paper.

8. This is discussed further in Whittington (2008). There is obvious overlap between decision usefulness and stewardship, insofar as stewardship also is concerned with economic decisions, but there are important differences of emphasis. Decision usefulness when applied to investors and lenders typically emphasises the valuation of the entity in terms of predicting future cash flows. This ignores the interactive aspects of stewardship, as in corporate governance, where the shareholder is seen as a proprietor to whom the management of the entity is accountable for its past actions and who, by responding to such information (e.g. by appointing and rewarding senior

management) can influence future activities and cash flows, rather than passively predicting them. In this context, historic information can provide important feedback for stewardship, whereas the passive investor will be concerned with such information only if it assists in predicting future returns.

9. Here we use the term 'efficient' in the sense of informational efficiency, as in the Efficient Markets Hypothesis (Beaver 1981, Chapter 6). This is widely assumed to exist, in the semi-strong form, where the market price reflects all publicly available information.

10. Curiously, the IASB has chosen not to revisit the parallel problem of capital maintenance, which was at the heart of the 'inflation accounting' (more properly 'price change accounting') debates of the nineteen seventies and eighties (Tweedie and Whittington 1984, Chapter 12). This may reflect a desire to avoid reviving the controversies of the past.

11. For example, Giner and Arce (2014) study the role of lobbying by national standard setters in the due process for the development of IFRS 2, Share-Based Payments.

12. North America 3, plus 2 Australasians and one each from UK and South Africa.

A Critical Analysis of the Balanced Scorecard: Towards a More Dialogic Approach

David J. Cooper and Mahmoud Ezzamel

1   Introduction

Reliance on traditional management and accounting practices is believed to lead to incorrect operational and strategic decisions (Locke 1996). Eccles (1991), for example, notes how managers have been experimenting with new measures to deal with these changes. Since the first article by

We acknowledge the financial support of the Social Science and Humanities Research Council. We thank the late Norman Macintosh for encouraging us to collaborate. Earlier versions were presented at the University of Alberta, the European Accounting Association Congress, the 'Governing by Numbers' conference at the University of Edinburgh and at the University of Strathclyde. We appreciate the research assistance of Olio Muchinsky and discussions with Barbara Townley, Sandy Qu and Daniel Martinez. We benefitted also from comments by Wai-Fong Chua, Niels Dechow, Ken Euske, the late Anthony Hopwood, Megan McDugauld, Andrea Mennicken, Paolo Quattrone, and Keith Robson.

D.J. Cooper (✉)
School of Business, University of Alberta, Edmonton, Alberta, Canada

M. Ezzamel
Cardiff Business School, University of Cardiff, Cardiff, Wales

IE Business School, Madrid

© The Author(s) 2016
J. Haslam, P. Sikka (eds.), *Pioneers of Critical Accounting*,
DOI 10.1057/978-1-137-54212-0_11

Kaplan and Norton (1992), the BSC has received much attention from academics, the management accounting profession, the consulting industry, and practicing managers. It is seen as a response to this concern for alignment between accounting techniques and measures and the current management context.

It is not difficult to see why strategic performance measurement systems, such as the BSC, are popular (Cooper et al. 2015). The BSC is presented as a technique that has been derived from the practice of leading companies. Kaplan and Norton have actively promoted the BSC and encouraged explicit modeling of organizations. Our concern is that most research and writing on the BSC has been on the technical aspects of its design and use, with insufficient attention paid to an evaluation of its fundamental approach to managing and organizing. In this chapter we examine its core assumptions.[1] We emphasize that the assumptions about managing organizations are not inevitable-—there could be alternative management assumptions, approaches and techniques. Only by presenting alternatives can managers choose which techniques and approaches best suit the circumstances of the organization (including which versions of the BSC or other strategic performance measurement systems to use). This choice process can be described as deciding on the means to achieve given purposes.

Further, as Lowe and many others have argued, a discussion of values (the purposes of management) needs to be an integral part of the choice of control systems generally (e.g. Chua et al. 1989; Lowe and McInnes 1971). It is only by considering both means and ends that managers will know whether they are doing the right things, as well as doing the things they do in an efficient manner.

This chapter asks a fundamental question: What consequences does the BSC have on understandings of the nature of managing, organizations and society? We provide a critical commentary on the seemingly ubiquitous mode of managing that has become known as 'managing by numbers' (Ezzamel et al. 1990; Porter 1995). While there is much of value in managing based on evidence and facts,[2] we aim to highlight complexity and power effects of such facts, such as whose facts are legitimate and what is occluded by such an approach. We seek both to highlight the role of power in fact production and to create space for other forms of rationality to be debated and adopted. We contend, however, that the manner by which 'managing by numbers/ facts/ evidence' has been discussed in the accounting literature and embraced in practice has marginalized consideration of alternative approaches to management (e.g. intuition, emotion, commitment, a public interest perspective). As the BSC is one of the most important developments in the 'managing by numbers' approach, we use it to illustrate our analysis. We show that the BSC can reinforce a view of organizations as hierarchical, capable of being managed as mechanisms, and managed for the ultimate benefit of a narrow set of interests. This view is not only presented as descriptive, but also becomes the basis for prescriptions—that organizations should be managed in this manner. However, we also suggest that the BSC can be used differently—encouraging and promoting dialogue and debate and offering a possibility for more democratic organizational processes.

It would be naïve to believe that strategic performance measurement systems like the BSC are, by themselves, likely to dramatically change our view of organizations or society, and how they can be best managed. What such techniques do is to help institutionalize certain ways of looking at, and understanding, the nature of management and organization (Meyer and Rowan 1977). By examining the core assumptions of such techniques we can appreciate the taken for granted assumptions about how organization and management function. There is a growing and substantial body of research that demonstrates how accounting and other techniques not only reflect views and cultures (Bourguignon et al. 2004), but also help to give specific shape and practical significance to such general views (Hopwood 1987; Miller and O'Leary 1990).

The purpose of our analysis is to indicate how accounting techniques, such as the BSC, help to construct and institutionalize specific ways of seeing and to spell out some of the economic, social, political and cultural effects that result from these ways of seeing and understanding. The BSC is conventionally regarded as a technical means to achieve almost any purpose or strategy—a neutral language/ measurement system to communicate and implement strategy. For us, techniques can fundamentally affect the purpose, strategy and indeed conception of an organization. Our critical analysis shows that the BSC is an example of management ideology and is based on empirical illustrations that relate not just to the writings of Kaplan and Norton but also how their ideas and writings have been taken up by teachers, consultants and organizations.

Exploring these assumptions and our proposed framework enables an analysis of the likely effects (e.g. on firm performance, resistance or acceptance) of adopting a management accounting technique, such as the BSC. Further, in testing the effects of the BSC, our framework would help cross sectional assessments (e.g. Ittner et al. 2003) of the success of the BSC, by specifying the conditions under which specific BSCs may lead to improved performance and which moderating variables affect the results (e.g. Chenhall 2005).[3]

It might be argued that assumptions do not matter- all that is important are predictions. This belief has become obsolete in the philosophy of science (Chalmers 1999), and can lead to seriously misleading or disabling management recommendations. For example, emphasizing a model's instrumental, or predictive, ability stresses results at the expense of understanding how these results were generated. Further, model assumptions have major ethical implications; assumptions are not neutral to the object being modeled, particularly when that object is human or a human construction such as an organization. If people are assumed to act mechanically to incentives, then their humanity and complexity can be ignored. Finally, model assumptions matter because they delineate the boundaries and conditions under which the model is expected to work best. For these and other reasons, assumptions matter; they have important consequences.

There is another reason we focus on the BSC. We see potential for using it as a mechanism to enhance more democratic and inclusive modes of management, which we refer to as a constrained dialogic BSC.[4] A constrained dialogical BSC would facilitate organizational debate about not only how the current organization operates and achieves results, but also facilitates a constructive and open discussion of objectives and strategy. Conventional uses of the BSC-—and the hierarchical way it is portrayed in most BSC writings—militate against such debate. One of the major virtues of the conventional BSC is that it has a focus on initiatives, or actions (Olve et al. 2003), and this feature enables a constrained dialogic BSC to balance dialogue and action, to avoid organizations being either talking shops or oriented toward action without reflection (Brunsson 2002). Tuomela (2005) indicates how one organization used a BSC to encourage more interactive controls, and to combine talk and action.

This chapter thus focuses both on the modes of thinking enshrined in the BSC and ways that these modes of thinking can be examined and assessed through greater dialogue. But we also are aware of the serious limitations of dialogue and the risk that the structures and taken for granted assumptions of the BSC can also subvert dialogue. Our arguments are based on careful readings of the writings of Kaplan and Norton, studies that have assessed the impacts of the BSC and our own experience researching the BSC and related performance measurement systems in multiple organizations (for profit and not for profit). Our approach is pragmatic, constrained but nevertheless progressive. Exploring assumptions enables the consideration of alternative views and thereby permits the possibility of improvement of management techniques—to make them more genuinely beneficial. It also allows us to move beyond action oriented towards the strategies imposed by capital markets and senior managers (Ittner and Larcker 2001; Ezzamel et al. 2008), to focus instead upon considering both the purposes and achievement of strategy.

After a brief description of the BSC, the chapter elaborates our version of critical analysis, which combines technical and social understandings and concerns in the context of sensitivity to issues of power and values. We then apply this analysis to examine the core assumptions of the BSC, before we draw together our main conclusions and offer some suggestions for a more dialogical use of the BSC. Our critical approach moves away from diagnostic controls and a heavy reliance on a scorecard approach, towards a strategic performance measurement system that facilitates organizational deliberation about beliefs, boundaries and interaction. This is more than the managerial extensions to 'interactive controls' (Simons 1995), 'clan controls' (Ouchi 1981) or 'enabling bureaucracies' (Adler and Borys 1996). Our approach seeks to integrate measures with other performance attributes not susceptible to sensible quantification, enables consideration of the categories and structure of the BSC, and facilitates a management approach that recognizes, and hopefully incorporates, other rationalities and values.

2   The BSC

The BSC has undergone a number of developments since the first article by Kaplan and Norton in 1992.[5] The BSC is presented as *the* tool that would remedy the problems of traditional budgeting systems. The BSC is presented as a comprehensive framework for a strategic management system that is not only derived from strategy but is translated back to strategy (Kaplan and Norton 1996a, p. 148).

Kaplan and Norton present the BSC as a translation of strategy into a collection of multiple financial and non-financial measures that are tied together in a series of cause and effect relationships that navigate the organization towards future competitive success. The measures cover four perspectives: financial, customer, internal-business process, and learning and growth. As their thinking and experience have evolved, Kaplan and Norton strengthen and clarify the link between the BSC and strategy. They suggest the use of strategy maps that cascade through the organizational hierarchy from its apex down to the level of the individual operator (Kaplan and Norton 2001, 2004a). The emphasis is increasingly on alignment (Kaplan and Norton 2004b, 2006) and top management leadership in implementation and use (Kaplan and Norton 2004a, 2008)

The diagram showing the architecture of the BSC (Kaplan and Norton 1996b; modified as Fig. 3–2 in ibid 2001) is a classic and powerful summary cited widely in many management accounting textbooks. This diagram begins with vision and strategy and proceeds through the four perspectives, with arrows linking all these parts to emphasize double-loop learning and balance between the perspectives. Moreover, associated with each perspective is a grid with four themes: objectives, measures, targets, and initiatives.

Different organizations and consultants emphasize different components and uses for the BSC, and might even use techniques that few others would recognize as part of a BSC. This, of course, is likely to be the case for any technique- users make it their own (Latour 1987). Nevertheless, it would be absurd to then argue that there is no commonality for a technique- in the case of the BSC we identify its link to strategy, its use of multiple perspectives, its emphasis on organizational mapping, some notion of balance and interaction between perspectives, its willingness to consider financial and non financial measures, and its commitment to a logic of goals—measures—targets and initiatives. It is these common features that we examine further in our critical analysis, where the purpose is to point out that the assumptions could be different and these differences could provide organizations with new ways of conceiving and using the BSC.

3   Critical Analysis

Our critical approach to examining the core assumptions, and their effects on our understanding of managing and organizations, combines technical and social understandings (see Table 1).

Table 1 Forms of analysis of the BSC

Issue	Social	Technical
Key questions	How does BSC affect the way we perceive, make sense of, and manage organizations? Implications for society?	How does BSC affect efficiency and profitability of organizations?
Conception of organization	Emphasizes disequilibria, discontinuity, and fuzzy boundaries	Stable, formal modeling is possible. Change within stable parameters
View of strategy	Questions what organizational strategy is. Emphasizes human, organization and society effects of the way BSC is conceived, formulated, and applied	Strategy is viewed as rationally developed and applied
Focus of strategy	All those affected by the BSC are significant stakeholders	Multiple constituencies are only important if they are calculated to eventually lead to shareholder benefit
Technology-people interaction	Human interests dominate	Technology and efficiency considerations dominate
Conception of performance	Questions the very idea of performance. Performance is contested	Multiple constituencies and dimensions of performance. Balance achieved by top managers

Critical analysis has a distinguished tradition in social science, raising questions about the fundamental and taken for granted assumptions of our everyday practices and systems for managing. We apply a critical analysis to the BSC in part because the technique is so influential and pervasive.[6] We demonstrate how this analysis of the BSC extends debates on organizations beyond questions of mechanisms of governance and the implementation of strategy, to questions about the focus of strategy and in whose interest the organization should operate. A critical analysis emphasizes the complex interactions between people and management techniques, allowing us to revisit the impact of the BSC on people and the impact of people on the BSC. Measurement systems, such as the BSC, impact modes of thinking and ways of behaving, which affects the way they are used.[7] A critical analysis sensitizes us to the variety of effects that different measurement systems have on the scope for engagement and dialogue in organizations. Measurement systems initiatives, such as the BSC, impact on the way employees define the meaning of their work and make sense of their work environment, construct and negotiate their interests, and shape their identities. A new measurement system offers employees a new representation of their effects on the world (Zuboff 1988). Such systems also have consequences for the allocation of organizational rewards, the psychic and material well being of all those connected to the organization, the distribution of wealth in society more generally, and the state of the environment. By examining some of the fundamental assumptions of the BSC we can shed light on the social impact of the technique that has generated so much technical attention.

The distinctions between a technical and social view can be illustrated by an example, using a hypothetical oil company. Let us assume the oil company is considering an investment in a new offshore facility, but it is known it will have significant ecological consequences. A technical analysis would proceed by conducting a (rational) cost benefit analysis, including any impacts the ecological consequences would have on the firm (reputation, legal liabilities, consumer boycotts etc). The assumption is that all relevant information and all appropriate trade offs can be made in terms of money and the Pareto criterion. The decision by senior managers to undertake the investment is then based on whether the calculations indicate that the proposed facility would add value to the owners. A social analysis would consider all possible stakeholders that are likely to be affected by such an investment. Like the technical analysis, a social analysis would rely on information about the likely effects of the investment, and recognize that different groups may have incentives to provide incorrect information. However, in a social analysis there may be disputes about what is relevant information and whether there is a universal means of measurement (such as money). Further, a social analysis would acknowledge that various stakeholders may have histories of mutual distrust and hostility, and that such histories may impact the information and possibilities of dialogue even if it may seem that would be in their self-interest to agree (Forester 2000). A resolution of competing assessments might be made through dialogue between all those involved, not simply a social cost benefit exercise where all costs and benefits are converted into money. Or, the analysis could reveal that a resolution was achieved through an exercise of power. In addition, a social analysis might go further and ask about the classification of a new offshore facility as an 'investment'. It could re-conceive the facility as, for example, a chance to build a local community, an opportunity to employ disadvantaged groups, a distraction from oil conservation, an economic benefit to the firm's owners, and so on (for a powerful example, relating to water policies, see Espeland 1998).

In contrast, consider Kaplan and Norton's discussion of Mobil, which they describe as "perhaps our best example of putting the five principles of a Strategy-Focused organization into practice." (2001, p. 29). They describe how strategy was translated to operational terms (covering the four BSC perspectives) and they end the chapter listing an impressive set of results attributed to the BSC. Yet, their discussion does not offer a substantial analysis of the links between the adoption of the BSC and these results, or any alternative explanations for the results. Their analysis is predominantly technical. Lacking any serious or social consideration of Mobil's history, its ownership structure, its competitive advantages, the trajectory of its life cycle, the state of the market and the social, political and economic climate in which it operates. There is no mention of how employees and unions reacted to, or interacted with, the BSC. There is no critical analysis, for example whether Mobil engages in activities that harm some stakeholders but benefit others.

Moving beyond their specific example, it seems that Kaplan and Norton would have little to say about an organization like Mobil enhancing their apparent performance through such activities as off-shore employment, expansion into cheaper, unregulated or tax-free zones, damage to the environment, and illicit actions around the world. The claimed benefits of the BSC cannot be fully assessed unless account is taken of the context of the organization, or of the alternative explanations for improved organizational performance (and, indeed, alternative assessments of performance). The universalistic appeal of the BSC[8] is based on the assumption that its adoption and use is the explanation for organizational performance. Yet, as we show in the next section, the assumptions normally underlying the BSC are consistent with the technical view outlined in Table 1. There does, however, seem to be a possibility of a BSC oriented towards a different set of assumptions, ones that are more aligned with the social view outlined in Table 1.

A critical analysis needs to recognize the mutuality between the technical and the social (Latour 1987). The value of integrating a technical and social analysis can be illustrated by considering how one might conduct a field study of the use of a BSC in an organization. For such a study, researchers would frame interviews and research questions around both the technical design and achievements of the BSC, as well as how the BSC helps to construct particular views of the nature of organization, strategy and performance. In so doing, such research would help us understand how specific organizations adapt the general ideas of the BSC for their specific purposes and context, and the effects of such adaptations on stakeholders (Qu and Cooper 2011; Busco and Quattrone 2015).

4   Assumptions of the BSC

In this section we identify and examine the core assumptions underlying the construction of the BSC and the manner by which the BSC tends to be used in practice. Our discussion of each assumption begins by indicating our view of the literature on the BSC and our experience of its application in practice.[9] We also briefly indicate how using a BSC dialogically can help critical reflection and assessment of assumptions and values, and stimulating consideration of other possibilities. This section identifies four key assumptions: the value of strategy and vision; the interests around which the BSC is constructed; the mechanical analogies used in BSC construction; and the (quantification) language used to construct the BSC.

4.1   The Value of Strategy and Vision

One of the key assumptions of the BSC is its explicit and direct connection with organizational vision and strategy. In Kaplan and Norton's work, the traditional control model built around the budgeting system is criticized for its failure to connect with organizational vision and strategy. Certainly, a common observation of practices in many organizations is the disjunction between the budget process and longer term planning processes (Mintzberg 1994; Pollitt and Bouckaert 2000). In contrast, the BSC is presented as the means by which strategy and vision are converted into desired outcomes (e.g. Kaplan and Norton 1996b, 2001, p. 73). It is depicted as the driver towards the 'strategy- focused organization', through the development and enactment of strategic maps (Kaplan and Norton 2001, 2004a). Strategy is premised to lie at the heart of the BSC (ibid, p. 9). Yet, curiously, there is little systematic evidence supporting a positive impact on organizational performance of a link between strategy and performance measures.

In the BSC, strategy is conceptualized as something that is both doable and deliverable, and the manager is assumed to have the necessary autonomy and opportunity to lead the organization in the desired direction. The focus is on 'execution' and implementation. Thus Kaplan and Norton suggest that the BSC should be viewed as more than a measurement system, as a way of successfully implementing new strategies (Kaplan and Norton 2001). Moreover, the strategic language implied by the BSC texts is based on SWOT analysis (strengths-weaknesses-opportunities-threats). The manager is entrusted with turning the threats facing the organization into opportunities, and recognizing and exploiting organizational strength to beat the competition (Kaplan and Norton 2001, p. 284).

A fundamental issue is that the value of strategic thinking and practices needs to be assessed rather than assumed; Mintzberg (1994) summarizes the evidence that shows that organizations do not necessarily benefit from strategic management, even when implemented as intended. Further, Kaplan and Norton offer a particular, but largely implicit, conceptualization of strategy and the manager; we draw attention to some implications of their conceptualization.

The conceptualization of strategy in the BSC has evolved over time. An emphasis on strategy maps and organizational modeling may suggest that the BSC is seen as a mechanism for developing strategy. Yet, Kaplan and Norton (2001, 2004a) focus on the BSC as a communicator of previously developed top management strategies, making strategy a continuous process, and developing strategy maps that link objectives in a cause-and-effect relationship. Whether the emphasis is formulation or implementation, the fundamental assumption is that these two processes can be meaningfully and usefully separated. This separation not only places unrealistic expectations (about the information and power of senior management), reinforcing a hierarchical model of the organization, but also represents employees as mere tools for executing the ideas of others. Further, alternative views of strategy emphasize its emergent nature; strategic intention often only becomes clear after observing how strategy implementation unfolds (Mintzberg et al. 1995).

A technical approach to the BSC assumes organizations as intensely competitive. It constructs a view of the world as hostile, confrontational and conflictual. In this scenario of competitive strategy, employees are expected to be "good corporate citizens" (Kaplan and Norton 2001, p. 96), embracing corporate objectives as if they were their own and seeing other organizations as hostile competitors. Possibilities for deviation from corporate priorities are assumed to be avoidable via the judicious use of reward structures and monitoring procedures, despite the voluminous evidence in the literature that such mechanisms never succeed in fully aligning the interests of employees with those of the organization. At the extreme, misalignment is viewed as resistance and disloyalty. The motive for forms of interaction between organizations, such as cooperative and trusting behaviour, strategic alliances and networking based on mutual benefit, is marginalized. Building alliances and cooperative networks is only regarded as rational when competitive advantage is likely. Being single-minded about pursuing competitive advantage may lead managers to focus their attention on winning the competition without considering the costs to employees, the community and the environment. The building and fostering of trust relations, which may result in lower, long-term, transactions costs (Ouchi 1979) would be an approach more consistent with a social view of the BSC. This would incorporate alternative views of the manager, for example as a 'coach', colleague or wise person, roles that may have more beneficial consequences for staff development and the minimization of intra-organizational conflict.

Further, the scope for action assumed to be enjoyed by the manager may be exaggerated in a technical approach: rather than being proactive in changing and shaping the environment, the manager may be so constrained by the infrastructure of past decisions, such as major investment decisions, as to only be in a position to react and respond to what organization history or the environment dictates (Williams et al. 1994).

The BSC has real potential, however, as a mechanism to enable widespread discussion of an organization's strategy. Rather than the top down view, a dialogic use of the BSC would encourage debate about the aims and objectives of the organization, and how sub- units can contribute to such aims. Used dialogically, the BSC would have the advantage of not separating planning and strategic thinking from knowledge and experience of operating the organization and making plans work. Implementation issues could be considered simultaneously with strategic development, thus contributing to better implementation of plans. The BSC would thus operate as a knowledge-sharing technology, enabling senior managers to develop and utilize their skills in coaching and facilitating discussion. Over-investment in debate and deliberation about alternatives and strategies would be limited, however, by the emphasis of the BSC on action plans.

4.2   In Whose Interest?

Kaplan and Norton argue that the four perspectives of the BSC identifies key stakeholders: shareholders (financial), customers, and employees (innovation and learning). They suggest that for some organizations, "one or more additional perspectives may be needed" (1996a, 34). Kaplan and Norton do not wish to commit themselves to a definitive list of stakeholders across all types of organization, yet they crucially state,

> …we don't think that all stakeholders are automatically entitled to a position on a business unit's scorecard. The scorecard outcomes and performance drivers should measure those factors that create competitive advantage and breakthroughs for an organization. (Kaplan and Norton 1996a, p. 35)

In contrast, other discussions of the BSC (e.g. Otley 1999) suggest its potential for improving the welfare of all organizational stakeholders. However, Kaplan and Norton (2001, pp. 102–103) criticize stakeholder scorecards for failing to show *how* the balanced goals are to be achieved. They consider the stakeholder scorecard as only a first step on the road to a strategy scorecard; a constituent will be considered a stakeholder only if it is calculated to "create competitive advantage". Kaplan and Norton (2004a, p. 11) consistently place the financial perspective, typically stated as 'long-term shareholder value', at the apex of their strategy maps.

A telling example of the dominance of shareholders in Kaplan and Norton's understanding of the BSC is provided by their discussion of a chemical company that wanted to create a new perspective to reflect environmental considerations. Kaplan and Norton responded "Keeping the environment clean is important. Companies must comply with law and regulations, but such compliance doesn't seem to be the basis for competitive advantage" (1996a, p. 35). Kaplan and Norton only acknowledged that environmental issues might be an additional perspective for that company when the chemicals company countered by stating that unless it demonstrates that it is an outstanding corporate citizen, its financial performance will be adversely affected. Kaplan and Norton believe that only shareholder (financial) advantage is the basis for deciding who counts as a stakeholder.

Kaplan and Norton argue that the BSC "guards against suboptimization" (1992, p. 73), but do not explain how this is achieved. It would seem that one of the four perspectives must be singled out as the main objective function, with the remaining perspectives acting as constraints. But which of the four perspectives is to have hierarchical priority over the others? How are trade-offs (balance) going to be incorporated into a multiple objective function? In contrast, using a BSC to encourage dialogue will enable serious discussion about multiple objectives, and perhaps allow a form of goal programming that is consistent with a conception of organizational objectives as a series of multiple constraints, producing a feasible set of action alternatives that would be satisfactory for all stakeholders (Simon 1964).

Jensen (2001) argues that the BSC is flawed because it fails to provide managers with a single score of how they have performed that reflects how they tradeoff between the four perspectives. He asserts that ultimately it is the change in long-term capital market value that managers and the institutional milieu use to assess the performance of corporations. At the heart of this discussion lies Kaplan and Norton's emphasis upon the notion of *balance* in the BSC. They specifically stress balance between: internal and external measures (e.g. those relating to shareholders and customers compared to those related to internal processes and learning and growth); past (lag, financial) and future (lead, mainly non-financial) measures; and outcomes and performance drivers (Kaplan and Norton 1996a, p. 10). Yet, Jensen's argument about the necessity for managers in capitalist economies to make tradeoffs undermines this claimed balance between the different measures, and also across the four perspectives of the BSC. Perhaps more critically, the lack of a substantive discussion of stakeholder groups by Kaplan and Norton may explain the frequency with which we can detect the underlying shareholder orientation being treated as pre-eminent for private sector organizations. For example, consider the diagrams (2004, pp. 8, 11, 31, 37, 39, 44, 50, 51, etc.; 2001, pp. 70–71, 82, 96, 98, 101, 110, 119, and 125–130) where the three non-financial perspectives *lead to* the financial perspective, the latter clearly situated at the top of the strategic maps as long-term shareholder value.

The preeminence given to shareholders by Kaplan and Norton can be questioned on both moral and instrumental grounds. Garvey and Swan make the moral argument that, "a more explicitly 'political' view of corporate objectives is appropriate, since members of the firm besides shareholders are affected by executive decisions" (1994, p. 148). Similarly, Kay and Silberston note that in the UK,

> [t]he 1985 Companies Act…imposes on directors an explicit duty to strike a balance between their interests and those of other members. (1995, p. 88)

Berle, co-author of a seminal book on US managerial and shareholder capitalism, offers a poignant statement:

> What contributions do they [stockholders] make, entitling them to heir-ship of half the profits of the industrial system…? Stockholders toil not, neither do they spin, to earn that reward. They are beneficiaries by position only. Justification for their inheritance must be sought outside classic economic reasoning. (1968, p. xxiiii)

In emphasizing the predominance of shareholder interests can also be challenged on more instrumental grounds. Kaplan and Norton's version of the BSC reinforces a particular version of Anglo-American capitalism, a version increasingly challenged on both moral and instrumental grounds, especially since the 2008 financial crisis (e.g. Arnold 2008; Merino et al. 2010). Different forms of capitalism have, at specific times, outperformed the Anglo-American model. Japanese and continental European capitalisms tend to emphasize the role of banks in capital formation and the rights of labour, while the South-East Asian 'tigers' relied on tight alliances between firms and often emphasize family connections (Whitley 1999). China currently offers a further economic model, where central political control informs economic activity. Bourguignon et al. (2004) argue that French capitalism relies on social hierarchy and honor. As Roberts and van den Steen (2001) observe, governance structures based on shareholder wealth maximization seem to out perform governance based on employee welfare only under highly specific conditions (see also Engelen 2002). Historical studies such as Gordon, Edwards and Reich (1982) show that the effectiveness and form of control systems in the USA depends on the specific version of capitalism and market conditions facing organizations. Barley and Kunda (1992) have also shown that different ideologies of control vary with the cycles of economic expansion and contraction. Kaplan and Norton do not consider the conditions that favour one version of capitalism over another. These examples suggest that on moral and instrumental grounds different stakeholders should be considered at the apex of the BSC.

Further, in a technical analysis, managers are cast as neutral agents with no specific allegiances; as dispassionate machines who are simply balancing the interests of other stakeholders. If managers were indeed neutral agents, they would adjust their ideologies and methods of control dependent on the most appropriate form of capitalism that exists in a particular time and place.[10] If managers wish to act as neutral agents, then they can structure the BSC to encourage debate and to understand the balance of forces between different stakeholders. A dialogic BSC would involve no pre-set hierarchy of perspectives, but instead facilitate discussion of different contributors to the organization in ensuring its survival and well being.

4.3   Models of Organization

Kaplan and Norton emphasize the importance of being explicit about modeling the organization in order to develop a useful performance measurement system. In their development of the BSC, an organization is regarded as a set of more or less independent variables linked to one another, producing clear and desirable results. It is a mechanical view that leads to an engineering perspective on management—pulling levers, pushing buttons, and lubricating points of friction, as if humans and machines are similarly predictable. If results vary from expectations, it is assumed that they are caused by human error or resistance. The organization is assumed to function as a hierarchical nest of mechanisms and causal chains. Pepper (1948) points out that the metaphor of mechanism includes both discrete mechanisms, such as levers, which stress independence of parts and management by contact, and consolidated mechanisms, such as electromagnetic fields, which stress interdependence and management at a distance. The possibility of consolidating mechanisms resonates with more contemporary models of organizations, which suggests the interdependence of parts and the value of employee empowerment and commitment. This model of the organization could form the basis of a BSC oriented towards empowerment and interdependence.

The discrete mechanism and linear modeling emphasis is very clearly stated in Kaplan and Norton's description of the BSC: "[t]he scorecard enables the strategic hypotheses to be described as a set of cause-and-effect relationships that are explicit and testable." (2001, pp. 75–76). This model of cause–effect ignores uncertainty as unknowability and ignorance. Externalities and complexities, typically the result of multiple effects and dynamic interactions, are not addressed in this modeling approach.

Kaplan and Norton offer multiple diagrams (e.g. 1996a, pp. 76, 77) that depict the BSC as a set of hierarchical relationships. Although they refer to double loop learning and emphasize the value of feedback, this model of the organization is not seriously developed. A preference for linear uni-directional modeling is also reflected in the subsequent academic literature that has sought to empirically test the effect of the BSC on firm performance (e.g. Huelsbeck et al. 2011; Tayler 2011). Mechanical analogy of the organization has the appeal of abstracting away from the daunting complexities of organizational reality. Within this model, the BSC becomes the framework that provides guidance, at every organizational level and for every individual, for intentional action towards desired outcomes.

Yet, as many commentators have noted, this discrete mechanical model has serious limitations (March and Simon 1958). While this model can be useful in stable conditions, in more turbulent situations it will create organizations incapable of adaptive and flexible behaviour, encourages mindless rule following, and produces undesirable consequences as the interests of organizational members can conflict with declared organizational goals, and result in dehumanizing effects on organizational members (Burns and Stalker 1961).

The discrete mechanical metaphor effectively denies alternative models of effective organization. However, any modeling of the organization should allow alternative scenarios to be considered (Midgley 2000). Organization theory has discussed several alternative models that emphasize adaptability, complex feedback loops, fragmentation and discontinuity (Morgan 1986). Of course, the BSC incorporates a measure of adaptation and complexity by emphasizing four perspectives rather than just the financial, and responds to the importance of feedback loops by emphasizing leading as well as lagging measures. However, the discrete mechanical organizational modeling suggested by most writings on, and applications of, the BSC does not take adequate account of the complexity and fragmentation of many organizations.

There is also an implicit assumption of stability underlying the design of the BSC: that a model developed from the perspective of the present will be relevant to the future. By seeking to reproduce the future in the image of the present, the BSC creates an artificial sense of stability and certainty in the world of management. Embracing simple, linear models may deceive managers and lead to poor organizational results.

Finally, for any modeling approach to be taken seriously, it must provide a careful specification and articulation of the boundaries of the system being modeled. To provide an example, in defining health costs in a hospital, the BSC might focus on costs within health institutions, but exclude private or community costs. Another example relates to costs and benefits in motor vehicle design: consumer welfare attached to vehicle safety is not compared to the possible decline in the profits of the manufacturer, unless we make the heroic assumption that safety concerns are captured in market prices or that the benefits to the manufacturer are actually used to compensate consumers who suffer as a result of poor safety. Such externalities are not admitted into the design of the technical BSC. These problems may be endemic to all modes of organization modeling; even the most sensitive and thoughtful modeler may become trapped in the assumptions and specifications of the model. At the very least, however, this limitation should be explicitly admitted so that the boundaries of the model are made clearer to its users. The technical version of the BSC seems insufficiently conscious of its own boundaries and limits.

A more dialogical approach to modeling organizations and management would enable better quality deliberation and decision making, ensuring that practice is reflective about the boundaries and values implicit in the models chosen (Jackson 2001). Using a BSC to facilitate discussion between managers about what alternative forms of models are appropriate would help to both flesh out alternative models, as well as identify ways that these models might be assessed and applied. It is not wise to presume *ex ante* which variables should be incorporated into a model of the organization, the linearity (or otherwise) of relationships between variables, the nature of feedback loops, or the temporal and spatial stability of the model. Using a BSC dialogically would facilitate discussion of the validity of alternative models, but enable more learning and adaptation.

4.4   Language and Quantification

Kaplan and Norton present the BSC as *the* language of strategy. They argue that, "[T]he Balanced Scorecard provides a framework to describe and communicate strategy in a consistent and insightful way." (2001, p. 10). This translation of strategy, or the language of strategy (ibid, pp. 67–69), deploys both the descriptive and numeric: each measure is first expressed linguistically (first translation of strategic vision) and subsequently quantified (numeric translation of strategic vision).

The technical view of the BSC assumes that any language can accurately reflect reality, for example, a numeric quantification captures the relevant attributes of the described measure, which, in turn, is assumed to be a faithful translation of strategic vision. This is am inadequate understanding of the relationship between language and reality. Language is a medium that structures our way of seeing and making sense of the world (language is constitutive of the world), and the system of linguistic signs is not neutral but hierarchical (Rorty 1980). Language, such as that employed in the BSC, is a linguistic form of expression that is imbued in a hierarchy that accords higher priority to certain 'signs' compared to others. Such hierarchies are so embedded into organizational language that they become internalized by managers in a manner that occludes the hierarchy implied and discourages reflexive thinking. The technical BSC does indeed offer a language, albeit sparse and limited, providing a numerical map that highlights only the features that senior management wishes to emphasize. Such maps fail to represent issues important to other stakeholders.

The BSC can be seen as a continuation of the approach of "managing by numbers", advocated by Johnson and Kaplan (1987). The appeal of quantification underpins the other assumptions of the technical version of the BSC: quantifying strategic vision; mechanical analogy and modeling via quantification; and quantification of stakeholders' potential to create value. Kaplan and Norton (1996a, p. 2) construe numbers as "a full battery of instrumentation" to be used to steer organizations through "the journey toward excellent future outcomes." This focus upon measuring and managing by numbers is captured in the original article proposing the BSC (1992): "What you measure is what you get". Each of the perspectives in the BSC is represented by numeric performance measures. As Kaplan and Norton argue, "[w]hat measures would prompt them [organizations] to do the right things? The answer turned out to be obvious. Measure the strategy!" (2001, p. 3). The danger is that if an organizational attribute is not a number it is assumed either to be unimportant or it cannot be managed. Indeed, Malina and Selto (2004) suggest that specific attributes of quantification (such as objectivity, reliability, timeliness) are the basis for identifying those measures in a BSC that have managerial salience and persist over time.

The assumed value of quantification appears in much of the literature on the BSC and permeates managerial thinking, even when modified by warnings that measurement is so powerful in motivating action that managers need to be sure they are measuring the right things. A number is an abstraction of what it is intended to represent. Like all abstractions, converting a quality into a quantity decouples the representation from the reality it is intended to represent. The management accounting literature, from multiple theoretical perspectives, recognizes the limits of measurement and the possibilities of goal displacement (e.g. Feltham and Xie 1994; Hartmann 2000; Hopwood 1973; Townley 1995). A focus on quantification seems to be related to a lack of creativity and 'paralysis by analysis'.

The accounting literature has not extensively explored alternatives to managing by numbers. This is understandable since calculation is often considered to involve number, and quantification and objectivity are often assumed to be linked (Porter 1995). Yet calculations are made on a number of different bases. Many studies (Gerboth 1973; Huy 1999; Frost et al. 2000) have shown that intuition, emotion, caring and compassion can be important parts of organizational decision making. Such elements cannot be meaningfully measured but are important parts of management, especially in knowledge organizations. A critical analysis can consider the role of faith, intuition, emotions, compassion, loyalty, and commitment (Frost et. al. 2000) in managing. These non quantified elements can be appreciated in some circumstances, rather than be cast as irrational (Chua 1996). Tradition, history, culture and the social context may also be part of managing (Cooper et al. 2015). Using the BSC in a dialogic manner would allow debate about the validity of measurement, the assumptions inherent in different forms of quantification, and the possibility that goals and targets would be better expressed in terms of qualities rather than quantities. It would enable non quantitative discourses to be taken seriously, to recognize the significance of non numerical evidence and help to ensure that such voices would not be drowned out by the language of those who think and act based on number.

If we are to have a better understanding of organizational complexities, multiple languages and maps, employing differing scales and focuses, are needed. By allowing a dialogue based on a BSC framework, multiple maps could be articulated and presented, allowing for differing projections to be made. To pursue the analogy, maps can highlight geology, demography, political borders, social and ethnic groups, land use, etc. No doubt, many organizations using current versions of the BSC produce multiple scenarios, but by making dialogue a central component of a BSC, more complex languages and viewpoints can be expressed and considered. In the past, such devices as semi-confusing information systems (Hedberg and Jonsson 1978) and retrospective sense making (Weick 1979; Boland 1978; Boland and Tenkasi 1985) have been suggested to encourage creative management and re-thinking of organizations. Our suggestion for a dialogic BSC is less dramatic than such suggestions, but will nevertheless help organizations respond to uncertainty, complexity and the knowledge economy.

5   Conclusion: Towards Constrained Dialogue

In this conclusion we build on our critical analysis and awareness of the assumptions of the BSC to elaborate our suggestions about a more dialogical use of the BSC. A constrained dialogic view integrates the features of a technical and social view of the BSC. It sees potential in the BSC to both promote substantive communication about the purposes of the organization and its strategy, while also ensuring that the technical concerns with efficiency and effective action are given serious consideration. This will help to overcome the pragmatic and ethical limitations of either a technical or a social version of the BSC. We acknowledge that our proposal has limitations (some of which we discuss below) that will need to be addressed in applications of the approach.

Our proposal develops from some of the findings of Townley et al. (2003). That study highlights initial managerial enthusiasm associated with the introduction of a strategic measurement system that emphasized a social view. This reaction gave way to cynicism, distrust and alienation when senior managers insisted on a more technical vision of the BSC. Managers experienced the negative effects of producing numbers for the hierarchy, of forcing their understanding of the organization into the language of measurement and results, and of seeing the complexity of organizational life distorted by a requirement from senior management to force that complexity into the standardized schedules that are so pervasive in BSC-type systems. For them, their ethic of trying to do a good job and act responsibly was undermined by a requirement that they describe and justify their work through standardized templates and present their performance in ways to make their boss 'look good'. For senior management, a technical approach to a performance measurement system had the advantage of providing a formalized and universal description that enabled them to feel they could rationally control the whole organization. The dissatisfaction and deteriorating performance effects, tempted senior managers to manage appearances and to do things they knew were undesirable for the organization as a whole.

Other studies confirm the problems of a technical view (eg., Ittner, Larcker and Meyer 2003; Carmona and Gronlund 2003; Wiersma 2009). Treating management techniques, such as the BSC, as a neutral, technical, mechanism will almost certainly create and reinforce the problems we have identified earlier. In our view, focusing on reforming either the technical or the social side of the BSC would yield few benefits. In contrast, we argue that conceptualizing the BSC as *both* a technical and a social mechanism would make it possible for the BSC to be developed in more beneficial ways, as a technology to enable serious, respectful debate that is oriented to action. Researchers, consultants, and managers might use the BSC to promote dialogue about the strategy of the organization and the most appropriate means of achieving it. We are suggesting a more expansive conception of communication than proposed by Kaplan and Norton (2004a) or Malina and Selto (2001), where dialogue and debate take place in a situation of democratic engagement and where the very terms of dialogue are themselves open for debate and revision.

Our conception of communication requires a commitment to take seriously the contributions of all parties in communication, including the possibility that those with less resources and authority may have something important to say, for example about the appropriate model of the organization, what the goals and objectives should be, and how particular organizational languages may disadvantage some points of view and actions, while privileging others. The validity of a dialogue should be assessed according to the norms of communicative action and discourse ethics (Habermas 1984, 1996). "Argumentation insures that all concerned in principle take part, freely and equally, in a cooperative search for truth, where nothing coerces anyone except the force of the better argument" (Habermas 1990, p. 198).

This approach to communication has been operationalized in the literature on democratic deliberation. Chambers argues that:

> ...deliberative democracy focuses on the communicative processes of opinion and will- formation that precede voting. Accountability replaces consent as the conceptual core of legitimacy. (2003, p. 308)

Communication is thus a process of deliberation and techniques such as deliberative opinion polling (Fishkin 1995) have been extensively used to facilitate discussion. It should be stressed that the purpose of deliberation is to improve information sharing, change preferences, broaden perspectives, encourage toleration and understanding between individuals and groups, and generally promote a more communitarian attitude to organizations and life more generally. The evidence suggests these aspirations are at least in part realized by the techniques of deliberation. Vaivio (2004) shows how the interactive use of non financial measures in a BSC type system can lead to the discovery of tacit knowledge and making that knowledge explicit.

In trying to apply the approach in organizations, it is important to recognize that most exercises of deliberative democracy are in the area of public policy and don't apply to corporations. Habermas (e.g. 1996) focusses on legal institutions such as the courts and legislatures. We suggest that our proposals for constrained dialogue can similarly be applied to public sector organizations and management. We further argue that they should apply to large public corporations, whose impact affects large elements of society. But in such organizations we recognize that constrained dialogue means that the decision making authority of top managers is not threatened; in such organizations, the focus of dialogue is information sharing (lateral as well as hierarchical) and opinion formation, not on producing a decision.[11]

A dialogic approach to the BSC would provide a structure for debate. This is both a strength and weakness. Structuring dialogue should stimulate and enable discussion about the assumptions of the BSC. It would facilitate dialogue about alternative models, organizational purposes, the value of strategizing and quantification in particular contexts. However, we are also very aware that any structure imposes a language and a set of categories for debate, which risks limiting the range of argument and enabling symbolic violence (Oakes et al. 1998). The BSC framework could encourage participants in dialogue to think and speak in the language of the BSC, notably in terms of goals, measures, targets, initiatives, the four most common perspectives, and so on. Consequently, the technology of the BSC should itself be recognized as a valid subject for discussion and challenge- for example whether a dialogic form of BSC encourages excessive talk, and insufficient action. The idea that the BSC itself is open for debate[12] can be considered a form of 'double loop learning'- the organization can learn and grow by examining the value of the techniques it uses (Tuomela 2005).

Our suggestion for a more dialogic BSC runs the risk of promoting debate and discussion at the expense of action, giving priority to the social view in Table 1. Current versions of the BSC, in emphasizing the technical view of Table 1, risk promoting action without thought and reflection. The action orientation of the current BSC—where initiatives and action plans flow from a gap between expected outcomes and targets—should militate against an over-emphasis on debate. A constrained dialogic approach offers the possibility of a balance between debate and action.[13] Our suggestion requires reflexive thinking and a willingness to consider alternative languages and models of organization. It is important to move away from a model of management that emphasizes action orientated towards the strategies imposed by senior managers, towards management that considers both ends and means of action. To facilitate rational debate and action about means and ends, the BSC should be combined with two neglected components of intelligent management: genuine communication and dialogue, and more open means of managing and living with uncertainty.

Diversity within organizations must be acknowledged explicitly, suggesting that all members of an organization should be free to participate in the dialogue about the BSC. While this seems somewhat romantic and naive, practitioners of democratic deliberation have shown it can be implemented in contexts where participants have a history of mutual hostility and distrust (Forester 2000). We acknowledge systemic sources of differential power between different participants (based, for example, on ethnicity, gender and class). Yet a dialogic approach, while constrained by formal authority and legal obligations, offers a structure and mechanism to introduce genuine and respectful debate into organizations (Ezzamel and Willmott 1993; Townley et al. 2003), enhance organizational democracy and enable more socializing forms of accountability (Roberts 1991). Alternative voices can be heard, a broader base of stakeholders can be acknowledged, action based on a more democratic vision of the organization can be carried out, and power imbalances can be recognized and differential benefits compensated for.

Managers may also need to find more intelligent ways to acknowledge and deal with uncertainty. Too often, the appeal to managers of new techniques such as the BSC is the promise of clarity, simplicity and controllability. Management techniques may appear deal with uncertain situations and complex realities, and quantification can provide a sense of control in the face of uncertainty (van Gusteren 1976). The appeal of the BSC may also be its assumption that everything that is worthwhile in an organization can be measured. Acknowledging managerial judgment, the inevitability of error and anxiety, and the importance of emotion would be major steps in making the BSC more useful to organizations. Such acknowledgment is more likely with dialogue and serious communication. The challenge is to encourage managers to use their judgment to acknowledge the unique and unexpected. One way to move away from a view of management as able to control most things is to re-consider the limits of management- a more humble conception of management would acknowledge that organizational performance is determined by wider social and economic structures. Another possible way of coping with complexity and uncertainty is through an emphasis on empathy, understanding, emotion, care and compassion. Other suggestions have included the value of ritual, with its potential to mystify or mask what is difficult to comprehend, thereby re-assuring people that things are in control. Whatever approach is adopted, dialogue offers space for learning, development and tolerance.

Kaplan and Norton have developed and promoted a measurement technique that is intended to help organizations thrive in an uncertain, competitive and knowledge intensive environment. Such environments call for more emphasis on empowerment and employee commitment. Simons (1994, 1995) proposes that in such environments organizations need greater use of all 'four levers of control', where managers "involve themselves regularly and personally in discussions with their subordinates" (1995, p. 85). A dialogic BSC, combining a technical and social approach, would provide opportunities for deliberation around organizational values, be more inspirational and share information and harness creativity, in short help to make practical Simons' concern for a balance between control and empowerment (1995).

The technical and social views presented in Table 1 are not alternatives; both are important for any comprehensive understanding of the BSC. Accordingly, we a constrained dialogic approach to the BSC is a way to integrate the technical and social. Our suggestions for developing a more dialogical approach call not just for a better balance between all those who contribute to an organization's success, not just for a better balance between acting and thinking, not just for a better balance between strategic discussions about organizational ends and means of achieving those ends, but also for a more serious commitment to drawing on and respecting the knowledge of all those who are involved with the organization. A more balanced and equitable scorecard should lead to better organizational performance, broadly conceived.

Notes

1. Norreklit (2000, 2003) offers useful reviews of some of the assumptions of the Balanced Scorecard. Our chapter differs from her work in two important respects. First, her paper focuses on the logic of two types of causality, between measures and between the BSC and strategic management. In contrast, our chapter considers a wider range of BSC assumptions. Second, she focuses on coherence as a means of reforming the BSC, while we acknowledge and critique a view of coherence as non-political and instead seek to challenge the use of the BSC to address social and political issues.
2. Indeed, some of the arguments we employ in the chapter are manifestations of the approach of 'managing by numbers' and the importance of evidence, thereby attesting to their usefulness.
3. We are not proposing a contingency view of the BSC, where the specific form of the assumptions of the BSC would depend on the state of the organization's environment (Chenhall 2003). It might be possible to interpret the technical version of the BSC offered by Kaplan and Norton as representing a configuration that may be best suited (in terms of organizational performance) to stable conditions and a social view as more appropriate in rapidly changing and uncertain environments (Waterhouse and Tiessen 1978; Tiessen

and Waterhouse 1983). However, there are significant problems with a contingency view, as outlined by Cooper (1983) and Neimark and Tinker (1986). First, the contingency literature has been unable to identify independent (contingent) variables that might determine effective management approaches (Hartman 2002; Chenhall 2003). None of the proposed contingent variables appear to have a strong effect, and each of these independent variables tend to lead to different predictions. Second, if different contingency variables are identified, it is unclear what their joint (interactive) effect will be on the appropriate management system. Finally, a contingency view relies on the existence of a universal measure of organizational performance yet this presupposes that there is agreement on whose interests the organization does or should operate. Without a unique objective, there is no criterion to select between forms of management.

4. In the final section of this chapter we elaborate on this approach. At this point, we refer to greater debate and articulation of different points of view and sharing of information in a context of minimal power differences and mutual respect. This, optimistic approach is constrained since it also recognizes legal and other constraints that result in an organizational authority having the power to determine ultimate actions.

5. It is not our intention here to trace the stages of BSC development, or in the inevitable changes in focus (see Free and Qu 2011). Our discussion is based on a synthesis of the general and enduring arguments of Kaplan and Norton.

6. We acknowledge that our analysis and discussion applies to many other management techniques.

7. Martinez and Cooper (2015) examine how measurement systems impact modes of thinking in international development, including ways of understanding accountability.

8. This may seem surprising since the BSC is presented as flexible and open; different organizations will populate the mission and values, goals and measures according to their own strategies and needs. Yet despite the potential for customization, the BSC, as a management technique, is presented as applicable to all organizations.

9. We also have conducted numerous field studies of performance measurement systems in manufacturing, retail, NGO and government organizations. Some reference to these studies is made in the appropriate parts of the chapter, but we have avoided providing a 'list' of what might be classified as empirical examples precisely because such illustrations run the risk of making the same error that we accuse of others in decontextualizing and providing insufficient information for such illustrations.

10. We doubt this view of managers as neutral agents. In a 'pure' capitalist system shareholders are dominant and managers, in order to survive in such a legal and market context, inevitably behave in a partisan manner, partly because they believe in the ideology of the system and partly because their own financial welfare is tied to shareholder interests (Nichols 1969).

11. We recognize that Habermas's appeal to rational discourse is subject to considerable debate and dispute. We acknowledge it relies on modernist (and maybe also Western and gendered) ideals of rationality and consensus. These ideals have been persuasively critiqued and stimulated alternative approaches such as agonistic deliberation (e.g. Mouffe 2000), which have been taken up by critical accounting scholars (e.g. Bebbington et al. 2007; Brown 2009; Brown and Dillard 2013). We are not (yet) willing to give up on modernist ideals (see also Bond 2011).

12. Many aspects of an issue (e.g. who participates, the appropriate process of deliberation, what issues are to be covered) can be included, and revised, in the deliberative process.

13. While Olve et al. (2003) also discuss dialogue in relation to the BSC, they seem to use the term as a synonym for discussion. The conception of dialogue that we offer is based and rooted in the considerable literature on democratic deliberation.

Reimagining the Corporation: The Relevance of Legal, Economic and Political Imaginaries

Hugh Willmott and Jeroen Veldman

1 Introduction

There are, we contend, few issues in management and organization studies (MOS) more critical than understanding the modern corporation. Today, 'corporate governance' and 'corporate responsibility' are business buzzwords that are becoming increasingly significant objects of study. Yet what 'corporate' means, and the contemporary (re)formation and significance of corporations, are rarely the focus of academic study (for an exception, see Crouch 2001, in particular Chap. 3). Our intention here is to shed some light on the concept of 'the modern corporation' and, in doing so, to make a timely contribution to a transformation in how corporate practices are understood, taught, and enacted.

What is a corporation? Although MOS is the context in which much 'management' is accomplished and where many structures and processes

H. Willmott (✉) • J. Veldman
Cass Business School, City University London, London, UK

© The Author(s) 2016   **231**
J. Haslam, P. Sikka (eds.), *Pioneers of Critical Accounting*,
DOI 10.1057/978-1-137-54212-0_12

of organizing are located, it would seem as if this question has limited relevance. Within MOS, the purpose, regulation, governance, and responsibility of corporations are, of course, taken up for examination where various conceptions of the corporation are more or less implicitly invoked. There is also some residual awareness and appreciation of debates about 'the modern corporation', associated with issues of 'ownership and control' (Berle and Means 2007[1932]), 'the managerial revolution' (Burnham 1962[1941]), and 'the visible hand' (Chandler 2002). The 'financialization' of corporations may soon be added to such background understandings (Davis 2011; Epstein 2005; Fligstein 1993). But, to our knowledge, these indications of interest in the modern corporation have not resulted in the development of a research program, a stream of research in standing working groups, or even a track within MOS conferences dedicated specifically to interrogating and researching the corporate form.[1] Indeed, it would appear that the study of the corporation has been quietly ceded to other specialisms, such as business history, law, economics, and political science where its representation(s) reflect the distinctive presuppositons and interpretive frameworks of those disciplines.[2]

2   The Corporation and Imaginaries

What, then, is the corporation? Our approach to answering this question, which is broadly consistent with a stream of work in MOS that addresses the significance of (competing) imaginaries (Davis 2009; Perrow 2002) presumes that the nature and the meaning of the corporation are inescapably contested; and that various imaginaries have been constructed to render the corporate form meaningful, real and consequential. We identify three imaginaries that, we contend, have framed and influenced properties and capacities vested in the modern corporation: the legal, the economic and the political.[3] As will become clear, our view is that that these imaginaries are intertwined, with the effect that they often mutually reinforce and contradict one another. Although analytically distinguishable, they are practically enmeshed.[4] The political imaginary, we will suggest, is a condition of possibility of legal and economic imaginaries that have routinely obscured the primacy of the political.

We adopt the term 'imaginary' to convey the understanding that (i) we have no direct access to the phenomena, including the phenomenon of 'the corporation' itself, which we seek to examine and explicate; (ii) imaginaries are developed to construct, interpret, and scrutinize social phenomena; (iii) imaginaries exert performative effects insofar as they are (partially and selectively) enacted and institutionalized. Whereas the legal and economic imaginaries directly evoke distinct conceptions, and prompt particular enactments, of the corporate form, the political imaginary, as we conceive of it here, is a condition of possibility of the other two imaginaries. Moreover, and relatedly, the political imaginary makes possible the casting of a reflective glance at those conditions as well as a forward anticipation of their consequences. The primacy accorded to the political is pithily stated by Ireland when he relates the rise of the corporate legal form in the nineteenth century to a shift of power to an emergent industrial and financial bourgeoisie:

> [The] emergence and development of [the corporate legal form] was not the economically-determined product of efficiency-driven evolution. It was, rather, in significant part the product of the growing political power and influence of the financial property owning class. The same is true of its recent reinforcement and entrenchment, and of the attempts to extend its global reach. (Ireland 2010, p. 853)

The key point to be drawn from Ireland's analysis is that the (continuous) social (re)construction of the corporate form is accomplished within relations of power which are a condition, but also a consequence, of such constructions.

3   The Modern Corporation

Modern economic organization is heavily dependent upon a distinctive conception of the public limited liability share corporation. This corporate form is "one of the most successful inventions in history, as evidenced by its widespread adoption and survival as a primary vehicle of capitalism over the past century" (Butler 1988, p. 99). At the apex of the contemporary corporate form stands the huge, multinational firm and its subsidiaries that have come to attract increasing criticisms for their efforts to avoid taxes, the excessive salaries paid to executives and their damaging impacts upon the environment.[5] Many of the potentially problematic effects of the corporate form—notably, with regard to its capacity to concentrate wealth and power and its capacity to circumvent inheritance tax—have been acknowledged since the early thirteenth century (Post 1934; Micklethwait and Wooldridge 2005). In recognition of this status, the corporate form was held under sovereign control until the late eighteenth century (McLean 2004) when pressures to expand and fund imperialist geopolitical ambitions slowly but steadily divorced the corporate form from direct political control by the sovereign (Johnson 2010; Neocleous 2003). In the nineteenth century, political restrictions were further questioned and loosened. Relaxations and occasional tightening of state-mediated political restrictions have ebbed and flowed in the twentieth and twenty-first centuries (Bowman 1996). Following the financial crash of 2007 and 2008, for example, the activities and tax affairs of major financial corporations have reemerged as an object of significant public interest, contestation, and calls for improved regulation (Veldman and Willmott 2016).

Historically, arguments for efficiency and/or improved access to capital (Chandler 2002) have been invoked to promote and to account for the displacement of partnerships by the modern limited liability corporation (Guinnane et al. 2007). Similarly, it has been argued that contemporary accounts of corporate governance foreshadow an end of history for corporate law (Hansmann and Kraakman 2000). In such teleological accounts (see Khurana 2007), a dominant (e.g. economic) imaginary is seen to foster an 'optimal' or inevitable organizational form (Ireland 2010, pp. 837–838), thereby obfuscating deep disagreements regarding the processes—evolutionary or contested—through which corporations developed during the nineteenth and twentieth centuries (Carroll et al. 2012; Johnson 2010). Those disputes have their echoes in contemporary debates about the relative merits of the incorporated, limited liability conception of the corporate form in comparison to other possibilities, such as cooperatives or partnerships. Key to grasping and interrogating the corporate form within the political imaginary, is an appreciation of the dynamics of contestation in which diverse parties (e.g. investors, industrialists, policy-makers, labor representatives, NGOs, etc), acquire and mobilize material and symbolic resources in struggles to institutionalize, deinstitutionalize, and reinstitutionalize preferred versions of the corporate form (Bowman 1996; Johnson 2010; Nace 2003). Traces of this dynamic are evident in the diverse attributes invoked to characterize the corporate form, such as 'entity', 'subject', 'agent', 'aggregation of individuals', 'nexus of contracts'. We now take a closer look at the genesis of these notions.

4 The Legal Imaginary

The role of the state in the establishment of modern corporations is seminal and remains significant today. A charter provided by the state initially enabled distinct, corporate entities to undertake a (very limited) range of activities—such as building roads or canals—where these activities were assessed to yield substantial public benefit.[6] In contrast to other not-for-profit corporations, the *chartered business* corporation was permitted to make a private profit for investors in it, but their liabilities were also typically *unlimited* well until the nineteenth century. The granting of a charter thus facilitated private funding of the provision of public goods in a way that, in principle, retained close public oversight of such business ventures—by granting a charter that could be retracted, and by making partners ultimately responsible for losses. From these beginnings, the history of the corporation has been one of contestation—with regard *inter alia* to the granting of limited liability to corporations and the justification for placing limits on the range of activities undertaken by chartered corporations, as well as to concerns about corruption associated with the granting of monopolies, and the respective merits of the legal form of the partnership versus the corporation (Horwitz 1985; Johnson 2010).

The partnership, as a legal form, is distinguished by the indivisibility of its assets and the partners who invest directly in it. Since there is no separation between the assets of the entity and those who own it, partners are jointly liable for the actions of each of the partners; the assets of the partnership can be seized by the partners' creditors[7]; and partner's shares carry considerable residual liabilities, making it challenging to sell such a share. As all partners are directly exposed to these types of liability, there is a material incentive for them, regardless of whether they are practicing partners or passive investors, to pay close attention to the actions of partners; and to pay attention to the liabilities (e.g. debts) of fellow partners as well as those of the partnership (Veldman and Willmott, fc, management chapter in CUP book). Moreover, because the partnership would be dissolved at the death or exit of a partner, the time horizon for a partnership and its operations in nineteenth century UK environment would be limited, typically about 15 years.

The *public limited liability joint stock corporation* is constructed in the legal imaginary as a separate legal entity that holds the assets and liabilities. The importance of this legal 'entity' in the legal imaginary can hardly be overstated, as it endows the corporation with a perpetual legal status and representation—independent of the investors, managers, or partners—that was not previously available to partnerships. Over time,[8] this legal 'entity', has also been endowed with attributions of ownership, rights, and protections in the capacity of legal 'subject', 'person', or even 'citizen'. Moreover, the legal entity has been endowed with an (agential) capacity[9]—a capacity which, importantly, enables it to contract in its own name and to own other such entities. This last capacity is highly significant for the development of capitalism as it has enabled, as a consequence of processes of acquisition and merger, economic activity to become concentrated within a small number of very large corporations (Chandler 2002; Hannah 2010). It is the modern corporate form, and not the partnership form, which has come to exert a powerful, monopoly-like influence over many areas of economic activity nationally and, increasingly, globally.[10]

Apart from such direct attributions of perpetuity, agency, ownership, rights, and protections, the notion of the 'entity' is also important. That is because, in contrast to the partnership, in the *public limited liability joint stock corporation* it is the legal entity that 'holds' the assets and liabilities of the corporation. This provides the basis for a very specific idea of ownership and liability in which the personal assets and liabilities of shareholders are divorced from the assets and liabilities of the corporation.

Since the assets, patents, investments, and liabilities are 'held' by the 'entity', they are "locked-in" and cannot be touched by the shareholders. The full separation of shareholders from the corporation's assets and liabilities means that shareholders cannot simply get hold of the assets that are 'held' by the entity. The legal entity thus provides a reciprocal protection against other shareholders, which means that passive shareholders especially are, in principle, far better protected against direct expropriation by other (controlling) shareholders than they would be in the partnership.

The attribution of assets and liabilities to the entity is accompanied by an assumption that the assets it holds are to be used for the benefit of 'the corporation'. Because the legal entity stands in for 'the corporation' as a whole, the assumption is that the legal entity represents the interests of the corporation per se. The notion that the legal entity or corporation has interests, separate from the controlling shareholders or the executive managers, is of particular interest to minority shareholders as it protects them against the imposition of single-focus strategies by controlling shareholders and executive managers; and it directs executive managers to use corporate assets in a way that will serve the corporation as a 'going concern'. Such notions of a going concern arguably focus on directing corporations in relation to long-term strategies for ongoing wealth creation (Biondi et al. 2007).

The assurances that, in contrast to the partnership, the corporation will not be dissolved at the exiting of every shareholder-partner; that corporate assets cannot be easily embezzled by individual (majority) shareholders; and that the assets held by the corporate entity will be used for the development of the corporation as a going concern, rather than for executive remuneration or shareholder payouts—all of these factors are not just of interest to minority shareholders, but also to other constituencies, notably creditors, but also employees, who depend on such notions for the protection of the implicit aspects of their contracts. In short, the legal imaginary of a corporate 'entity' provides important protections to a variety of constituencies (Deakin 2012).

It was also the notion that the corporate entity, and not the shareholders, holds corporate assets and liabilities which provided the basis for a general application of limited liability for private corporations in the mid-nineteenth century (Djelic 2013; Handlin and Handlin 1945). The development of limited liability was followed by the removal of residual liabilities from shares, such as the requirement that shareholders could be called upon to provide extra capital. Removing those requirements led to the development of fully paid up shares that made possible the liquid trading of shares in a secondary share market. The shares traded by the end of the nineteenth century are entirely different from the shares that partners had previously held in the partnership, as they function as financial 'coupons'. They do not carry residual liabilities and they are formally detached from onerous ownership functions as management or control. Again, the contrast with the partnership form is instructive. Partners are subject to liabilities, including those incurred by fellow partners. In contrast, the grant of limited liability to the corporation and the development of the new ideas of shares "[…]permits a man to avail himself of acts if advantageous to him, and not to be responsible for them if they should be disadvantageous; to speculate for profits without being liable for losses" (Edward Cox 1856, cited in Ireland 2010, p. 844).

The overall picture is that the modern corporate form is altogether a very different legal and organisational construct to that of the partnership form. The legal imaginary of the legal 'entity' establishes a fundamental distinction between the corporation and the stockholders. This distinction is the basis for many legal and economic privileges and protections, but it also creates a highly specific institutional background for the conceptual creation, justification, and legitimation of the corporate form.

Contrary to what advocates of agency theory and shareholder value may assume or conjecture (to be discussed below), the legal imaginary challenges the widely rehearsed wisdom that the corporate form is 'owned' by, and is therefore at the disposal of, its shareholders as a prioritized constituency whose interests it is obliged to pursue and promote (Allen 1992, p. 265; Crouch 2011, p. 136). Crucially, in the legal imaginary, the legal entity implies a structural separation of the functions of ownership, management, and control so that shareholders do not and cannot 'own' the corporation.[11] Shareholders do enjoy a limited set of rights, and in UK Company Law this includes the formal and potentially substantial responsibility of electing boards of directors. But their legitimate influence does not extend to exercising any direct rights over the assets of the corporation. Nor are shareholders legally the primary residual claimants of corporate revenues or assets. If bankruptcy strikes, it is the creditors who have the first claim in the legal imaginary. This works the other way around as well: if a breach of health and safety regulation occurs and a penalty is exacted, the fine is not levied on the assets of investors or the managers. Instead, such charges are exacted upon the assets of the corporation. In addition to a structural separation from claims to direct ownership, this means that, in principle, shareholders have limited options to exercise pressure on boards in relation to the determination of strategic issues. That is because such actions place in jeopardy the justification for the benefits of the separate legal entity, most notably limited liability.

In combination, the radical divergence from the partnership form provided by the legal entity; the specific properties and protections provided by this legal entity; and the specific ownership and control structure it puts in place, serves to explains why, in the legal imaginary, shareholders are not seen as having direct or primary claims on the corporation. Instead, the corporate form, *qua* entity, can have multiple 'owners' or 'stakeholders'; and these stakeholders may have a variety of 'investments' in its formation, development, and continuation (Biondi et al. 2007; Ireland 2005, 2009, 2010; Robé 2011; Stout 2012). It is for this reason that, in the legal imaginary, the *legal* duty of CEOs, board members and senior executives is *not* to act exclusively or primarily on behalf of shareholders or to maximize shareholder value. Instead, the legal obligation is to act "in the best interests of the company" (Parkinson 2003, p. 493)—a duty that extends to all those deemed to have an investment in the corporation (Biondi et al. 2007; Robé 2011; Veldman and Willmott 2015 (HR)). As conceived within the legal imaginary, the corporation *qua* legal entity has "responsibilities to a *range* of constituents, including shareholders as well as employees [including managers], customers, creditors, and the general public" (Ciepley 2013, p. 147, emphasis added).[12]

This understanding of the corporation as a legal entity is not overturned by an economic imaginary that, as we will see shortly, focuses on efficiency or social utility. It is not overruled by the idea that shareholders are the principal beneficiaries of the limited liability corporate form on the grounds that they provide a more productive, but also more risky, class of corporate assets, in the form of capital. Nor, however dominant it may become, does the idea that the use of equity capital leads to optimal social utility (see Aglietta and Rebéroux 2005) defeat the point that the structural conditions which provide the legitimacy for the corporation in the *legal* imaginary are directly connected to the idea of an 'entity' that holds ownership over corporate assets.

5   The Economic Imaginary

The economic imaginary poses an alternative to, but does not override or overturn the legal imaginary. As we saw in the previous section, the legal imaginary of the corporate form provided a very specific notion of an 'entity' that produced beneficial outcomes to the company and the shareholders, including a host of direct attributions of agency, ownership, rights, and protections; a perpetual time horizon for the legal recognition of the company; significant expansion of de facto time horizons for the company and its operations; significant safeguards for shareholders and creditors by setting the conditions for a specific ownership and control structure; provision of conditions for the application of limited liability; and provision of a liquid status for stocks, and thereby the conditions for the creation of a liquid stock market. Were the economic imaginary to reject the legal entity altogether, these advantages would be at risk. For this reason, in the economic imaginary, the 'entity' is retained, but is backgrounded and domesticated as an inconsequential 'legal fiction'. In this process, the economic imaginary shifts attention *away from* the legal imaginary, where the role of executives is to safeguard and expand the assets of the corporation on behalf of a wide range of stakeholders; and it shifts attention *towards* the material interests and right of control ascribed to investors (Aglietta and Rebérioux 2005).

The economic imaginary accords greatest significance to the superior efficiency of the corporation as an organizational form (Hanssman and Kraakman 2000)—for example, in terms of reduced transaction costs compared to markets. Rational economic justifications for the modern corporation, as advanced by the economic imaginary, also underscore how, for example, perpetuity and the ownership of assets by the legal entity provide distinct benefits. In comparison to the partnership, there is, as noted in the previous section, less need to maintain substantial but unproductive liquid resources, with the beneficial outcome that those resources are available for investment in productive processes, thereby reducing the cost of capital in relation to prospective returns. As a consequence of shares being tradable, the joint stock company is, as also noted above, seen to bring the benefit of greater liquidity. Moreover, and again in comparison to the partnership form, the recurring liquidation and exchange of firm assets introduced by the partnership form is avoided. Higher returns can be expected as less provision must be made for claims upon assets.

In the economic imaginary, these economic advantages are calculated comfortably to offset the downside of surrendering any direct legal claim on the assets of the modern corporation. Nonetheless, *in the absence of limited liability*, shares are less easily tradable on account of carrying a residual risk. Under these conditions shareholders are obliged to safeguard the value of their shares by expending time and effort in understanding and monitoring the business (like members of a partnership). *Limited liability*, then, makes investment in the business corporation more appealing than investment in a partnership because it reduces transaction costs in relation to share ownership and share trading.

The economic imaginary identifies benefits of limited liability, but it also highlights a significant drawback. This can be illustrated by the post-1970s economic imaginary that raises questions about the 'value' received by 'shareholders'. In this imaginary, concerns have been expressed about shareholders' dependence upon the competence, in addition to the loyalty, of salaried executive managers who are identified as their 'agents'. When managers are salaried employees, and not owners, they may be seen to lack sufficient incentive to prioritise returns to investors. Instead, they may merely 'satisfice' performance and/or engage in job-securing or empire-building projects. That managers are imagined to lack sufficient inducement to safeguard and maximize the interests attributed to shareholders points to the presence of an 'agency problem', for which the favoured solution developed within the economic imaginary is the introduction of incentives in the form of stock options and (short-term) performance-related bonuses. The introduction and/or raising of these incentives is intended to align executive decision-making with the maxi-mization of shareholder value (Khurana 2007).

In this contemporary (principal-agent) economic imaginary, there are three inter-related departures from the legal imaginary. *First,* the corporation is typically cast as a 'nexus of contracts': a nexus of on-going contractual relations among the self-interested, atomistic individuals who comprise its factors of production (Bratton 1989). Imagining the corporation as a continuous process of contract negotiation, and as a nexus that seamlessly extends into a broader market, means that non-market forms of coordination, such as hierarchy and processes of learning, become comparatively less important. Relatedly, less weight is given to a conception of management as a materially and symbolically privileged element in possession of obligations as well as rights, as defined by a vertical division of labor. Another feature of this first departure from the legal imaginary is the rejection of a view of managers as impartial experts or mediators who apply their expertise to make informed, well-balanced decisions in the interest of wider sets of stakeholders (Veldman and Willmott, fc, management).

Second, according to the agency-theoretic economic imaginary, the most critical aspect of corporate governance concerns the contract between shareholders (principals) and directors and executives (agents) (Bratton 1989; Jackson 2000). This informs a dyadic view of corporate governance in which parties other than investors, directors, and executive officers are largely external to a conception of the corporation and its governance. The point is well made by Johnson (2012, p. 1160) when he observes that:

> Other parties…are regarded as secondary, instrumental participants, and are remitted to contract law or other legal regimes dealing with creditors' rights, employees' rights, consumer protection, or environmental concerns, and so on.

Regardless of the importance of their contribution to a flourishing, dynamic enterprise, the significance of groups other than shareholders and boards is structurally marginalized in the economic imaginary of corporate governance.

Table 1 Key features of the legal and economic imaginaries

	Legal imaginary	Economic imaginary
Ownership	Held by legal entity	Held by legal fiction, but attributed to shareholders as prioritized constituency
Fiduciary duties	To 'the company'	To 'the shareholders'
Limited liability	Historical addition conditional upon the establishment of a legal entity	Necessary to fulfill the potential of the corporation as a vehicle for the comparatively riskless expansion of private wealth

A third departure from the legal imaginary is the recasting of firm relations within the contemporary, agency-theoretic economic imaginary "in terms of discrete, bilateral contracts. [It] deemphasizes the entity [...] To find the firm's essence, [it] looks solely to the behaviour of individual economic actors" (Bratton 1988/9, p. 428). By focusing exclusively on the action of economic 'individuals' as it simultaneously de-emphasises the legal entity, the economic imaginary disregards the central features and issues of the legal imaginary. The distinctive economic benefits of the corporate form are celebrated as teleological outcomes of legal innovation, while the tradeoffs which came with the legal imaginary—notably, the separation of ownership from the ownership of assets that are vested in the legal entity—are downplayed or simply ignored. On the basis of this displacement of the legal imaginary, the economic imaginary of the corporation lends spurious (academic) credibility to the assertion that "public companies should be run predominantly, if not exclusively, in their [the shareholders'] interests" (Ireland 1999, p. 49).

The key features of the legal and economic imaginaries are summarised in Table 1.

6   The Political Imaginary

It is when the claims of the economic imaginary are considered from the perspective of the political imaginary that they are seen to rely upon the displacement of the legal imaginary—a practice that has been characterized as intellectual shamanism (Ireland 2005, p. 81; Bratton 1989; Robé 2011). Charges of 'intellectual shamanism' point to the contested terrain of the corporate form and its governance. They invite reflection upon the relations of power through which representations of the corporation are advanced, warranted and challenged. For those who invoke the political imaginary

> [...] it is important that scholars of corporate governance do not permit deeply political processes to be passed off as the products of a politically neutral, purely economic logic or allow the distributional dimensions of corporate governance to be spirited off the agenda... (Ireland 2005, p. 81, emphasis added).

The political imaginary gives primacy to relations of power, formulated primarily in terms of class, and of contests between fractions of capital, in which legal and economic elements are conceived as a medium as well as an outcome of relations of domination and subjugation. Within the political imaginary, the key to understanding the historical emergence and subsequent development of the corporate form is neither economic efficiency nor refinements, or teleological accounts, of legal theory. Rather, the emergence and development of the corporate form is understood to be a condition and a consequence of shifts in power relations between, and also within, groups that mobilise available resources, as they establish, consolidate or transform relations of domination from which they endeavour to gain material and symbolic advantage (see Johnson 2010; Wilks 2013).

The political imaginary supports, for example, an account of the modern corporate form in which its emergence is linked directly to the priorities of a *rentier* class. This account is specifically informed by the understanding that the partnership form was appropriate and viable for all but a few business ventures prior to the early nineteenth century (Johnson 2010; Mclean 2004). Historically, the exception of incorporation was granted only where a public benefit was clear; where the risks were exceptionally high; and/or where the activities of the business could be readily routinized. It was only in such exceptional circumstances, as Adam Smith (1998[1776]) argued, that the rewards of the corporate form, in terms of prospective public benefits, would conceivably outweigh the risks of 'negligence and profusion' invited by the risks of replacing the partnership with the corporate form. From the perspective of the political imaginary, the risk takes multiple forms. In addition to executives' potential misuse of the investments made by many stakeholders in the corporation, there is also the risk of the prospective irresponsibility of investors who, as a consequence of their option to dispose of their shares in a secondary market when performance dips, are disinclined to take a close interest in how corporations are run. Moreover, such risks are, by default, increased by a lack of (potential for) oversight and control by other parties—the public, the state, supranational political units, etc.—with a direct interest in determining the direction and purpose of corporations (Veldman 2013; Veldman and Willmott 2016). In recent years, there have been numerous individual and systemic examples of 'negligence and profusion', as anticipated by Smith, that have shown what is at stake for diverse stakeholders.

Specifically, the political imaginary invites consideration of how (i) the development of the modern corporate form was not a result of received legal and political wisdom and always retained a very unsatisfactory theoretical status; and, therefore, was never a 'natural' step in a process of organisational evolution or a teleological development toward a more effective organization of finance and ownership (Roy 1999); (ii) the host of properties and protections that have benefitted *rentier* shareholders foremost rest on a conception of the corporation as an organisational form that potentially presents significant risks to broad sets of stakeholders; and (iii) the corporate form, along with the properties and protections it provides, has historically been an object of contestation for that reason (see Bowman 1996; Johnson 2010). This introduces the questions why central features of the modern corporate form, such as the corporate concession, which presents political risks when applied to private ventures, was nevertheless deemed fit to be freely obtainable; why limited liability was granted as a generally accessible privilege, even though this was a highly contested grant at the time; and why the 'entity' was endowed with such broad attributions of agency, ownership, rights, and protections on the basis of questionable theoretical justifications.

Both informed by and in pursuit of such concerns, the political imaginary focuses on the group or groups that wield sufficient influence and/or stand to benefit most from the development of the modern, limited liability corporate form. We contend that, prior to its establishment, investors could risk their fortunes by forming or joining[13] partnerships but, crucially, mitigating the personal risks associated with joining the partnership necessitated their close and questioning involvement in management (Veldman and Willmott, management, fc). The other limitation of partnerships is that, for investors, they yielded slim returns as rates were pegged by usury laws (until 1854) while alternatives, such as gilts, also offered unexciting returns. It was members of the growing class of (*unlimited* liability) shareholders who, during the early nineteenth century, were rapidly expanding in numbers and influence, who found the prospect of the *public limited liability corporate form* highly attractive as it offered a large number of legal and economic advantages in comparison to the partnership (Johnson 2010). The subsequent creation of a liquid market in shares meant that if the actual or anticipated yield became less attractive, there was always the option to sell the coupons (Veldman and Willmott, fc, management). In turn, the increased tradability of these coupons facilitated the distribution of capital across a portfolio of investments, and thereby further reduced investor risk. In short, the establishment of the modern corporate form, with the protection afforded by limited liability, enabled *rentier* investors, at least in principle,[14] to secure comparatively risk-free returns on their capital by enjoying capital appreciation and/or dividends without the demands, costs, risks, or responsibilities of overseeing, or even inquiring into, how their gains were generated.

This analysis does not deny or exclude the appeal of limited liability for stimulating rapid economic growth or the positive material benefits of expansion for an emergent middle class of comparatively privileged (white collar) wage workers—that is, managers (Chandler 2002; Djelic 2013; Pollard 1968). But it does emphasise how the 'push' for the development of this new organisational form was aligned most directly with the material interests of an emergent class of investors, and with the agency of politicians and professionals who served to articulate and advance their concerns and priorities (Johnson 2010). Nor does this analysis disregard how the position of the modern corporate form and its creation of the conditions for modern shareholding remains politically contingent as well as historically dynamic (Djelic 2013). There are no guarantees that the situation will be maintained, as occasional calls for the mutualization and nationalization of corporate assets attest. Nor, finally, does the present analysis ignore how, as circumstances change, calls for restrictions upon speculative investment activity may prove politically irresistible, resulting in a (re)imposition of regulations to redress what is regarded as their earlier, and excessive, relaxation.

Instead, this analysis invites consideration of the *effects* of the development of the modern corporate form, and to understand these in relation to the interests of a range of stakeholders. The capacity of the corporate form to transform economies showed itself most dramatically between 1890 and 1910, when the UK and US economies consolidated to a massive degree (Chandler 2002; Hannah 2010). This consolidation led to a strong dispersal of shareholding positions and drew in increasing numbers of comparatively small shareholders (Johnson 2010), resulting in a degree of 'socialization' of the ownership of the corporation (Roy 1997). The increasing dilution of strong blockholding positions actualised the theoretical split between the functions of ownership, control, and management that the legal changes of the mid-nineteenth century made possible (Veldman and Willmott, fc). As a consequence of the dilution of the capacity of shareholders to exercise direct control, and with an increased ability for executive managers to obtain funding from sources other than share markets, executive managers were correspondingly empowered to take control over these emerging corporate empires. A 'managerial revolution' (Berle and Means 1932; Burnham 1962[1941]) was perceived to be the outcome of these *de jure* and de facto shifts of control to executive managers.

In whose name or on whose authority these executive managers operated was, and remains, a contested question. The dilution of the capacity (and willingness) of shareholders to exercise control and oversight meant that these managers were increasingly seen to have the capacity to prioritize and pursue objectives—self-interested as well as public-interested—that departed from those attributed to shareholders.[15] For Berle and Means (2007[1932]), the legitimacy for the corporate form itself, the oligopolistic reconstitution of the economy it had helped to bring about, and the lack of oversight by shareholders were reasons to argue that managerial control over these corporations required explication and justification (Moore and Rebérioux 2007). It was anticipated that, with the advent of 'managerial capitalism', the attention of managers would shift, progressively and irreversibly, toward a broad 'public purpose' conception of the corporation whose goals, and, concomitantly, its proceeds would be directed to mitigation of a broad range of issues (Berle 1954, 1959; Drucker 2006[1946]; Kaysen 1957).

This was the backdrop to the emergence of a broad consensus, institutionalised in a post-War settlement, where a selective embrace of Keynesianism became reflected in increased state subsidization and intervention in the private sector (e.g. the expansion of a military-industrial complex, see Marens 2012). It has been suggested that the effects of this settlement were such that, by the 1960s, even in the US "little was left of the classical corporation. Its internal dealings with shareholders and its debtor-creditor relations were substantially regulated by the federal securities acts. Its labor relations were regulated by the new federal labor laws. Its relations in the general market with consumers and suppliers became increasingly regulated by the antitrust laws[…]" (Hovenkamp quoted in Tsuk 2003, p. 1897). Such was the appeal of the idea that the corporate form could be harnessed to provide positive outcomes for a wide range of stakeholders, and such was the myopia or complacency of the left (Bowden 2001), that between the 1940s and the 1970s, the relevant political challenge was not considered to be the reform of company law to cement these changes as the latter seemed irreversible (Ireland 2009). Rather, the focus was on the fuller realisation of the benefits of the 'managerial revolution'. This vision involved the selection and development of a cadre of scientific and impartial corporate executives, trained in newly established business schools, to represent the interests of multiple stakeholders (Drucker 2006[1946]; Khurana 2007).

That the realization of the 'managerial revolution' and the trumpeted redirection of corporate purpose and value was shallowly rooted if not wholly illusory became evident in the 1970s. The allegiance of executives to managerialism was tested in the 1970s and subsequent decades when a "perfect storm" developed comprising a mounting fiscal crisis, diminishing returns to investors, and disillusionment with what was increasingly construed as the smothering attention of a bloated and unsustainable nannying state. In the face of these developments, there were some calls for a strengthening, or further extension of, the 'managerial revolution' but these were drowned out by those who seized upon economic decline and fiscal crisis presented as a long-awaited awaited opportunity to re-establish market discipline and revitalise shareholder primacy.

Proponents of the counter-managerial revolution attributed flagging growth to the dampening effects of Keynesian full employment policies, disempowering welfare provision, and extensive state ownership. From the 1980s, this rhetoric led to extensive deregulation and liberalization. In combination with the dismantling of Bretton Woods,[16] international capital flows increased and accelerated, thereby hastening the concentration of shareholding in financial institutions, investment funds, including pension funds, hedge funds and sovereign wealth funds—all of which were a condition and a consequence of a rapid expansion and domination of financial markets (Davis 2009; Epstein 2005; Krippner 2012).

What, then, were the effects of this counter-revolution upon the modern corporation? Concerned to reassert the discipline of the market, a dyadic conception of corporate governance has been generated, inspired by agency theory, that, in effect, is attentive only to the relation between shareholders and boards. To refocus managerial attention on the interests of shareholders, a number of means have been mobilised, such as stock options and other forms of financial incentives (e.g. performance bonuses), in addition to performance measures (e.g. shareholder value metrics). Seeking a closer alignment between 'agents' (corporate managers) and 'principals' (shareholders), these inducements have been introduced to (re)impose market discipline as a remedy for weak economic performance. As corporate managers were returned to an early nineteenth century position of recalcitrant but tractable servants of shareholders (Veldman and Willmott, fcmanagement) the degree of autonomy that had been enjoyed by executives during the post-War years was drastically reduced as the tiller of economic development passed from executives and state bureaucrats to the rentier investors (Ireland 2010).

The politico-economic reorientation of corporate governance with shareholder demands became increasingly visible in the post-1970s era, as an overriding concern with shareholder value (Lazonick and O'Sullivan 2000, p. 16) came together with the widespread use of leveraged buy-outs and M&As to restructure the corporate landscape. In combination with the increasing use of corporate profits for dividends and stock buybacks, these developments produced a massive redistribution of social wealth. From the 1950s through to the mid-1970s, companies, on average, directed 45% of their after-tax profits to dividend payments. Even in 1981, corporations still directed a little less than half their profits to shareholders.[17] Yet, between 1990 and 1995, nonfinancial corporations paid out 78% of their after-tax profits as dividends (Henwood in Newfield 2008, p. 128)—a trend that shows little sign of reversing. For the US, between 2003 and 2012 dividend payouts went to 37%, and share buybacks constituted 54%, giving a total of 91%.[18] For the 86 largest companies that appear in the S&P Europe 350 Index, the equivalent figure is 89% during 2001–2010, with dividends payout at 63% and share buybacks at 26%.[19]

In sum, the political imaginary highlights the contingency of the development of the corporate form and attends to the distribution of the benefits derived from this specific legal construct. Keynes (2007[1936]) declared that finance should be the servant, not the master. In its post-1940s incarnation, the modern corporate form broadly complied with this injunction: shareholder interests were accommodated but not exclusively privileged, while a technocratic and public-spirited idea of managerial control over these massive institutions that had transformed the UK and US economies was supported by a broad range of actors (Khurana 2007). From the 1970s onwards, the sidelining of a legal imaginary that had provided the basis for the exercise of managerial control meant that effective power over the corporation shifted to (mostly institutional) market parties, such as pension funds, hedge funds, private equity funds, and sovereign wealth funds. As a result, the corporate form, once again, became harnessed to the priorities of shareholders, notably in the pursuit of short-termist private wealth accumulation.

7   Concluding Remarks

We began with the claim that, in management and organization studies (MOS), there are few issues more critical than the modern corporate form. Corporations are potent enablers of collective action. Whatever the corporation is conceived, or imagined, to be, informs how corporate practices are established, enacted, taught, legitimized and changed. Multiple and competing imaginaries, we have argued, are influential in the constitution of the corporate form—an influence that is evident in its theoretical instability, the shifts between different imaginaries, and in the practical effects that follow those shifts.

Engaging a political imaginary helps to explicate how, in the legal 'imaginary', the corporate form is conceived as a construct that features as an 'entity', 'subject', or 'person'; and it illuminates how the legal imaginary has produced a very specific legal and organisational form which creates very specific privileges as a consequence of the attribution of perpetuity, ownership, agency, rights, and protections. The political imaginary also attends to how the legal imaginary of the corporate form provides ways to advance and represent the claims made by different parties (see Biondi et al. 2007; Deakin 2012). Most importantly, the political imaginary recalls how, in the legal imaginary, the corporation cannot be understood as a simple asset over which a particular group (e.g. partner-shareholders, rentiers, or managers) can legitimately claim ownership or control. That is because, legally, the corporation is an 'entity' that holds ownership in and by itself (Robé 2011). Because the very condition for the creation of the assets ascribed to the 'entity' is the contribution(s) made by diverse stakeholders (e.g. as suppliers, creditors, employees, etc.), both past and present (Biondi et al. 2007; Deakin 2012; Williams and Zumbansen 2011), the separate legal entity is conceived to represent "a network of social and productive relationships" (Ireland 1999, p. 56; see also Gindis 2009). The (re)production of this 'network' (ibid) depends on the participation of a wide diversity of stakeholders in the creation and reproduction of those assets (see Paranque and Willmott 2013). Attributing assets to a corporate entity serves, in this instance, to recall how *corporate assets are indivisibly social, and not private, property.*

The political imaginary helps to show how, in the economic imaginary, the legal status and effects of the corporate form are formally acknowledged but substantively disregarded as it is relegated to the status of a 'legal fiction'. The displacement of the legal imaginary by the economic imaginary has practical significance as it obscures the basis for the separation of (i) ownership of shares from (ii) ownership of assets and from (iii) corporate control (Ireland 1999; Bratton 1989; Ireland 1996; Robé 2012). More specifically, the displacement derogates the role of executives as the 'trustees' of institutional assets and ignores how their fiduciary duties are towards 'the company', not (just) to 'the shareholders' (Armour et al. 2003, p. 537). More broadly, the displacement of the legal imaginary removes the basis for the legal and economic benefits of the corporate form (e.g. limited liability) and the justifications for those benefits.

By exposing the contingency and partiality of the dominant, economic imaginary, the political imaginary debunks the latter's apparent self-evidence and neutrality, making it vulnerable to radical challenge rather than supine endorsement (Veldman and Wilmott 2016). It challenges corporate governance theory and policy that: identifies shareholders as the sole 'principal' to whom managers are held accountable (Veldman and Willmott fc, management); commends incentive structures (e.g. stock options) established by 'principles' (shareholders) to control their 'agents' (executives) leading to a myopic focus on short-term results (Davis 2009); and frames enhancement of corporate governance exclusively and limitedly in terms of the capacity for monitoring and control by (institutional) shareholders by extending financial information flows, by improving the role and training of non-executive directors, and by separating the roles of the chairman and the CEO, etc. (Veldman and Willmott 2015, HR). It also challenges corporate governance theory and policy that discounts non-explicit aspects of contracts for all other stakeholders, specifically under takeover conditions (Aglietta and Rebérioux 2005; Deakin 2015; Tsagas 2014). And, moreover, the political imaginary illuminates how the focus of the economic imaginary on shareholder value as a proxy for social utility (Aglietta and Rebérioux 2005) condones the exploitation of tax loopholes (Palan et al. 2010) and regulatory arbitrage (Overbeek et al. 2007); and shows how this focus also ratchets up the payouts for shareholders and managers through the raising of dividends and stock buybacks (Lazonick 2000) at the expense of other constituencies and interests.

To counter these developments, it is necessary to question and resist the diverse but interdependent elements of an economic imaginary that assigns control over the corporate form to shareholders, and thereby promotes the priorities of a dominant class which has harnessed the corporate form for its own ends—that is, the private appropriation of corporate wealth (Aglietta and Rebérioux 2005; Lazonick and O'Sullivan 2000). The genius of the contemporary economic imaginary resides mainly in its subversion and reversal of the reforms associated with an earlier debate on the corporation, exemplified in elements of Berle and Means' *The Modern Corporation*—a debate that temporarily opened up a broader, more inclusive perspective on issues of ownership, control, accountability, responsibility, and the purpose of corporate governance (Moore and Rebérioux 2007).

Engaging the political imaginary draws attention to how the contemporary economic imaginary is central to the systemic exclusion of voices other than shareholders and directors from the theory and practice of corporate governance. It attends to how the dominance of the economic imaginary has been instrumental in the production and widespread naturalisation of externalised costs (e.g. pollution and global warming) that improve the corporate bottom line, and so strengthen short-term shareholder returns but also contribute directly to the major problems facing the world today, including massive and growing economic inequality, largely unchecked environmental degradation, and rapid climate change. Studying the nature and governance of corporations, as outlined above, can assist proponents of MOS to engage critically with these issues.

Notes

1. Here we make a distinction between (i) 'the corporation', which is widely conceptualized as a collection of individuals, and the assets attributed to it; and (ii) 'the corporate form' as its (imaginary) representation (e.g. in the legal or economic spheres).

2. Whilst there is a measure of agreement about its rise to dominance and economic influence from the end of the nineteenth century (Chandler 2002; Guinnane et al. 2007; Horwitz 1985; Roy 1999) there are marked differences of understanding about the nature and significance of the corporate form amongst specialists in legal studies (Freund 1897; Dewey 1926; Ireland 2003; Laufer 1994; Lederman 2000; Naffine 2003; Wells 2005), economics (Jensen and Meckling 1983, p. 14), corporate governance (Bratton and McCahery 1999, p. 5), political science (Bowman 1996; Ciepley 2013), and organization theory (Schrader 1993, p. 1).

3. We acknowledge that additional imaginaries might be identified— such as the moral imaginary that, today, animates the social responsibility attributed to corporations, in addition to conditioning both the legal and economic imaginaries. We also acknowledge that in the use of the concept of the 'political imaginary', we focus on the political aspects of the contemporary concept of the corporate form, rather than its development in relation to the direct political constitution of and control over the corporate form that determined the development of the concept up until the start of the nineteenth century (Veldman 2011). Finally, we acknowledge that different legal systems and historical developments place different constraints on the concept of incorporation. A rich scholarly field has developed around these differences, comparing the resultant governance systems and their relative effects (Guinnane et al. 2007; Gourevitch and Shinn 2005). However, there are two arguments which suggest that these differences are marginal compared to some underlying similarities. *First*, the contemporary concept of incorporation has developed in a strikingly similar way all over the world in almost exactly the same time-frame (Bowman 1996; Guinnane et al. 2007). As Bowman (1996, p. 291) argues: "the corporate reconstruction of the world political economy in the late twentieth century(…)appears to be modelled on the corporate transformation of North American society in the early-to-mid-twentieth century." Although national and regional differences can be found in the precise understanding of incorporation, the major points by which incorporation diverges from other, forms of business representation in legal systems

worldwide are unwavering. *Second*, as we make clear in the economic imaginary section below, the adoption of a contractual model of the corporation has, after the 1970s, spread a uniform understanding of incorporation across the world. This has, in turn, made it almost impossible to conduct business internationally without acknowledging and accepting the assumptions behind the Anglo-American concept of incorporation (see also Guinnane et al. 2007, p. 690). For these two reasons, we consider the contemporary concept of 'incorporation' to be internationally embraced: a specific form of incorporation, characterized as the modern western limited liability share corporation, which emerged principally from Anglo-American legal and economic origins in the nineteenth and twentieth century.

4. Our notion of the imaginary is loosely compatible with Laclau's (1990) concept of the (social) 'imaginary' which, for him, 'structures the field of intelligibility' and is therefore 'the condition of possibility for the emergence of any object' (ibid, p. 64). In our case, the corporate form is the emergent object which is articulated within the legal, economic and political fields of intelligibility.

5. By the end of the twentieth century, about half of the world's trade was conducted between such firms (Kobrin 2006, p. 220). Twenty-nine corporations then appeared in the list of the world's largest economies (Chandler and Mazlish 2006; Goodwin 2006, p. 135); and these firms alone hold 90% of all technology and product patents worldwide (Dine 2006, p. 152).

6. It is relevant to note that the corporate form was granted to other entities, such as town, universities, colonial settlements etc. before it was bestowed upon private ventures (Arrighi 2010; Gindis 2009). This enabled such entities to make contracts in their own name, and against assets assigned to them, rather than in the name of individuals (see Maitland 2003; Post 1934; Williston 1888).

7. Upon the retirement or departure of a partner, there is a substantive or formal liquidation of assets to which partners have priority access, depending upon whether a new partner can be found to purchase the departing partner's share of the assets.

8. It is relevant to note that the corporate form did not appear overnight. Initially, it was barely distinguishable from the partnership but

over a period of approximately 50 years, it took on a distinctive identity that is central to 'the modern doctrine of separate corporate personality, with its reified corporations and "complete separation" of shareholders and the company' (Ireland 2010, p. 847).

9. This 'entity' has become consolidated in the legal imaginary as a reified singular construct with attributions of agency, ownership, and rights and by the end of the nineteenth century was understood as a full legal 'subject' or even 'person'. Anthropomorphic imagery is widely engaged in both American (Ciepley 2013; Johnson 2012) and British (Wells 2005) contexts. On the basis of such imagery, the corporate form has been endowed in the USA with a large set of amendment rights (Veldman and Parker 2012). There are, of course, questions to be raised about a legal imaginary which conceives of the corporation as a discrete entity or 'subject' with powers of agency, ownership, etc. abstracted, or differentiated, from its members. In this paper, however, we focus on the performative effects of different imaginaries, and thereby contribute to a debate about the consequences of these imaginaries, rather than devote more attention to their ontological or epistemological justification.

10. It has also enabled the profusion of opaque international control and finance structures (Palan et al. 2010), and unclear attributions of liability (Ackroyd and Murphy 2013).

11. See https://themoderncorporation.wordpress.com/company-law-memo/ for a statement written and supported by leading company lawyers to this effect.

12. In conceptions of the corporate form which prevailed from the 1930s until the 1970s the legal imaginary led to the view of the corporate form as a 'quasi-public' type of representation (Berle and Means 2007[1932]) which implicitly incorporated a stakeholder conception of governance (Drucker 2006[1946]; Kaysen 1957).

13. Opportunities for joining partnerships, which promised the highest economic returns, were restricted, since most were able to fund desired expansion by ploughing back profits or by borrowing at capped rates.

14. In practice, rentier investors often continued to be exposed to fraud, in part because they declined to take any active interest in the businesses in which they invested (Johnson 2010).

15. But, as Ireland (nd, p. 16) cautions, while managers enjoyed more room to maneuver, they could not afford to ignore or marginalize shareholders or substantially redefine their established markers of performance. Even when external pressures were relaxed, executives willingly imposed similar disciplines upon themselves by developing multi-divisional management structures in which decentralized profit centers competed for capital.

16. The 'Bretton Woods' agreement was established in 1944 as a basis for reforming an international economic system amongst leading capitalist nations. It created rules and institutions (e.g. International Monetary Fund, IMF) which obliged states which ratified the agreement to peg their currency to the US dollar, and for the IMF to 'manage' imbalances. In 1971, the USA terminated unilaterally the convertibility of the US$ into gold, resulting in the end of the Bretton Woods agreement as the US$ effectively became the reserve currency of choice and currencies floated instead of being tied to the US$.

17. http://www.washingtonpost.com/opinions/harold-meyerson-in-corporations-its-owner-take-all/2014/08/26/0c1a002a-2ca7-11e4-bb9b-997ae96fad33_story.html.

18. https://hbr.org/2014/09/profits-without-prosperity and http://www.washingtonpost.com/opinions/harold-meyerson-in-corporations-its-owner-take-all/2014/08/26/0c1a002a-2ca7-11e4-bb9b-997ae96fad33_story.html.

19. http://www.theguardian.com/commentisfree/2012/aug/27/shareholder-payouts-holding-back-prosperity.

Big Four Accounting Firms: Addicted to Tax Avoidance

Prem Sikka

Tony Lowe was very concerned about the direction, control and social accountability of accountancy profession. In particular, he was concerned that major firms were increasingly devoted to pursuit of private profits at almost any cost and warned that "It is quite usual to regard business enterprises as expendable social artefacts because their responsiveness to human needs is a precondition of their survival. The accounting profession in the longer run is unlikely to be exempt from such social evolutionary processes" (Lowe and Tinker 1977, p. 273).

The above is a reminder of the likely future of accountancy firms. It is highly pertinent to the current times, as entrepreneurial accountancy firms have expanded beyond their traditional jurisdiction of accounting, auditing and a variety of consultancy activities into money laundering (Mitchell et al. 1998a, b), tax evasion and tax avoidance (Sikka 2008; Mitchell and Sikka 2011; Sikka and Willmott 2013). Such practices

P. Sikka (✉)
Essex Business School, University of Essex, Colchester, Essex, UK

© The Author(s) 2016   **259**
J. Haslam, P. Sikka (eds.), *Pioneers of Critical Accounting*,
DOI 10.1057/978-1-137-54212-0_13

boost accountancy firm profits and enlarge the list of satisfied clients, but they also bring the firms into conflict with the state and citizens as without adequate tax revenues the state cannot invest in social infrastructure, redistribute wealth, or deliver the social settlement mandate through the ballot-box.

This chapter provides a glimpse of the role of the Big Four accounting firms (PricewaterhouseCoopers (PwC), Deloitte and Touche, KPMG and Ernst & Young) in crafting and implementing tax avoidance schemes. This is appropriate because tax avoidance can be hugely lucrative for big accounting firms. The US Senate Permanent Subcommittee on Investigations (2005) concluded that "the tax shelter industry had moved from providing one-on-one tax advice in response to tax inquiries to also initiating, designing, and mass marketing tax shelter products… dubious tax shelter sales were no longer the province of shady, fly-by-night companies with limited resources. They had become big business, assigned to talented professionals at the top of their fields and able to draw upon the vast resources and reputations of the country's largest accounting firms…" (p. 9). After investigating documents leaked by whistleblowers, the International Consortium of Investigative Journalists (ICIJ) concluded that "Big 4 firms are central architects of the offshore system—and key players in an array of cross-border transactions that raise legal and ethical questions" (Hudson et al. 2014). The tax avoidance practices of the Big Four firms are increasingly on the radar of parliamentary committees (US Senate Permanent Subcommittee on Investigations 2003, 2005; UK House of Commons Committee of Public Accounts 2013a, 2015).

The remainder of this chapter is structured as follows. The second section shows that in the remorseless pursuit of private profits, the Big Four firms have prioritised profits over people. Fines and even prison sentences for antisocial practices seem to be treated as just another business cost as the tax avoidance business continues relentlessly. The third section provides examples of a variety of tax avoidance schemes and strategies developed, marketed and implemented by the Big Four firms. Many of these have been declared to be unlawful by the courts. The fourth and final section summarises the chapter and considers the relevance of Tony Lowe's legacy for engaging with big accountancy firms.

1   Profits Before People

The glossy brochures and websites of the Big Four firms seek to disarm critics with claims of ethical business conduct (Sikka 2010), but rarely provide a glimpse of their actual practices. The Big Four firms have a history of involvement in facilitating tax avoidance and have devoted extensive organisational resources to designing and marketing this highly profitable trade (Brooks 2013; Rostain and Regan Jr. 2014). In 2013, the firms became the subject of a hearing into their tax avoidance practices by the UK House of Commons Committee of Public Accounts. Just before the hearing the Committee received evidence from a former senior PwC employee stating that the firm's policy was that it would sell a tax avoidance scheme which had only a 25% chance of withstanding a legal challenge, or as the Committee chairperson put it "you are offering schemes to your clients—knowingly marketing these schemes—where you have judged there is a 75% risk of it then being deemed unlawful" (UK House of Commons Committee of Public Accounts 2013a: Ev4).. The other three firms admitted to "selling schemes that they consider only have a 50% chance of being upheld in court" (p. 5).

The Big Four firms have been under scrutiny in the USA too. The US Senate Permanent Subcommittee on Investigations (2005) concluded that "KPMG devoted substantial resources and maintained an extensive infrastructure to produce a continuing supply of generic tax products to sell to clients, using a process which pressured its tax professionals to generate new ideas, move them quickly through the development process, and approve, at times, illegal or potentially abusive tax shelters…Ernst & Young sold generic tax products to multiple clients despite evidence that some…were potentially abusive or illegal tax shelters…PricewaterhouseCoopers sold generic tax products to multiple clients, despite evidence that some…were potentially abusive or illegal tax shelters" (pp. 6–7). A former Commissioner of the US Internal Revenue Service (IRS) noted that "the low point came when we discovered that a senior tax partner at KPMG (one of the Big Four, which by virtue of their prominence set standards for the others) had advocated—in writing—to leaders of the company's tax practice that KPMG make a "business/strategic decision" to ignore a particular set of IRS disclosure rules. The reasoning was that the IRS was unlikely to discover the underlying transactions and that even if we did, any penalties assessed could be absorbed as a cost of doing business" (Everson 2011). The US authorities pursued KPMG, which admitted "criminal wrongdoing[1]" and paid a fine of $456 million. In March 2013, Ernst & Young paid a fine of $123 million to avoid prosecution over "the wrongful conduct of certain partners and employees[2]". A number of KPMG and Ernst & Young former partners and employees have received prison sentences (Rostain and Regan Jr. 2014).

The above has provided a brief glimpse of the zeal with which the Big Four firms have sought to increase their profits. The next section provides examples of the kind of schemes manufactured by each of the firms.

2   The Business of Tax Avoidance

2.1   Deloitte & Touche

After the 2007–2008 banking crash, many western banks were bailed out by governments. Most of the distressed banks were audited by the Big Four firms. Despite collecting huge fees, the audited accounts did not provide any clues about the impending crisis (Sikka 2009). The same firms have also boosted their income by crafting schemes to enable bankers to avoid taxes. In one particularly notorious example (see Deutsche Bank Group Services (UK) Ltd v Revenue & Customs [2011] UKFTT 66 (TC)), Deloitte designed a scheme for the London office of Deutsche Bank to enable its staff to avoid income tax and National Insurance Contributions (NIC) on bonuses adding up to £92 million. More than 300 bankers participated in the scheme which operated through a Cayman Islands registered investment vehicle. In 2011, the scheme was declared to be unlawful by the courts. The judge in the case said that "the Scheme as a whole, and each aspect of it, was created and coordinated purely for tax avoidance purposes" (Para 112, Deutsche Bank Group Services (UK) Ltd v Revenue & Customs [2011] UKFTT 66 (TC)).

Complexity is a great resource for the tax avoidance industry as it uses complex financial instruments to make profits vanish. One such scheme was designed by Deloitte and challenged by HMRC in the case of Explainaway Ltd & Ors v Revenue & Customs [2011] UKFTT 414 (TC) (24 June 2011). The scheme in question was designed to avoid the corporation tax that would otherwise have arisen on the disposal of certain shares. By following the steps designed by Deloitte, the company entered into a series of paper transactions, sales of shares, futures, and derivatives contracts to generate a loss. The scheme was rejected by the First-Tier Tribunal and again by the Upper Tribunal in Explainaway Limited v HMRC [2012] UKUT 362 (TCC) because there was no real loss.

In 2013, the UK Supreme Court ruled (on a scheme "which was designed to minimise the overall liability to VAT of a group of companies involved in motor breakdown insurance" (paragraph 1 of WHA Ltd & Anor v Revenue and Customs [2013] UKSC 24). The hearing was the culmination of a class action brought by Deloitte to demand VAT refunds for its clients. Some of events went back to the 1970s and Deloitte claimed that the motor industry has been overcharged VAT by possibly as much as £2 billion. Deloitte brought a test case against the UK government on behalf of Warranty Holdings Limited (trading as WHA Limited). The case related to an insurance company which entered into a series of complex transactions with Gibraltar-based companies to enable it to reclaim VAT on motor breakdown insurance sold to UK motorists. Gibraltar is part of the EU for trade purposes, but for VAT purposes it is treated as a non-EU jurisdiction. As the services were supplied in Gibraltar, the company argued that the VAT on its supplies is exempt from VAT. In 2003 the Special Commissioners ruled in favour of the company. In 2004, HMRC appealed to the Court of Appeal (WHA Ltd & Anor v Customs & Excise [2004] EWCA Civ 559), which in turn sought guidance from the European Court of Justice, which sent the matter back to the Court of Appeal. On 17 July 2007, the Court of Appeal ruled (WHA v HM Revenue & Customs [2007] EWCA Civ 728) in favour of the tax authorities. The chief reason was that the arrangements were mainly designed for tax avoidance. Nevertheless, the matter went to the Supreme Court and in 2013, it unanimously ruled (WHA v HM Revenue & Customs

[2013] UKSC 24) in favour of HMRC. A press release issued by HMRC said that the scheme was "designed to avoid VAT on car repairs that could have cost the Exchequer £600 million a year[3]".

Deloitte became embroiled in the acquisition of the German telecoms operator Mannesman by London-based Vodafone. Deloitte were auditors of Vodafone until 2014. The acquisition was financed by a €35bn debt parked in Vodafone's Luxembourg subsidiary, VIL Sarl. Under the deal, Mannesmann paid interest on debt to VIL Sarl and thereby reduced its taxable profits and tax bill in Germany. The interest received by VIL Sarl avoided tax and was not booked in the UK. The UK tax authorities argued that the transactions were "wholly artificial arrangements intended to escape the United Kingdom tax normally payable" (see Vodafone 2 v Revenue and Customs [2008] EWHC 1569 (Ch) (04 July 2008)). The dispute related to some £6 billion of income recorded in Luxembourg from activities in Germany and Greece (UK House of Commons Committee of Public Accounts 2011: Ev123). Vodafone's 2010 annual accounts (note 6) filed at Companies House, audited by Deloitte, disclosed that "HMRC are enquiring into the establishment and activities of certain Group holding companies in Luxembourg to determine whether they constitute 'wholly artificial arrangements', which the Group maintains that they do not. The Group carries provisions of £2.2 billion in relation to the potential tax exposure at 31 March 2010 (2009: £2.2 billion)". Deloitte were also advising Vodafone on tax matters and played a key role in the resolution of tax disputes with HMRC. The Guardian newspaper reported[4] that during Vodafone's tax negotiations HMRC chairman Dave struck up a close relationship with Andrew Cruickshank, Deloitte's senior British partner. They had 48 meetings between 2007 and 2011, including meetings about Vodafone. In 2010, the dispute was settled with Vodafone paying a lump sum of £800,000 with a further £450,000 spread over five years (Brooks 2013). A report by the National Audit Office said that the settlement was "reasonable", but criticised HMRC for failing to follow its own procedures, which included keeping notes of key meetings, consulting independent experts and seeking legal advice (National Audit Office 2012). In May 2013, Dave Hartnett joined Deloitte & Touche as a specialist advisor (UK House of Commons Committee of Public Accounts 2013b).

2.2   Ernst & Young

Former HMRC chairman Dave Hartnett has described Ernst & Young as probably the most aggressive, creative, abusive provider] of avoidance schemes" (Mitchell and Sikka 2011, p. 12), but that has not deterred the firm from crafting ingenious schemes. The case of Iliffe News and Media Ltd & Ors v Revenue & Customs [2012] UKFTT 696 (TC) (01 November 2012) reported that Ernst & Young devised a tax avoidance scheme for its audit client, a highly profitable media company. The company owned a number of newspaper titles and was advised to treat its mastheads as a new asset. These were all transferred to the parent company for a nominal sum, and then immediately leased back to the subsidiaries for annual royalties. The tax tribunal noted that over a five year period, the subsidiaries paid royalties of £51.6 million. This intragroup transaction did not result in any transfer of cash to an external party, but the subsidiaries claimed tax relief on the royalty payments. The company's board minutes, as reproduced in the court papers, noted that "[Ernst & Young] had confirmed that if the newspaper titles and/or mastheads were registered as trade marks in the ownership of [INML], it was possible for the latter [i.e. INML] to charge the newspaper companies a fee for the use of the former in a tax efficient manner that would significantly lessen the transparency of reported results. It was agreed to progress this matter in consultation with [E&Y]" (paragraph 54 of Iliffe News and Media Ltd & Ors v Revenue & Customs [2012] UKFTT 696 (TC) (01 November 2012)). The tax avoidance scheme was rejected by the courts.

Ernst & Young manufactured a tax avoidance scheme to enable Debenhams and 90 major retailers to avoid VAT and increase their profits. The scheme was described by a UK treasury spokesperson as "one of the most blatantly abusive avoidance scams of recent years" (cited in Mitchell and Sikka 2011, p. 26). The court judgment in Debenhams Retail PLC v Customs and Excise [2003] UKVAT V18169 noted that in its marketing of the £4 million VAT avoidance scheme to Debenhams, Ernst & Young referred to the scheme as "a very lucrative tax planning opportunity... an ongoing opportunity "unless legislated against by Customs"...counteracting measures would take "a number of years" to enact...Due to the level of potential profit opportunity available there is a desire to introduce the scheme as quickly as possible" (paragraph 39). The scheme was designed to change the terms on which "the Debenhams Group accepts credit cards in order to produce a position whereby less VAT is paid than was paid previously and for no other reason" (para. 5). The outward sign of this scheme was a statement printed on customers' credit card receipts. It read "I agree that 2.5% of the above value is payable to Debenhams Card Handling Services Ltd (DCHS) for card handling services. The total amount I pay remains the same". As financial services were exempt from VAT, Ernst &Young advised its clients to claim that 2.5% of the proceeds were not subject to VAT, and therefore the output tax payable to the Treasury would be less. Ernst & Young informed Debenhams that "Customs would need a legislative change to stop this". The tax tribunal concluded that the transactions in the scheme "were carried out solely for the purpose of avoiding tax…The arrangement was wholly artificial" (para. 117). The matter went to the High Court which ruled (Debenhams Retail Plc v Commissioners of Customs and Excise (2004) EWHC 1540 (Ch)) in Debenhams' favour. HMRC then took the case to the Court of Appeal (Debenhams Retail Plc [2005] EWCA Civ 892) which outlawed the scheme. The presiding judge referred to the scheme as "Tweedledum in Alice in Wonderland: I know what you're thinking about, but it isn't so, no how" (para. 45). This scheme alone could have deprived the treasury of up to £500 million of tax revenues per year.

Ernst & Young mass marketed a scheme involving loans between companies in a group. The scheme was described by a UK legislator as "purely artificial" (UK House of Commons Committee of Public Accounts (2013: Ev9). The loans involved a series of complex transactions whose ultimate aim was to enable the company making the interest payment to claim tax relief on this expense, whilst enabling the company receiving the interest to avoid tax. This scheme was sold to Greene King, a leading pub retailer and brewer. The company is audited by Ernst & Young. In the matter of Greene King, tax relief on payments of £21.3 million was at stake and the agreement, as the tax tribunal noted, required that Ernst & young would take a percentage of the tax saved by adoption of its scheme. The scheme was thrown out by the First-Tier Tribunal in its judgement in Greene King Plc & Anor v Revenue & Customs [2012] UKFTT 385

(TC) (14/06/2012). HMRC argued that "it was "blindingly obvious" that the motivation, or main motivation, of the scheme was tax avoidance" (para 120 of the judgment). The company appealed against the decision, but it was once again thrown out by the judgment in Greene King Plc & Anor v Revenue And Customs [2014] UKUT 178 (TCC) (22 April 2014).

3   KPMG

The US case of Salem Financial Inc. v United States, No. 10-192T (Ct. Fed. Cl. Sept. 20, 2013) shows how the Big Four firms market avoidance schemes at a global scale, playing one country's tax system against another's. In this example, KPMG collaborated with Barclays PLC to mass market a tax avoidance scheme to several global corporations, including AIG, Microsoft, Prudential, Wachovia, Wells Fargo, Bank of New York Mellon, and Branch Banking & Trust (BB&T). The scheme marketed during the period 2002–2007, known as the Structured Trust Advantaged Repackaged Securities (STARS), involved a series of complex transactions to buy an asset, set up a trust and then issue securities to investors. The main objective was to generate a series of foreign tax credits which could then be offset against the US tax liability of the companies. The US tax authorities disputed a deduction of $892 million for BB&T and argued[5] that the scheme was designed to "subvert the foreign tax credit rules and generate illicit tax benefits to be shared among the transaction's participants".

The court judge explained (see of Salem Financial Inc. v United States, No. 10-192T (Ct. Fed. Cl. Sept. 20, 2013)) that STARS required BB&T to establish a trust containing approximately $6 billion in revenue-producing bank assets. The monthly revenue from the trust was then cycled through a UK trustee, an act that served as a basis for UK taxation. Although the revenue was immediately returned to BB&T's trust, the assessment of UK taxes generated UK tax credits that were shared 50/50 between Barclays and BB&T. A $1.5 billion loan from Barclays to BB&T was also part of the structured transaction, although the loan was not necessary to the objective of generating foreign tax credits. Barclays' monthly payment to BB&T represented BB&T's share of the tax credits, and had the effect of reducing the interest cost of BB&T's loan. KPMG was the principal marketer of STARS, and provided BB&T with advice as to the viability and profitability of the transaction. The court judgement noted that as discussions between KMPG and BB&T progressed, BB&T became concerned that if challenged, the IRS may determine that STARS lacked economic substance. KPMG advised BB&T that the possibility of a court finding BB&T to have engaged in a sham transaction was "so remote as to not need to be considered". KPMG further advised that even if STARS was found to lack economic substance, BB&T would nevertheless be allowed a deduction for the U.K. taxes. The judge concluded that "KPMG's overarching advice was that BB&T should engage in an economically meaningless transaction to achieve foreign tax credits for taxes BB&T had not in substance paid" (p. 61 of Salem Financial Inc. v United States, No. 10-192T (Ct. Fed. Cl. Sept. 20, 2013), The tax avoidance scheme was thrown out by the court and the judge said that the scheme was "driven solely by the sham circular cash flows of the Trust" (p. 49) and that "the conduct of those persons from BB&T, Barclays, KPMG…who were involved in this and other transactions was nothing short of reprehensible" (p. 3).

Another KPMG scheme to enable P&O to artificially generate a tax credit of £14m was thrown out by the tax tribunal in the case of Peninsular & Oriental Steam Navigation Company v Revenue & Customs [2013] UKFTT 322 (TC) (29 May 2013). At the time, KPMG were both auditors and tax advisers to the P&O group. The scheme involved a series of transactions between the UK and Australian subsidiaries to boost tax credits on dividend income. The judges said that the "scheme was designed and implemented for no reason other than tax avoidance" and contrived transactions were "all part of an elaborate trick designed to exploit [tax legislation]….P&O and its subsidiaries played out a scripted game of charades" (para. 69 of the judgment).

A mass marketed KPMG scheme became the subject of litigation in the case of Spectrum Computer Supplies Ltd v Revenue and Customs Commissioners; Kirkstall Timber Ltd v Revenue and Customs Commissioners [2006] STC (SCD) 668. The scheme enabled companies and their employees to avoid UK NIC and income tax by paying their directors with the debts of the company instead of cash. The companies had no prior relationship with KPMG and were introduced to the firm through their accountants. KPMG had developed arrangements whereby bonuses were satisfied by the assignment to employees of trade debts owed to the employer. KPMG spoke to a number of clients, including Spectrum, in relation to such possible arrangements (para 5 of Spectrum Computer Supplies Ltd & Anor v Revenue & Customs [2006] UKSPC SPC00559 (22 August 2006)). Kirkstall were told that KPMG were marketing a method for paying directors a form of bonus which would save Kirkstall national insurance contributions (para. 7). Clients had to sign up to a duty of confidentiality about the scheme. In subsequent presentations, KPMG explained the steps necessary for implementing the schemes. The tax authorities disallowed the reliefs claimed by the schemes and the case was referred to a tax tribunal which upheld the position of the tax authorities. The subsequent appeal was referred to Special Commissioners and they stated that "Our decision on PAYE in Spectrum is that the assignment of book debts constituted a payment, but that they did not constitute trading arrangements...Our decision in principle in the Kirkstall appeals is that the assignment of the book debts was not a payment in kind for National Insurance Contributions purposes; that it constituted a payment for PAYE; but that they did not constitute trading arrangements" (paras. 31 and 32 of Spectrum Computer Supplies Ltd & Anor v Revenue & Customs [2006] UKSPC SPC00559 (22 August 2006)).

4   PricewaterhouseCoopers

PricewaterhouseCoopers (PwC) is credited[6] with developing Ireland as a tax haven and particularly with refining a scheme which subsequently became known as the Double Irish Dutch Sandwich (International Monetary Fund 2013). The scheme uses complex corporate structures to exploit tax treaties and tax rate differentials and arbitrage global tax systems. The essence of the technique is to shift profits to low/no tax jurisdictions through royalty payments for the use of intellectual property, transfer pricing techniques, intragroup loans and other internal transactions. Variants of the Double Irish have enabled global corporations to avoid taxes in many countries.

Links with governments and industry enable the Big Four firms to create new business opportunities. In May 2012, the BBC's Panorama programme[7] showed how PwC devised schemes to enable multinational corporations, such as GlaxoSmithKline (GSK) and Northern & Shell,[8] to move profits to offshore tax havens via Luxembourg. The schemes involved a variety of intergroup loans, contrived interest payments, and transfer pricing arrangements to reduce profits in the UK (and other countries) and avoid corporate taxes. According to the Panorama Programme, GSK created a new subsidiary in Luxembourg in 2009. In 2010, the new subsidiary lent £6.34bn to another GSK company in the UK. In return, GSK paid nearly £124 million in interest to its Luxembourg subsidiary. The company was effectively paying interest to itself. No cash left the GSK group of companies, but it had tax effects. In the UK at that time, the corporation tax rate was 28%. By paying interest, the UK taxable profits were reduced by £124 million, and resulted in a lower tax liability. In Luxembourg, PwC negotiated a secret deal to levy tax on that £124m at effectively less than 0.5%, or about £300,000. In the UK, the tax on £124 million would have been £34.7 million. According to Panorama, PwC also negotiated Luxembourg tax deals for Northern & Shell. It too received loans from Luxembourg-based subsidiaries and thus saved on the payment of taxes in the UK.

Panorama showed that schemes were approved by senior government officials from the Luxembourg government. In November 2014, the full scale of such arrangements was brought to public attention by a whistleblower in what became known as the Luxembourg Leaks (or Luxleaks). The leaked information, publicly available on the website of the International Consortium of Investigative Journalists (http://www.icij.org/project/luxembourg-leaks) refers to some 28,000 pages of tax agreements, returns and other papers relating to over 1,000 businesses. The papers provide details of tax avoidance schemes crafted by PwC[9] and relate to giant global corporations. Most notably, the 28,000 pages, which are publicly available, make no mention of ethics, morality, or the possible social impact of lost tax revenues.

PwC mass marketed a scheme which relied on complex financial transactions, but in essence assumed that due to deficiencies in legislation profits on loan notes would not be taxable. Amongst others, it was sold to Vocalspruce Limited, at that time a subsidiary of FTSE-listed group Brixton plc. The scheme was challenged by HMRC in the lead case of Vocalspruce Ltd v Revenue & Customs [2012] UKFTT 36 (TC) (21 December 2011). In this case, the loan notes were exchanged between the parent company and its subsidiary and then translated into shares to generate profits, and steps were taken to make the profits non-taxable. The tax tribunal rejected the scheme and the company and its tax advisers launched an appeal. The Upper Tribunal (Vocalspruce Ltd v HMRC [2013] UKUT 276 (TCC) (19 June 2013)) rejected the scheme. Undeterred, the company and its advisors took the case to the Court of Appeal where judges described the scheme as "fiction" (Vocalspruce Ltd v The Commissioners for HMRC [2014] EWCA Civ 1302 (30 October 2014)) and rejected it. The case had implications for other buyers of the scheme too, who collectively had to pay £62 million.[10]

5   Summary and Discussion

This chapter began by citing a warning from Tony Lowe (Lowe and Tinker 1977) that the accountancy profession's legitimacy and survival ultimately depends on ethical and socially responsible behaviour. Lowe's scrutiny of the role of accounting practices in corporate frauds and collapses led to the conclusion that the profession deserves a share of the responsibility for the poor quality of industrial/financial management, and needs to pay attention to the social context of its practices. Such advice has not been heeded by some influential parts of the accountancy establishment. If anything, the profession has developed even more anti-social practices. The design and marketing of tax avoidance schemes is an example of the new profit maximising tools that have been used by the Big Four firms to undermine social welfare.

This chapter has presented some evidence of the involvement of Big Four accounting firms in tax avoidance. Their trade enables corporations and wealthy individuals to avoid taxes, and has serious implications for the relationship between citizens and the state. Due to a lack of tax revenues, many hard won social rights relating to education, pensions and social welfare are being eroded. The state's capacity to make social investment or meet social settlement mandated through democratic processes is being neutered. This has considerable potential to cause social unrest and instability. Despite the widespread media coverage of the nefarious practices of the Big Four firms, there has been little firm action by the professional accountancy bodies. For example, no accountancy firms in the UK have ever been disciplined or fined for selling tax avoidance schemes, even after they have been declared unlawful by the courts. When challenged, the chief executive of the Institute of Chartered Accountants in England & Wales (ICAEW) said, "You ask whether any of the major firms has been the subject of an adverse disciplinary finding in relation to advisory work on taxation. I can confirm that no such findings have been made either by ICAEW or by the Financial Reporting Council, which as you know, has responsibility for considering cases affecting the public interest[11]".

Tony Lowe had argued that an irresponsible profession faces public opprobrium, retribution, and ultimately oblivion. Intoxicated by ever-rising profits and sheltered by political patronage and self-regulation, albeit in a statutory context, major firms have assumed they were somehow immune to public scrutiny (Mitchell and Sikka 2011). Such assumptions are increasingly challenged by negative press coverage and critical reports from civil society organisations (for example, Christian-Aid 2008, 2009; Action-Aid 2010; Harari et al. 2012). The rising public visibility of these antisocial practices probably persuaded the UK House of Commons to launch its own inquiry into the role of the Big Four firms in tax avoidance (UK House of Commons Committee of Public Accounts 2013, 2015). This was preceded by hearings by a US Senate Committee (US Senate Permanent Subcommittee on Investigations 2003, 2005). Unlike the UK, the findings of the US hearings were followed by other government agencies and resulted in fines for the firms and prison sentences for some of their personnel. However, so far, this does not appear to have significantly dulled their appetite for profiting from the sale of tax avoidance schemes, a crucial part of their business models. They are unlikely to voluntarily dilute their tax avoidance trade. Perhaps, the continuing spectre of public disquiet, parliamentary hearings and critical media coverage would persuade governments to take punitive action against major accounting firms. Such a scenario also presents opportunities for critical academics to intervene in public affairs and craft new policies to enable people to live fulfilling lives, a role which Tony Lowe consistently advocated for scholars.

Notes

1. US Department of Justice press release, KPMG to Pay $456 Million for Criminal Violations in Relation to Largest-Ever Tax Shelter Fraud Case, 29 August 2005; http://www.justice.gov/opa/pr/2005/August/05_ag_433.html.
2. US Department of Justice press release, Manhattan U.S. Attorney Announces Agreement With Ernst & Young LLP To Pay $123 Million To Resolve Federal Tax Shelter Fraud Investigation, 1 March 2013; http://www.justice.gov/usao/nys/pressreleases/March13/EYNPAPR.php.
3. HMRC press release, Car warranty tax scheme scuppered, 13 May 2013; http://www.mynewsdesk.com/uk/hm-revenue-customs-hmrc/pressreleases/car-warranty-tax-scheme-scuppered-864800.
4. The Guardian, Deloitte appoints official criticised over 'sweetheart' tax deals, 27 May 2013; http://www.theguardian.com/business/2013/may/27/deloitte-appoints-dave-hartnett-tax.
5. US Justice Department press release, Justice Department prevails in "stars" tax shelter case, court imposes over $100 million in penalties, 20 September 2013 (http://www.justice.gov/tax/2013/txdv131054.htm).
6. Bloomberg, Man Making Ireland Tax Avoidance Hub Proves Local Hero, 28 October 2013; http://www.bloomberg.com/news/2013-10-28/man-making-ireland-tax-avoidance-hub-globally-proves-local-hero.html.
7. BBC News, Major UK companies cut secret tax deals in Luxembourg, 11 May 2012; http://www.bbc.co.uk/news/business-17993945.

8. Northern & Shell business empire includes newspapers (such as, Daily Express, Sunday Express, Daily Star, Star on Sunday), magazines (such as, OK!, New!, Star, TV Pick) and TV stations (such as, Channel 5, 5*, 5USA, Television X, Red, Hot TV).

9. Also see The Guardian, Luxembourg tax files: how tiny state rubber-stamped tax avoidance on an industrial scale 5 November 2014, http://www.theguardian.com/business/2014/nov/05/-sp-luxembourg-tax-files-tax-avoidance-industrial-scale; BBC News, Disney and Skype 'used Luxembourg tax deals', 10 December 2014, http://www.bbc.co.uk/news/world-europe-30412293.

10. HMRC press release, HMRC wins in court have protected over £1 billion, 18 July 2013; https://www.gov.uk/government/news/hmrc-wins-in-court-have-protected-over-1-billion.

11. Letter dated 20 December 2012 from ICAEW to Austin Mitchell (Austin Mitchell stepped down from the UK House of Commons in May 2015).

References

Accounting Standards (formerly Steering) Committee. (1975). *The corporate report*. London: ICAEW.

Action-Aid. (2010). *Calling time: Why SABMiller should stop dodging taxes in Africa*. London: Acton-Aid.

Adler, P., & Borys, B. (1996). Two types of bureaucracy: Enabling and coercive. *Administrative Science Quarterly, 41*, 61–89.

Agger, B. (2004). *The virtual self. A contemporary sociology*. Oxford: Blackwell.

Aglietta, M., & Rebérioux, A. (2005). *Corporate governance adrift: A critique of shareholder value*. Cheltenham: Edward Elgar.

Agyemang, G., & Lehman, C. (2013). Adding critical accounting voices to migration studies. *Critical Perspectives on Accounting, 24*(4/5), 261–272.

Allen, W. (1992). Our schizophrenic conception of the business corporation. *Cardozo Law Review, 14*(2), 261–281.

Amel-Zadeh, A., & Meeks, G. (2013). Bank failure, mark to market and the financial crisis. *Abacus, 49*(3), 308–339.

Andersen, N. (2003). *Discursive analytical strategies: Understanding Foucault, Koselleck, Laclau and Luhmann*. Bristol: Policy Press.

Andre, P., Cazavan-Jeny, A., Dick, W., Richard, C., & Walton, P. (2009). Fair value accounting and the banking crisis; shooting the messenger. *Accounting in Europe, 6*(1), 3–4.

Angier, N. (1999). *Woman: An intimate geography*. Boston: Houghton Mifflin.

© The Author(s) 2016
J. Haslam, P. Sikka (eds.), *Pioneers of Critical Accounting*,
DOI 10.1057/978-1-137-54212-0

275

Angier, N. (2007). *The canon.* Boston: Houghton Mifflin.

Annisette, M. (2003). The colour of accountancy: Examining the salience of 'race' in a professionalization project. *Accounting, Organizations and Society, 28*(7/8), 639–674.

Annisette, M., & Trivedi, V. (2013). Globalization, paradox and the (un)making of identities: Immigrant chartered accountants of India in Canada. *Accounting, Organizations and Society, 38*(1), 1–29.

Anthony, R. (1965). *Planning and control systems: A framework for analysis.* Boston: Harvard University.

Antonio, R. (1981). Immanent critique as the core of critical theory: Its origins and developments in Hegel, Marx and contemporary thought. *British Journal of Sociology, 32*(3), 330–345.

Armour, J., Deakin, S., & Konzelmann, S. (2003). Shareholder primacy and the trajectory of UK corporate governance. *British Journal of Industrial Relations, 41*(3), 531–555.

Armstrong, P. (1994). The influence of Michel Foucault on accounting research. *Critical Perspectives on Accounting, 5*(1), 25–55.

Arnold, P. (2009). Global financial crisis: The challenge to accounting research. *Accounting, Organizations and Society, 34*(6), 803–809.

Arrighi, G. (2010). *The long twentieth century: Money, power, and the origins of our times.* London: Verso.

Arrington, C. E., & Francis, J. (1989). Letting the chat out of the bag: Deconstruction, privilege and accounting research. *Accounting, Organizations and Society, 14*, 1–28.

Arrington, C. E., & Schweiker, W. (1992). The rhetoric and rationality of accounting research. *Accounting, Organizations and Society, 17*, 511–533.

Ashby, W. R. (1956). *An introduction to cybernetics.* London: Chapman and Hall.

Ashby, W. R. (1958). Requisite variety and its implications for the control of complex systems. *Cybernetica, 1*(2), 83–99.

Bakan, J. (2004). *The corporation—The pathological pursuit of profit and power.* London: Constable and Robinson Ltd.

Ball, R., & Brown, P. (1968). An empirical evaluation of accounting numbers. *Journal of Accounting Research, 6*, 159–177.

Barley, S., & Kunda, G. (1992). Design and devotion: Surges in rational and normative ideologies of control in managerial discourse. *Administrative Science Quarterly, 37*, 363–399.

Barter, N., & Bebbington, J. (2010). *Pursuing environmental sustainability* (Research report 116). London: ACCA.

Barth, M., & Landsman, W. (2010). How did financial reporting contribute to the banking crisis? *Accounting Horizons, 19*(3), 399–423.

Battilana, J., & Dorado, S. (2010). Building sustainable hybrid organizations: The case of commercial microfinance organizations. *Academy of Management Journal, 53*(6), 1419–1440.

Beaver, W. (1968). The information content of annual earnings announcements. *Journal of Accounting Research, Supplement, 6*, 67–92.

Beaver, W. (1981). *Financial reporting: An accounting revolution.* Englewood Cliffs: Prentice-Hall.

Bebbington, J. (2007). *Accounting for sustainable development performance.* London: CIMA.

Bebbington, J., & Gray, R. (2001). An account of sustainability: Failure, success and a reconception. *Critical Perspectives on Accounting, 12*(5), 557–587.

Bebbington, J., & Larrinaga-Gonzalez, C. (2014). Accounting and sustainable development: An exploration. *Accounting, Organizations and Society, 39*(6), 395–413.

Bebbington, J., Gray, R., Hibbitt, C., & Kirk, E. (2001). *Full cost accounting: An agenda for action.* London: ACCA.

Bebbington, J., Brown, J., & Frame, B. (2007a). Accounting technologies and sustainability assessment models. *Ecological Economics, 61*(2), 224–236.

Bebbington, J., Brown, J., Frame, B., & Thomson, I. (2007b). Theorizing engagement: The potential of a critical dialogic approach. *Accounting, Auditing & Accountability Journal, 20*(3), 356–381.

Beer, S. (1959). *Cybernetics and management.* London: English University Press.

Beer, S. (1966). *Decision and control.* London: John Wiley.

Beer, S. (1972/1981). *Brain of the firm.* London/Chichester: Allen Lane, Penguin/John Wiley.

Beer, S. (1974). *Designing freedom.* Toronto: CBC Learning.

Beer, S. (1975). *Platform for change.* London: John Wiley.

Beer, S. (1979/1995). *The heart of enterprise.* London: John Wiley.

Beer, S. (1985). *Diagnosing the system for organizations.* Oxford: University Press.

Beer, S. (2004). World in torment: A time whose idea must come. *Kybernetes, 33*(3/4), 774–803.

Bennett, J. (2008). Research for life: Paradigms and power. *Feminist Africa, 11*, 1–12.

Bennett, M., & James, P. (Eds.). (1999). *Sustainable measures: Evaluation and reporting of environmental and social performance.* Sheffield: Greenleaf.

Berle, A. (1954). *The 20th century capitalist revolution.* New York: Harcourt, Brace.

Berle, A. (1959). *Power without property: A new development in American political economy*. New York: Harcourt, Brace and World.

Berle, A. (1968). Property, production and revolution. Preface to A. Berle., & G Means (Eds.), *The modern corporation and private property*, revised edition. New York: Harcourt, Brace and World.

Berle, A., & Means, Gardiner C. (1932/2007). The modern corporation and private property. London: Transaction Publishers.

Bernstein, R. (1976). *The restructuring of social and political theory*. Philadelphia: University of Pennsylvania Press.

Berry, A., et al. (1985). Management control in an area of the NCB: Rationales of accounting practices in a public enterprise. *Accounting, Organizations and Society, 10*(1), 3–8.

Bhaskar, R. (1975). *A realist theory of science*. London: Verso.

Bhaskar, R. (1979). *The possibility of naturalism*. London: Routledge.

Bhaskar, R. (1989). *Reclaiming reality: A critical introduction to contemporary philosophy*. London: Verso.

Biondi, Y., Canziani, A., & Kirat, T. (2007). *The firm as an entity: Implications for economics, accounting and the law*. Oxon: Routledge.

Bisoux, T. (2010, July/August). Taking care. *BizEd*, 20–24.

Bititci, U., Turner, T., & Ball, P. (1999). The viable business structure for managing agility. *International Journal of Agile Management Systems, 1*(3), 190–199.

Blackburn, N., Brown, J., Dillard, J., & Hooper, V. (2014). A dialogical framing of AIS-SEA design. *International Journal of Accounting Information Systems, 15*(2), 83–101.

Boland, R. (1978). The process and product of system design. *Management Science, 24*(9), 887–898.

Boland, R. (1989). Beyond the objectivist and the subjectivist: Learning to read accounting as text. *Accounting, Organizations and Society, 14*, 591–604.

Boland, R., & Tenkasi, R. (1995). Perspective making and perspective taking in communities of knowing. *Organization Science, 6*(4), 350–372.

Bond, S. (2011). Negotiating a 'democratic ethos': Moving beyond the agonistic–communicative divide. *Planning Theory, 10*, 161–186.

Boulding, K. (1974). In L. Sigell (Ed.), *Collected papers: Toward a general social science*. Boulder: Colorado Associated University Press.

Bourdieu, P. (1990). *In other words: Essays towards a reflexive sociology*. Oxford/Palo Alto: Polity Press/Stanford University Press.

Bourdieu, P. (2004). *Science of science and reflexivity*. Chicago: University of Chicago Press.

Bourdieu, P. (2007). *Sketch for a self-analysis*. Cambridge: Polity Press.

Bourdieu, P. (2010). *Sociology is a martial art*. New York: The New Press.

Bourdieu, P., & Wacquant, L. (1992). *An invitation to reflexive sociology*. Chicago/Oxford: University of Chicago Press/Polity Press.

Bourguignon, A., Malleret, V., & Norreklit, H. (2004). The American balanced scorecard versus the French tableau de bord: The ideological dimension. *Management Accounting Research, 15*(2), 107–134.

Bove, P. (1992). *In the wake of theory*. Hanover: Wesleyan University Press.

Bowman, S. (1996). *The modern corporation and American political thought: Law, power, and ideology*. Pennsylvania: Pennsylvania State University Press.

Bratton, W., Jr. (1989). The new economic theory of the firm: Critical perspectives from history. *Stanford Law Review, 41*(6), 1471–1527.

Braverman, H. (1974). *Labor and monopoly capital*. New York: Monthly Review Press.

Broadbent, J. (2002). Critical accounting: A view from England. *Critical Perspectives on Accounting, 13*(4), 433–449.

Broadbent, J., & Kirkham, L. (2008). Glass ceilings, glass cliffs or new worlds?: Revisiting gender and accounting. *Accounting Auditing, and Accountability Journal, 21*(4), 465–473.

Broadbent, J., & Laughlin, R. (1997). Developing empirical research in accounting: An example informed by a Habermasian approach. *Accounting Auditing and Accountability Journal, 10*(5), 622–648.

Broadbent, J., & Laughlin, R. (1998). Resisting the 'new public management': Absorption and absorbing groups in schools and GP practices in the UK. *Accounting, Auditing and Accountability Journal, 11*(4), 403–435.

Broadbent, J., & Laughlin, R. (2013). *Accounting control and controlling accounting*. Bingley: Emerald.

Broadbent, J., Laughlin, R., & Read, S. (1991). Recent financial and administrative changes in the NHS: A critical theory analysis. *Critical Perspectives on Accounting, 2*, 1–30.

Brooks, R. (2013). *Britain became a tax haven for fat cats and big business*. London: Oneworld.

Brown, J. (2009). Democracy, sustainability and dialogic accounting technologies: Taking pluralism seriously. *Critical Perspectives on Accounting, 20*(3), 313–342.

Brown, J. (2010). Accounting and visual cultural studies: Potentialities, challenges and prospects. *Accounting, Auditing & Accountability Journal, 23*(4), 482–505.

Brown, J., & Dillard, J. (2012). Agonistic pluralism and imagining CSEAR in the future. *Social and Environmental Accountability Journal, 32*(1), 3–16.

Brown, J., & Dillard, J. (2013a). Agonizing over engagement: SEA and the "death of environmentalism" debates. *Critical Perspectives on Accounting, 24*(1), 1–18.

Brown, J., & Dillard, J. (2013b). Critical accounting and communicative action: On the limits of consensual deliberation. *Critical Perspectives on Accounting, 24*(3), 176–190.

Brown, J., & Dillard, J. (2014). Integrated reporting: On the need for broadening out and opening up. *Accounting, Auditing & Accountability Journal, 27*(7), 1120–1156.

Brown, J., & Dillard, J. (2015). Dialogical accountings for stakeholders: On opening up and closing down participatory governance. *Journal of Management Studies, 52*, 961–985. doi:10.1111/joms.12153.

Brown, J., Dillard, J., & Hopper, T. (2015). Accounting, accountants, and accountability regimes in pluralistic societies: Taking multiple perspectives seriously. *Accounting Auditing and Accountability Journal, 28*(5), 626–650.

Brunsson, N. (2002). *The organization of hypocrisy: Talk, decisions and actions in organizations*. Malmo: Liber.

Burchell, S., Clubb, C., Hopwood, A., Hughes, J., & Nahapiet, J. (1980). The roles of accounting in organizations and society. *Accounting, Organizations and Society, 5*(1), 5–27.

Burchell, D., Clubb, C., & Hopwood, A. (1985). Accounting in its social context: Towards a history of value added in the United Kingdom. *Accounting, Organizations and Society, 10*, 381–414.

Burkett, E. (2015, June 6). What makes a woman? *New York Times*.

Burnham, J. (1941/1962). *The managerial revolution*. Bloomington: Indiana University Press.

Burns, T., & Stalker, G. (1961). *The management of innovation*. London: Tavistock.

Burrell, G., & Morgan, G. (1979). *Sociological paradigms and organisational analysis*. London: Heinemann Educational.

Busco, C., & Quattrone, P. (2015). Exploring how the balanced scorecard engages and unfolds: Articulating the visual power of accounting inscriptions. *Contemporary Accounting Research, 32*(3), 1236–1262.

Butler, H. (1989). The contractual theory of the corporation. *George Mason University Law Review, 11*(4), 99–123.

Camfferman, K., & Zeff, S. (2006). *Financial reporting and global capital markets*. Oxford: University Press.

Camfferman, K., & Zeff, S. (2015). *Aiming for global accounting standards*. Oxford: University Press.

Canning, J. (1929). *The economics of accountancy.* New York: Ronald Press.

Carenys, J. (2010). Management control systems: A historical perspective. *International Bulletin of Business Administration, 37*(7), 37–54.

Carmona, S., & Gronlund, A. (2003). Measures vs. actions: The balanced scorecard in Swedish law enforcement. *Operations & Production Management, 23*(12), 1475–1496.

Carroll, A., Lipartito, K., Post, J., Werhane, P., & Goodpaster, K. (2012). *Corporate responsibility: The American experience.* Cambridge: Cambridge University Press.

Chabrak, N., & Craig, R. (2013). Student imaginings, cognitive dissonance and critical thinking. *Critical Perspectives on Accounting, 24*(2), 91–104.

Chalmers, A. (1999). *What is this thing called science?* Brisbane: University of Queensland Press.

Chambers, R. (1966). *Accounting, evaluation and economic behaviour.* Englewood Cliffs: Prentice-Hall.

Chambers, S. (2003). Deliberative democratic theory. *Annual Review of Political Science, 6*, 307–326.

Chandler, A. D. (2002 [1977]). *The visible hand: The managerial revolution in American business.* Cambridge: Harvard University Press.

Checkland, P. (1999). *Systems thinking, systems practice: Soft systems methodology: A 30-year retrospective.* Chichester: John Wiley.

Chenhall, R. (2003). Management control systems design within its organizational context: Findings from contingency-based research and directions for the future. *Accounting Organizations & Society, 28*(2/3), 127–168.

Chenhall, R. (2005). Integrative strategic performance measurement systems, strategic alignment of manufacturing, learning and strategic outcomes: An exploratory study. *Accounting, Organizations and Society, 30*(5), 395–422.

Chenhall, R. (2007). Theorizing contingencies in management control systems research. In C. Chapman, A. Hopwood, & M. Shields (Eds.), *Handbook of management accounting research* (Vol. I). Oxford: Elsevier.

Childe, S., Maull, R., & Bennet, J. (1994). Frameworks for understanding BPR. *International Journal of Operations and Production Management, 14*(12), 22–34.

Christenson, C. (1983). The methodology of positive accounting. *The Accounting Review, 58*, 1–22.

Christian-Aid. (2008). *Death and taxes: The true toll of tax dodging.* London: Christian-Aid.

Christian-Aid. (2009). *False profits: Robbing the poor to keep the rich tax-free.* London: Christian-Aid.

Chua, W. F. (1986). Radical developments in accounting thought. *The Accounting Review, 61*(4), 601–632.

Chua, W. F. (1988). Interpretive sociology and management accounting research – A critical review. *Accounting Auditing and Accountability, 1*, 59–79.

Chua, W. F. (1996). Teaching and learning only the language of numbers-monolingualism in a multilingual world. *Critical Perspectives on Accounting, 7*(1/2), 129–158.

Chua, W. F., Puxty, A., & Lowe, T. (1989a). Ideology, rationality and the management control process. In W. F. Chua, E. A. Lowe, & A. Puxty (Eds.), *Critical perspectives in management control* (pp. 115–139). London: Macmillan.

Chua, W. F., Lowe, E. A., & Puxty, A. (Eds.). (1989b). *Critical perspectives in management control*. Basingstoke: Macmillan.

Churchman, C. W. (1968). *The systems approach*. New York: Dell.

Chwastiak, M. (2013). Profiting from destruction: The Iraq reconstruction, auditing and the management of fraud. *Critical Perspectives on Accounting, 24*(1), 32–43.

Ciancanelli, P. (1992). M[othering] view on: The construction of gender: Some insights from feminist psychology. *Accounting, Auditing, and Accountability Journal, 5*(3), 133–136.

Ciancanelli, P., Gallhofer, S., Humphrey, C., & Kirkham, L. (1990). Gender and accountancy: Some evidence from the UK. *Critical Perspectives on Accounting, 1*(2), 117–144.

Ciepley, D. (2013). Beyond public and private: Toward a political theory of the corporation. *American Political Science Review, 107*, 1–20.

Clegg, S., & Dunkerley, D. (1980). *Organizations, class and control*. London: Routledge and Kegan Paul.

Collins, G. (2009). *When everything changed: The amazing journey of American women from 1960 to the present*. New York: Little Brown and Co.

Conant, R., & Ross Ashby, W. (1970). Every good regulator of a system must be a model of that system. *International Journal of Systems Science, 1*(2), 89–97.

Connerton, P. (Ed.). (1973). *Critical sociology*. Harmondsworth: Penguin.

Connolly, W. (1987). *Politics and ambiguity*. Madison: University of Wisconsin Press.

Coontz, S., & Henderson, P. (Eds.). (1986). *Women's work, men's property*. London: Verso.

Cooper, D. (1983). Tidiness, muddle and things: Commonalities and divergences in two approaches to management accounting research. *Accounting, Organizations and Society, 8*(2/3), 269–286.

Cooper, C. (1992). The non and nom of accounting for (M)other nature. *Accounting, Auditing, and Accountability Journal, 5*(3), 16–39.

Cooper, C. (2001). From women's liberation to feminism: Reflections in accounting academia. *Accounting Forum, 5*(3), 214–245.

Cooper, D. (2014). On the intellectual roots of critical accounting: A personal appreciation of Tony Lowe (1928–2014). *Critical Perspectives on Accounting, 25*(4–5), 287–292.

Cooper, C., & Coulson, A. (2014). Accounting activism and Bourdieu's 'collective intellectual' – Reflections on the ICL case. *Critical Perspectives on Accounting, 25*(3), 237–254.

Cooper, D., & Ezzamel, M. (2013). Globalization discourses and performance measurement systems in a multinational firm. *Accounting, Organizations and Society, 38*(4), 288–313.

Cooper, D., & Sherer, M. (1984). The value of corporate accounting reports: Arguments for a political economy of accounting. *Accounting, Organizations and Society, 9*(3/4), 207–232.

Cooper, D., Ezzamel, M., & Qu, S. Q. (2015a). *Popularizing a management accounting idea: The case of the balanced scorecard.* Unpublished paper, University of Alberta.

Cooper, D., Ezzamel, M., & Robson, K. (2015b). *The multiplicity of performance management systems: Heterogeneity in multinational corporations and management sense-making.* Unpublished paper, University of Alberta.

Corporate Reform Collective. (2014). *Fighting corporate abuse: Beyond predatory capitalism.* London: Pluto Press.

Cox, E. (1857). *The new law and practice of joint stock companies, with and without limited liability.* By Edward W. Cox.... Etc: Law Times Office.

Crane, A., Palazzo, G., Spence, L., & Matten, D. (2014). Contesting the value of 'creating shared value'. *California Management Review, 56*(2), 130–153.

Crouch, C. (2011). *The strange non-death of neo-liberalism.* Cambridge: Polity.

Dambrin, C., & Lambert, C. (2012). Who is she and who are we? A reflexive journey in research into the rarity of women executives in accountancy. *Critical Perspectives on Accounting, 23*(1), 1–16.

Davis, G. (2009). *Managed by the markets: How finance re-shaped America.* Oxford: Oxford University Press.

Davis, S., & Albright, T. (2004). An investigation of the effect of BSC implementation on financial performance. *Management Accounting Research, 15,* 135–153.

Davis, S., Menon, K., & Morgan, G. (1982). The images that have shaped accounting theory. *Accounting, Organizations and Society, 7,* 307–318.

Dawe, A. (1970). The two sociologies. *British Journal of Sociology, 21*(2), 207–218.

De Botton, A. (1997). *How Proust can change your life*. London: Picador.

Deakin, S. (2012). Corporation as commons: Rethinking property rights, governance and sustainability in the business enterprise. *The Queen's LJ, 37*(2), 339–381.

Dey, C., Russell, S., & Thomson, I. (2011). Exploring the potential of shadow accounts in problematizing institutional conduct. In S. Osbourne & A. Ball (Eds.), *Social accounting and public management: Accountability for the common good* (pp. 64–75). Abingdon: Routledge.

Dierkes, M. (1979). Corporate social reporting in Germany: Conceptual developments and practical experience. *Accounting, Organizations and Society, 4*(1/2), 87–107.

Dillard, J. (1991). Accounting as a critical social science. *Accounting Auditing and Accountability Journal, 4*(1), 8–28.

Dillard, J. (2002). Dialectical possibilities of thwarted responsibilities. *Critical Perspectives on Accounting, 13*(5–6), 621–642.

Dillard, J., & Brown, J. (2012). Agonistic pluralism and imagining CSEAR into the future. *Social and Environmental Accountability Journal, 32*(1), 3–16.

Dillard, J., & Brown, J. (2014). Taking pluralism seriously within an ethic of accountability. In S. Mintz (Ed.), *Accounting for the public interest: Perspectives on accountability, professionalism and role in society*. New York: Springer.

Dillard, J., & Reynolds, M. (2008). Green owl and the corn maiden. *Accounting Auditing and Accountability Journal, 21*(4), 556–579.

Dillard, J., & Roslender, R. (2011). Taking pluralism seriously: Embedded moralities in management accounting and control systems. *Critical Perspectives on Accounting, 22*(2), 135–147.

Dillard, J., & Ruchala, L. (2005). The rules are no game: From instrumental rationality to administrative evil. *Accounting Auditing and Accountability Journal, 18*(5), 608–630.

Dillard, J., & Yuthas, K. (2013). Critical dialogics, agonistic pluralism, and accounting information systems. *International Journal of Accounting Information Systems, 14*, 113–119.

Dillard, J., Ruchala, L., & Yuthas, K. (2005). Enterprise resource planning systems: The physical manifestation of administrative evil. *International Journal of Accounting Information Systems, 6*(2), 107–128.

Ditz, D., Ranganathan, J., & Banks, R. (1995). *Green ledgers: Case studies in environmental accounting*. Baltimore: World Resources Institute.

Djelic, M.-L. (2013). When limited liability was (still) an issue: Mobilization and politics of signification in 19th-century England. *Organization Studies, 34*(5–6), 595–621.

Douzanis, C. (2013). *Philosophy and resistance in the crisis.* Cambridge: Polity.

Drucker, P. (2006[1946]). *Concept of the corporation.* New Brunswick: Transaction Publishers.

Durden, C. (2008). Towards a socially responsible management control system. *Accounting Auditing and Accountability Journal, 21*(5), 671–694.

Eccles, R. (1991). The performance measurement manifesto. *Harvard Business Review January-February, 69,* 131–137.

Eisler, R. (1987). *The chalice and the blade: Our history, our future.* Cambridge, MA: Harper & Row.

Emerson, J. (2006). Moving ahead together: Implications of a blended value framework for the future of social entrepreneurship. In A. Nicholls (Ed.), *Social entrepreneurship—New models of sustainable social change.* Oxford: Oxford University Press.

Engelen, E. (2002). Corporate governance, property and democracy: A conceptual critique of shareholder ideology. *Economy and Society, 31*(3), 391–413.

Epstein, G. (2005). *Financialization and the world economy.* Cheltenham: Edward Elgar.

Espeland, W. (1998). *The struggle for water: Politics, rationality and identity in the American Southwest.* Chicago: University of Chicago Press.

Everett, J. (2002). Organizational research and the praxeology of Pierre Bourdieu. *Organizational Research Methods, 5*(1), 56–80.

Everett, J. (2016). Accounting research and Bourdieu's "Scholarship with commitment". In R. Roslender (Ed.), *Routledge companion to critical accounting.* London: Routledge.

Everson, M. (2011, June 18). Lawyers and accountants once put integrity first. *New York Times.* http://www.nytimes.com/2011/06/19/opinion/19everson.html

Ezzamel, M., & Willmott, H. (1993). Corporate governance and financial control: Recent reforms in the UK public sector. *Accounting Auditing and Accountability Journal, 6*(3), 110–133.

Ezzamel, M., Hoskin, K., & Macve, R. (1990). Managing it all by numbers: A review of Johnson and Kaplan's 'relevance lost'. *Accounting and Business Research, 20,* 152–166.

Ezzamel, M., Willmott, H., & Worthington, F. (2008). Manufacturing shareholder value: The role of accounting in organizational transformation. *Accounting, Organizations and Society, 33*(2), 107–140.

Farjaudon, A.-L., & Morales, J. (2013). In search of consensus: The role of accounting in the definition and reproduction of dominant interests. *Critical Perspectives on Accounting, 24*(2), 154–171.

FASB. (2006, September). *SFAS 157: Fair value measurement.* Financial Accounting Standards Board, Norwalk.

Fay, B. (1987). *Critical social science.* Ithaca: Cornell University Press.

Fishkin, J. (1995). *The voice of the people: Public opinion and democracy.* New Haven: Yale University Press.

Fligstein, N. (1993). *The transformation of corporate control.* Cambridge: Harvard University Press.

Flyvbjerg, B. (2001). *Making social science matter.* Chicago: University of Chicago Press.

Forester, J. (2000). *The deliberative practitioner: Encouraging participatory planning practices.* Cambridge, MA: MIT Press.

Free, C., & Qu, S. Q. (2011). The use of graphics in promoting management ideas: An analysis of the balanced scorecard, 1992–2010. *Journal of Accounting & Organizational Change, 7*(2), 158–189.

Freire, P. (1970). *Pedagogy of the oppressed.* New York: Seabury.

French, M. (1986). *Beyond power: On women, men & morals.* London: Abacus.

Frost, P., Dutton, J., Worline, M., & Wilson, A. (2000). Narratives of compassion in organizations. In S. Fineman (Ed.), *Emotion in organizations* (pp. 25–45). London: Sage.

Gaffikin, M. (2005). The idea of accounting. In W. Funnell & R. Williams (Eds.), *Critical and historical studies in accounting* (pp. 1–24). Sydney: Pearson Education Australia.

Gaffikin, M. (2008). *Accounting theory: Research, regulation and accounting practice.* Sydney: Pearson Education Australia.

Gallhofer, S. (1998). The silences of mainstream feminist accounting research. *Critical Perspectives on Accounting, 9*(3), 355–375.

Gallhofer, S., & Haslam, J. (1991). The aura of accounting in the context of a crisis: Germany and the First World War. *Accounting, Organizations and Society, 16*(5/6), 487–520.

Gallhofer, S., & Haslam, J. (1993). Approaching corporate accountability: Fragments from the past. *Accounting and Business Research, 23*(91a), 320–330.

Gallhofer, S., & Haslam, J. (1995). Accounting and modernity. *Advances in Public Interest Accounting, 6*, 203–232.

Gallhofer, S., & Haslam, J. (1997). Beyond accounting: The possibilities of accounting and 'critical' accounting research. *Critical Perspectives on Accounting, 8*(1/2), 71–95.

Gallhofer, S., & Haslam, J. (2003). *Accounting and emancipation: Some critical interventions.* London/New York: Routledge.

Gallhofer, S., & Haslam, J. (2006). On the emancipatory potential of online reporting: The case of counter accounting. *Accounting Auditing and Accountability Journal, 19,* 681–718.

Gallhofer, S., & Haslam, J. (2007). Exploring social, political and economic dimensions of accounting in the global context: The international Accounting Standards Board and accounting disaggregation. *Socio-Economic Review, 5,* 633–644.

Gallhofer, S., & Haslam, J. (2008). The possibilities of accounting in the global context: Critical reflections on accounting and the Internet as a new technology of communication. In M. Lada & A. Kozarkiewicz (Eds.), *Rachunkowosc w otoczenik nowych technologii* (pp. 11–30). Beck: Warsaw.

Gallhofer, S., Haslam, J., & Yonekura, A. (2013). Further critical reflections on a contribution to the methodological issues debate in accounting. *Critical Perspectives on Accounting, 24*(3), 191–206.

Gallhofer, S., Haslam, J., & Yonekura, A. (2015). Accounting as differentiated universal for emancipatory praxis: Accounting delineation and mobilisation for emancipation(s) recognising democracy and difference. *Accounting Auditing and Accountability Journal, 28*(5), 864–874.

Gambling, T. (1974). *Societal accounting.* London: George Allen and Unwin.

Garvey, G., & Swan, P. (1994). The economics of corporate governance: Beyond the Marshallian firm. *Journal of Corporate Finance, 1,* 139–174.

Gerboth, D. (1973). Research, intuition, and politics in accounting inquiry. *Accounting Review, 48*(3), 475–482.

Gilman, S. (1939). *Accounting concepts of profit.* New York: Ronald Press.

Gindis, D. (2009). From fictions and aggregates to real entities in the theory of the firm. *Journal of Institutional Economics, 5*(1), 25–46.

Giner, B., & Arce, M. (2014). National standard-setters' lobbying: An analysis of its role in the IFRS 2 due process. In R. Di Pietra, S. McLeay, & J. Ronen (Eds.), *Accounting and regulation* (pp. 377–398). New York: Springer.

Gleeson-White, J. (2014). *Six capitals, the revolution capitalism has to have—or can accountants save the planet?* Sydney: Allen and Unwin.

Godsiff, P., & Maull, R. (2011). Operationalising and managing variety. *Paper presented at the 2011 Naples Forum on Service: Service Dominant Logic.*

Goodwin, N. (2006). The social impact of multinational corporations: An outline of the issues with a focus on workers. In A. Chandler & B. Mazlish (Eds.), *Leviathans: Multinational corporations and the new global history* (pp. 135–166). Cambridge: Cambridge University Press.

Gordon, D., Edwards, R., & Reich, M. (1982). *Segmented work, divided workers.* Cambridge: Cambridge University Press.

Gouldner, A. (1962). Anti-minotaur: The myth of a value-free sociology. *Social Problems, 9*(3), 199–213.

Gourevitch, P., & Shinn, J. (2005). *Political power & corporate control, the new global politics of corporate governance*. Princeton/Oxford: Princeton University Press.

Gray, R. (2010). Is accounting for sustainability actually accounting for sustainability…and how would we know? An exploration of narratives of organisations and the planet. *Accounting, Organizations and Society, 35*(1), 47–62.

Gray, R., & Bebbington, J. (2000). Environmental accounting, managerialism and sustainability: Is the planet safe in the hands of business and accounting? *Advances in Environmental Accounting and Management, 1*, 1–44.

Gray, R., & Bebbington, J. (2001). *Accounting for the environment* (2nd ed.). London: Sage.

Gray, R., & Laughlin, R. (2012). It was 20 years ago today: Sgt Pepper, accounting, *auditing and accountability journal*, green accounting and the blue meanies. *Accounting, Auditing & Accountability Journal, 25*(2), 228–255.

Gray, R., Owen, D., & Adams, C. (1996). *Accounting and accountability: Changes and challenges in corporate social and environmental reporting*. London: Prentice Hall.

Gray, R., Adams, C., & Owen, D. (2014). *Accountability, social responsibility and sustainability: Accounting for society and the environment*. London: Pearson.

Grenfell, M. (2010). Working with *habitus* and *field*: The logic of Bourdieu's practice. In E. Silva & A. Warde (Eds.), *Cultural analysis and Bourdieu's legacy*. London: Routledge.

Grey, C. (1994). Debating Foucault: A critical reply to Neimark. *Critical Perspectives on Accounting, 5*(1), 5–24.

Guinnane, T., Harris, R., Lamoreaux, N., & Rosenthal, J. (2007). Putting the corporation in its place. *Enterprise and Society, 8*(3), 687–729.

Habermas, J. (1974). *Theory and practice* (trans: Viertel, J.). London: Heinemann.

Habermas, J. (1984). *The theory of communicative action, Vol. I* (trans. McCarthy, T.). Boston/Cambridge, MA: Beacon Press/MIT Press.

Habermas, J. (1987). *The theory of communicative action, Vol. II* (trans. McCarthy, T.). Boston: Beacon Press.

Habermas, J. (1996). *Between facts and norms: Contributions to a discourse theory of law and democracy*. Cambridge, MA: MIT Press.

Habermas, J. (2004). *Theory and practice* (trans. Viertel, J). London: Heinemann Educational.

Haigh, N., & Hoffman, A. (2014). The new heretics: Hybrid organizations and the challenges they present to corporate sustainability. *Organization & Environment, 27*(3), 223–241.

Hammer, M. (1990). Re-engineering work: Don't automate, obliterate. *Harvard Business Review July/August, 68*, 104–122.

Hammond, T., & Oakes, L. (1992). Some feminisms and their implication for accounting practice. *Accounting Auditing and Accountability Journal, 5*(3), 52–70.

Handlin, O., & Handlin, M. (1945). Origins of the American business corporation. *The Journal of Economic History, 5*(1), 1–23.

Hannah, L. (2010 [1976]). *The rise of the corporate economy*. Oxon: Routledge.

Hansen, H., & Muhlen-Schulte, A. (2012). The power of numbers in global governance. *Journal of International Relations and Development, 15*, 1–11.

Hansmann, H., & Kraakman, R. (2001). End of history for corporate law. *The Geo. LJ, 89*, 439.

Harari, M., Meinzer, M., & Murphy, R. (2012). *Financial secrecy, banks and the big 4 firms of accountants*, Tax Justice Network. http://www.taxjustice.net/cms/upload/pdf/FSI2012_BanksBig4.pdf

Haraway, D. (1989). *Primate visions: Gender, race, and nature in the world of modern science*. New York: Routledge.

Hartmann, H. (1979). The unhappy marriage of Marxism and feminism: Towards a more progressive union. *Capital & Class, 3*(2), 1–33.

Hartmann, F. (2000). The appropriateness of RAPM: Toward the further development of theory. *Accounting, Organizations and Society, 25*(4–5), 451–482.

Hausmann, R., Tyson, L., & Zahidi, S. (2010). *The global gender gap report 2010*. Geneva: World Economic Forum.

Haynes, K. (2008). Moving the gender agenda or stirring chicken's entrails?: Where next for feminist methodologies in accounting? *Accounting Auditing and Accountability Journal, 21*(4), 539–555.

Hedberg, B., & Jonsson, S. (1978). Designing semi confusing information systems for organizations in changing environments. *Accounting Organizations & Society, 3*(1), 47–64.

Held, D. (1980). *Introduction to critical theory: Horkheimer to Habermas*. London/Berkeley: Hutchinson/University of California Press.

Held, D., & McGrew, A. (Eds.). (2000). *The global transformation reader: An introduction to the globalization debate*. Cambridge: Polity/Blackwell.

Hill, W. L., & Newa, J. (2004). I don't think poetry has anything to do with accounting. *Critical Perspectives on Accounting, 15*, 649–654.

Holvino, E. (2010). Intersections: The simultaneity of race, gender and class in organizational studies. *Gender Work & Organization, 17*(3), 248–277.

Hood, D. (2015, September 18). Losing sleep. Leaders of the accounting profession discuss its biggest nightmares. *Accounting Today*. http://www.accountingtoday.com/news/firm-profession/losing-sleep-75927-1.html

Hopper, T., & Powell, A. (1985). Making sense of research into the organizational and social aspects of accounting: A review of its underlying assumptions. *Journal of Management Studies, 22*(5), 429–465.

Hopwood, A. (1973). *An accounting system and managerial behaviour.* Farnbourgh: Saxon House.

Hopwood, A. (1987). The archaeology of accounting systems. *Accounting, Organizations and Society, 12*(3), 207–234.

Hopwood, A. (1989). Accounting and the pursuit of social interests. In W. F. Chua, E. A. Lowe, & A. Puxty (Eds.), *Critical perspectives in management control* (pp. 141–157). Basingstoke: Macmillan.

Horkheimer, M. (1947). *Eclipse of reason.* Oxford: Oxford University Press.

Horwitz, M. J. (1985). Santa Clara revisited: The development of corporate theory. *West Virginia Law Review, 88*, 173–224.

Hoskin, K. (1994). Boxing clever: For against and beyond Foucault in the battle for accounting theory. *Critical Perspectives on Accounting, 5*(1), 57–85.

Hoskin, K., & Macve, R. (1986). Accounting and the examination: A genealogy of disciplinary power. *Accounting, Organizations and Society, 11*, 105–136.

Hoy, D. C. (2005). *Critical resistance, from poststructuralism to post-critique.* Cambridge, MA: MIT Press.

Hudson, M., Chavkin, S., & Mos, B. (2014). Big 4 audit firms play big role in offshore murk, 5 November 2014, the International Consortium of Investigative Journalists. http://www.icij.org/project/luxembourg-leaks/big-4-audit-firms-play-big-role-offshore-murk. Accessed 25 May 2015.

Huelsbeck, D. P., Merchant, K. A., & Sandino, T. (2011). On testing business models. *The Accounting Review, 86*(5), 1631–1654.

Huy, Q. N. (1999). Emotional capability, emotional intelligence, and radical change. *Academy of Management Review, 24*, 325–345.

International Accounting Standards Board (IASB), London: Due Process Handbook (2015 revision) http://go.ifrs.org//Due-Process-Handbook; IASC Conceptual Framework (1989) *Framework for the Preparation and Presentation of Financial Statements;* IAS 24 (2009) *Related Party Disclosures (Revised);* IAS 37 (1998) *Provisions, Contingent Liabilities and Contingent Assets;* IAS 39 (1998), subsequently revised) *Financial Instruments: Recognition and Measurement;* IASB (2008) Amendments to IAS 32, *Financial Instruments: Presentation* and IAS 1, *Presentation of Financial Statements- Puttable Financial Instruments and Obligations Arising on Liquidation;* IASB (2014) *Agriculture: Bearer Plants* (Amendments to IAS 16 and IAS 41); IASB (2015) *Exposure Draft: Conceptual Framework for Financial Reporting.*IFRS 2 (2004) *Share-*

Based Payment; IFRS 3 (2004) *Business Combinations;* IFRS for SMEs (2009) *The International Financial Reporting Standard for Small and Medium-sized Entities;* IFRS 9 (2009, amended 2014) *Financial Instruments;* IFRS 13 (2011) *Fair Value Measurement;* IFRS 14 (2014) *Regulatory Deferral Accounts;* IFRS 15 (2014) *Revenue from Contracts with Customers.*

International Labor Organization. (2014, December). Global wage report 2014/15. International Labor Organization. http://www.ilo.org/global/publications/books/WCMS_324839/lang--en/index.htm

International Monetary Fund. (2013). *World economic and financial surveys – Fiscal monitor: Taxing times.* Washington, DC: IMF.

Ireland, P. (1999). Company law and the myth of shareholder ownership. *Modern Law Review, 62*(1), 32–57.

Ireland, P. (2005). Shareholder primacy and the distribution of wealth. *Modern Law Review, 68*(1), 49–81.

Ireland, P. (2009). Financialization and corporate governance. *Northern Ireland Legal Quarterly, 60*(1), 1–34.

Ireland, P. (2010). Limited liability, shareholder rights and the problem of corporate irresponsibility. *Cambridge Journal of Economics, 34*(5), 837–856.

Ittner, C., & Larcker, D. (2001). Assessing empirical research in managerial accounting: A value-based management perspective. *Journal of Accounting and Economics, 32*, 349–410.

Ittner, C., Larcker, D., & Meyer, M. (2003a). Subjectivity and the weighting of performance measures: Evidence from a balanced scorecard. *Accounting Review, 78*(3), 725–758.

Ittner, C., Larcker, D., & Randall, T. (2003b). Performance implications of strategic performance measurement in financial services firms. *Accounting, Organizations and Society, 28*, 715–741.

Jackson, G. (2000). Comparative corporate governance: Sociological perspectives. In J. Parkinson, A. Gamble, & G. Kelly (Eds.), *The political economy of the company* (pp. 265–288). Oxford: Hart.

Jackson, M. (2001). Critical systems theory and practice. *European Journal of Operations Research, 128*(2), 233–244.

Jacobsen, R. (1991). Economic efficiency and the quality of life. *Journal of Business Ethics, 10*, 201–209.

Jaggar, A. (1983). *Feminist politics and human nature.* Totowa: Rowman/Allanheld.

Jeacle, I. (2006). Face facts: Accounting, feminism and the business of beauty. *Critical Perspectives on Accounting, 17*(1), 87–108.

Jensen, M. (2001). Value maximization, stakeholder theory and the corporate objective function. *Journal of Applied Corporate Finance, 14*, 8–21.

Jermier, J. (2008). Exploring deep subjectivity in sociology and organizational studies: The contributions of William Catton and Riley Dunlap on paradigm change. *Organization & Environment, 21*(4), 460–470.

Johnson, P. (2010). *Making the market: Victorian origins of corporate capitalism.* Cambridge: Cambridge University Press.

Johnson, L. (2012). Law and legal theory in the history of corporate responsibility: Corporate personhood. *Seattle University Law Review, 35*, 1135–1164.

Johnson, H., & Kaplan, R. (1987). *Relevance lost: The rise and fall of management accounting.* Boston: Harvard Business School Press.

Jones, C. (1990). Corporate social accounting and the capitalist enterprise. In D. Cooper & T. Hopper (Eds.), *Critical accounts* (pp. 272–293). Basingstoke: Macmillan.

Jones, M., & Haigh, M. (2007). The transnational corporation and new corporate citizenship theory: A critical analysis. *Journal of Corporate Citizenship, 27*, 51–69.

Judt, T. (2010). *Ill fares the land.* New York: Penguin.

Kaplan, R., & Norton, D. (1992). The balanced scorecard: Measures that drive performance. *Harvard Business Review, 70*(1), 71–79.

Kaplan, R., & Norton, D. (1996a). *The balanced scorecard: Translating strategy into action.* Boston: Harvard Business School Press.

Kaplan, R., & Norton, D. (1996b). Using the balanced scorecard as a strategic management system. *Harvard Business Review, January-February, 74*, 75–85.

Kaplan, R., & Norton, D. (2001). *The strategy-focused organization: How balanced scorecard companies thrive in the new business environment.* Boston: Harvard Business School Press.

Kaplan, R., & Norton, D. (2004a). *Strategy maps: Converting intangible assets into tangible outcomes.* Boston: Harvard Business School Press.

Kaplan, R., & Norton, D. (2004b). Measuring the strategic readiness of intangible assets. *Harvard Business Review, 82*(2), 52–63.

Kaplan, R., & Norton, D. (2006). *Alignment: Using the balanced scorecard to create corporate synergies.* Boston: Harvard Business School Press.

Kaplan, R., & Norton, D. (2008). *The execution premium: Linking strategy to operations for competitive advantage.* Boston: Harvard Business School Press.

Kay, J., & Silberston, A. (1995). Corporate governance. *National Institute Economic Review, 153*(August), 84–97.

Kaysen, C. (1957). The social significance of the modern corporation. *The American Economic Review, 47*(2), Papers and proceedings of the sixty-eighth annual meeting of the American Economic Association: 311–9.

Kearins, K., Collins, E., & Tregidga, H. (2010). Beyond corporate environmental management to a consideration of nature in visionary small enterprise. *Business & Society, 49*(3), 512–554.

Kelan, E. (2010). Gender logic and (Un)doing gender at work. *Gender, Work and Organization, 17*(2), 174–194.

Kessler-Harris, A. (1981). *Women have always worked: An historical overview.* New York: McGraw Hill.

Keynes, J. M. (1936/2007). *The general theory.* London: Macmillan.

Khurana, R. (2007). *From higher aims to hired hands: The social transformation of American business schools and the unfulfilled promise of management as a profession.* Princeton: Princeton University Press.

Kim, S. (2004). Racialized gendering of the accountancy profession: Toward an understanding of Chinese women's experiences in accountancy in New Zealand. *Critical Perspectives on Accounting, 15*(3), 400–427.

Kim, S. (2008). Whose voice is it anyway? Rethinking the oral history method in accounting research on race, ethnicity and gender. *Critical Perspectives on Accounting, 19*(8), 1346–1369.

Kirkham, L. (1992). Integrating herstory and history in accountancy. *Accounting, Organizations and Society, 17*(3/4), 287–297.

Kirkham, L., & Loft, A. (1993). Gender and the construction of the professional accountant. *Accounting, Organizations and Society, 18*(6), 507–558.

Kirkham, L., & Loft, A. (2001). The lady and the accounts: Missing from accounting history? *The Accounting Historians Journal, 28*(1), 67–90.

Klein, N. (2007). *The shock doctrine: The rise of disaster capitalism.* New York/London: Henry Holt/Penguin.

Klir, G. (1967). *Cybernetic modelling.* London: Iliffe.

Knight, F. (1965). *Risk, uncertainty, and profit.* New York: Harper and Row.

Kobrin, S. (2006). Multinational corporations, the protest movement, and the future of global governance. In A. Chandler & B. Mazlish (Eds.), *Leviathans: Multinational corporations and the new global history* (pp. 219–236). Cambridge: Cambridge University Press.

Komori, N. (2008). Toward the feminization of accounting practice: Lessons from the experiences of Japanese women in the accounting profession. *Accounting Auditing and Accountability Journal, 21*(4), 507–538.

Krippner, G. (2012). *Capitalizing on crisis.* Harvard: Harvard University Press.

Kurunmaki, L. (1999). Professional vs financial capital in the field of health care – The redistribution of power and control. *Accounting, Organizations and Society, 24*(2), 94–124.

Laclau, E., & Mouffe, C. (1987). Post-Marxism without apologies. *New Left Review, I/166*, 79–106.

Laclau, E., & Mouffe, C. (2001/1985). *Hegemony and socialist strategy: Towards a radical democratic politics* (2nd ed.). London: Verso.

Ladd, D. (1963). *Contemporary corporate accounting and the public*. Homewood: Richard D Irwin.

Lamberton, G. (2000). Accounting for sustainable development—A case study of city farm. *Critical Perspectives on Accounting, 11*(5), 583–605.

Latour, B. (1987). *Science in action*. Milton Keynes: Open University Press.

Laughlin, R. (1987). Accounting systems in organizational contexts: A case for critical theory. *Accounting, Organizations and Society, 12*(5), 479–502.

Laughlin, R. (1991). Environmental disturbances and organisational transitions and transformations: Some alternative models. *Organisation Studies, 12*(2), 209–232.

Laughlin, R. (1995). Empirical research in accounting: Alternative approaches and a case for middle range thinking. *Accounting Auditing and Accountability Journal, 8*(1), 63–87.

Laughlin, R. (1999). Critical accounting: Nature, progress and prognosis. *Accounting Auditing and Accountability Journal, 12*, 73–78.

Laughlin, R. (2004). Putting the record straight: A commentary on 'methodology choices and the construction of facts: Some implications from the sociology of knowledge'. *Critical Perspectives on Accounting, 15*(2), 261–278.

Laughlin, R. (2007). Critical reflections on research approaches, accounting regulation and the regulation of accounting. *British Accounting Review, 39*, 271–289.

Laughlin, R. (2014). Tony Lowe and the interdisciplinary and critical perspective on accounting project: Reflections on the contributions of a unique scholar. *Accounting Auditing and Accountability Journal, 27*(5), 766–777.

Laughlin, R., & Broadbent, J. (1993). Accounting and law: Partners in the juridification of the public sector in the UK? *Critical Perspectives in Accounting, 4*, 337–368.

Laughlin, R., & Gray, R. (1988). *Financial accounting: Method and meaning*. London: Van Nostrand Reinhold.

Laughlin, R., & Lowe, E. A. (1990). A critical analysis of accounting thought: Prognosis and prospects for understanding an changing accounting systems design. In D. Cooper & T. Hopper (Eds.), *Critical accounts* (pp. 15–43). Basingstoke: Macmillan.

Laughlin, R., Lowe, E. A., & Puxty, A. (1986). Designing and operating a course in accounting methodology: Philosophy, experience and some preliminary empirical tests. *British Accounting Review, 18*(1), 17–42.

Lazonick, W., & O'sullivan, M. (2000). Maximizing shareholder value: A new ideology for corporate governance. *Economy and Society, 29*(1), 13–35.

Lederer, E. (2005, November 18). Violence and discrimination against women is a major cause of death. *Associated Press.* Accessed from www.sacredchoices. org

Lehman, C. (1992a). Herstory in accounting: The first eighty years. *Accounting, Organizations and Society, 17*(3/4), 261–285.

Lehman, C. (1992b). Fe[min]ists' account: Introduction. *Accounting Auditing and Accountability Journal, 5*(3), 4–15.

Lehman, C. (2012). We've come a long way! Maybe! Re-Imagining gender and accounting. *Accounting Auditing and Accountability Journal, 25*(2), 256–294.

Lehman, C., & Tinker, T. (1987). The 'real' cultural significance of accounts. *Accounting, Organizations and Society, 12*(5), 503–522.

Lennard, A. (2002). *Liabilities and how to account for them: An exploratory essay.* London: Accounting Standards Board.

Leonard, A. (1990/revised 2004). Coming concepts: The cybernetic glossary for new management, from http://www.anu.edu.au/iisn/activities/systems/ cybernetic_glossary.pdf

Lerner, G. (1986). *The creation of patriarchy.* Oxford: Oxford University Press.

Locke, R. (1996). *The collapse of the American management mystique.* Oxford: Oxford University Press.

Lodh, S., & Gaffikin, M. (1997). Critical studies in accounting research, rationality and Habermas: A methodological reflection. *Critical Perspectives on Accounting, 8*, 433–474.

Loft, A. (1986). Towards a critical understanding of accounting: The case of cost accounting in the UK, 1914–1925. *Accounting, Organizations and Society, 11*, 137–170.

Loft, A. (1992). Accountancy and the gendered division of labour: A review essay. *Accounting, Organizations and Society, 17*(3–4), 367–378.

Lowe, E. A. (1971a). On the definition of a 'system'. *Journal of Systems Engineering, 2*(2), 95–98.

Lowe, E. A. (1971b). On the idea of a management control system: Integrating accounting and management control. *Journal of Management Studies, 8*(1), 1–12.

Lowe, E. A. (1972). The finance director's role in the formulation and implementation of strategy: A framework for financial strategy. *Journal of Business Finance, 4*(4), 58–70.

Lowe, E. A. (1981). The management of purposive environmental enquiry: Suggestions for the development of MIS thinking. In M. Bromwich & A. Hopwood (Eds.), *Essays in British accounting research* (pp. 209–223). London: Pitman.

Lowe, A. (2004). Methodology choices and construction of facts: Some implications from the sociology of scientific knowledge. *Critical Perspectives on Accounting, 15*(2), 207–231.

Lowe, E. A., & McInnes, J. (1971). Control in socio-economic organisations: A rationale for the design of management control systems (section I). *Journal of Management Studies, 8*(2), 213–227.

Lowe, E. A., & Puxty, T. (1989). The problems of a paradigm: A critique of the prevailing orthodoxy in management control. In W. F. Chua, E. A. Lowe, & T. Puxty (Eds.), *Critical perspectives in management control*. Basingstoke: Macmillan.

Lowe, E. A., & Puxty, T. (1990). Accounting as social science: Some implications for teaching and research. *Directions, 12*(1), 54–72.

Lowe, E. A., & Shaw, R. (1968). An analysis of managerial biasing: Evidence from a company's budgeting process. *Journal of Management Studies, 5*(3), 304–315.

Lowe, E. A., & Soo, W. F. (1980). Organisational effectiveness: A critique and proposal. *Managerial Finance, 6*(1), 63–77.

Lowe, E. A., & Tinker, A. (1976a). The architecture of requisite variety Part 1. *Kybernetes, 5*, 145–154.

Lowe, E. A., & Tinker, A. (1976b). The architecture of requisite variety Part 2. *Kybernetes, 5*, 197–207.

Lowe, E. A., & Tinker, A. (1977a). Siting the accounting problematic: Towards an intellectual emancipation of accounting. *Journal of Business Finance and Accounting, 4*(3), 263–276.

Lowe, E. A., & Tinker, A. (1977b). New directions for management accounting. *Omega: The International Journal of Management Science, 5*(2), 173–183.

Lowe, E. A., & Tinker, T. (1989). Accounting as social science. In W. F. Chua, E. A. Lowe, & A. Puxty (Eds.), *Critical perspectives in management control* (pp. 47–61). London: Macmillan.

Lowe, E. A., et al. (1983). Simple theories for complex processes: Accounting policy and the market for myopia. *Journal of Accounting and Public Policy, 2*(1), 19–42.

Lowe, E. A., Gallhofer, S., & Haslam, J. (1991). Theorising accounting regulation in a global context: Insights from a study of accounting in the Federal Republic of Germany. *Advances in Public Interest Accounting, 4*, 143–177.

Machin, J., & Lowe, E. A. (1983). *New perspectives in management control.* London: Macmillan.

Macintosh, N. (2002). *Accounting, accountants and accountability: Postructural positions.* London: Routledge.

Mackintosh, I. (2014, December 9). Prepared remarks by Ian Mackintosh, Vice-Chairman of the IASB. *AICPA conference on current SEC and PCAOB developments,* Washington, DC.

Malina, M., & Selto, F. (2001). Communicating and controlling strategy: An empirical study of the effectiveness of the balanced scorecard. *Journal of Management Accounting Research, 13,* 47–90.

Malina, M., & Selto, F. (2004). Choice and change of measures in performance measurement models. *Management Accounting Research, 15*(4), 441–469.

Malsch, B., Gendron, Y., & Grazzini, F. (2011). Investigating interdisciplinary translations: The influence of Pierre Bourdieu on accounting literature. *Accounting Auditing and Accountability Journal, 24*(2), 194–228.

Mansell, S. (2013). *Capitalism, corporations and the social contract: A critique of stakeholder theory.* Cambridge: CUP.

March, J., & Simon, H. (1958). *Organizations.* London: John Wiley.

Marens, R. (2012). Generous in victory? American managerial autonomy, labour relations and the invention of corporate social responsibility. *Socio-Economic Review, 10*(1), 59–84.

Martinez, D., & Cooper, D. (2015). *Accountability and the disarticulation of a social movement: Assembling international development.* Unpublished paper, Alberta School of Business.

Mattessich, R. (1964). *Accounting and analytical methods: Measurement and projection of income and wealth in the micro- and macro-economy.* Homewood: Irwin.

Matuz, R. (1963). Accounting as a social science. *The Accounting Review, 38*(2), 317–325.

Maupin, R., & Lehman, C. (1994). Talking heads: Stereotypes, status, sex-roles and satisfaction of female and male auditors. *Accounting, Organizations and Society, 19*(4–5), 427–437.

McLean, J. (2004). The transnational corporation in history: Lessons for today. *Indiana Law Journal, 79*(2), 363–377.

Mennicken, A., & Miller, P. (2014). Michel Foucault and the administering of lives. In P. Adler, P. Du Gay, G. Morgan, & M. Reed (Eds.), *Oxford handbook of sociology, social theory and organization studies: Contemporary currents* (pp. 11–38). Oxford: Oxford University Press.

Merino, B. (1989). An analysis of the development of accounting knowledge: A pragmatic approach. *Paper presented at the studies in accounting as a human practice conference*, University of Iowa.

Merino, B., Mayper, A., & Tolleson, T. (2010). Neoliberalism, deregulation and Sarbanes-Oxley: The legitimation of a failed corporate governance model. *Accounting Auditing and Accountability Journal, 23*(6), 774–792.

Meyer, J., & Rowan, B. (1977). Institutionalized organizations: Formal structure as myth and ceremony. *American Journal of Sociology, 83*, 340–363.

Mickhail, G. (2013). *The MetaCapitalism spectacle*. Unpublished PhD thesis, University of Wollongong.

Micklethwait, J., & Wooldridge, A. (2005). *The company: A short history of a revolutionary idea*. London: Modern Library.

Midgley, G. (2000). *Systematic intervention: Philosophy, methodology and practice*. New York: Dordrecht.

Miller, P., & O'Leary, T. (1990). Making accountancy practical. *Accounting, Organizations and Society, 15*(3), 479–498.

Miller, P., Kurunmäki, L., & O'Leary, T. (2008). Accounting, hybrids and the management of risk. *Accounting, Organizations and Society, 33*(7), 942–967.

Milne, M., & Gray, R. (2013). W(h)ither ecology? The triple bottom line, the global reporting initiative, and corporate sustainability reporting. *Journal of Business Ethics, 118*(1), 13–29.

Milne, M., Tregigda, H., & Walton, S. (2009). Words not actions! The ideological role of sustainable development reporting. *Accounting Auditing and Accountability Journal, 22*(8), 1211–1257.

Mintzberg, H. (1983). The case for corporate social responsibility. *The Journal of Business Strategy, 4*(2), 3–15.

Mintzberg, H. (1994). *The rise and fall of strategic planning*. New York: Free Press.

Mintzberg, H., Quinn, J., & Ghoshal, S. (1995). *The strategy process*. London: Prentice-Hall.

Mitchell, A., & Sikka, P. (2011). *The pin-stripe mafia: How accountancy firms destroy societies*. Basildon: Association for Accountancy & Business Affairs.

Mitchell, A., Sikka, P., & Willmott, H. (1998a). Sweeping it under the carpet: The role of accountancy firms in moneylaundering. *Accounting, Organizations and Society, 23*(5/6), 589–607.

Mitchell, A., Sikka, P., & Willmott, H. (1998b). *The accountants laundromat*. Basildon: Association for Accountancy & Business Affairs.

Mitchell, M., Curtis, A., & Davidson, P. (2012). Can triple bottom line reporting become a cycle for "double loop" learning and radical change? *Accounting Auditing and Accountability Journal, 25*(6), 1048–1068.

Modell, S. (2007). Mixed methods research in management accounting research: Opportunities and obstacles. In M. Granlund (Ed.), *Total quality in academic accounting: Essays in honour of Kari Lukka*. Turku: Turku School of Economics and Business Administration.

Modell, S. (2009). In defence of triangulation: A critical realist approach to mixed methods research in management accounting. *Management Accounting Research, 20*(3), 208–221.

Modell, S. (2010). Bridging the paradigm gap in management accounting research: The role of mixed methods approaches. *Management Accounting Research, 21*(2), 124–129.

Modell, S. (2014). *Critical realist accounting research: Whence and whither?* Mimeo: Manchester Business School.

Molyneaux, C., & Jacobs, K. (2005). Waiting for Marxo: A short play in two acts. *Critical Perspectives on Accounting, 16*(8), 1059–1066.

Moore, M., & Rebérioux, A. (2007). The corporate governance of the firm as an entity, old issues for the new debate. In Y. Biondi, A. Canziani, & T. Kirat (Eds.), *The firm as an entity: Implications for economic, accounting and the law* (pp. 348–374). London: Routledge.

Morgan, G. (1983). Social science and accounting research: A commentary on Tomkins and Groves. *Accounting, Organizations and Society, 8*, 385–388.

Morgan, G. (1986). *Images of organization.* Newbury Park: Sage.

Morlidge, S. (2010). *The application of organisational cybernetics to the design and diagnosis of financial performance management systems.* Thesis, University of Hull.

Mouck, T. (1992). The rhetoric of science and the rhetoric of revolt in the 'story' of positive accounting theory. *Accounting Auditing and Accountability Journal, 5*, 35–56.

Mouffe, C. (1997). Decision, deliberation, and democratic ethos. *Philosophy Today, 41*(1), 24–30.

Mouffe, C. (1999). Deliberative democracy or agonistic pluralism? *Social Research, 66*(3), 745–758.

Mouffe, C. (2000a). *The democratic paradox.* London: Verso.

Mouffe, C. (2000b). Deliberative democracy or agonistic pluralism. *Institute for Advanced Studies (IHS), Vienna, Political Science Series 72.*

Mouffe, C. (2005). *On the political.* London: Routledge.

Mouffe, C. (2013). *Agonistics: Thinking the world politically.* London: Verso.

Murphy, J., & Ackroyd, S. (2013). Transnational corporations, socio-economic change and recurrent crisis. *Critical Perspectives on International Business, 9*(4), 336–357.

Nace, T. (2003). *Gangs of America.* San Francisco: Berrett-Koehler.

National Audit Office. (2012). *Settling large tax disputes*. London: TSO.

National Committee on Pay Equity. (2015). http://www.pay-equity.org. Accessed May 2015.

Neimark, M. (1990). The king is dead: Long live the king. *Critical Perspectives on Accounting, 1*(1), 103–114.

Neimark, M. (1994). Regicide revisited: Marx, Foucault and accounting. *Critical Perspectives on Accounting, 5*(1), 87–108.

Neimark, M., & Tinker, T. (1986). The social construction of management control systems. *Accounting, Organizations and Society, 11*(4/5), 369–395.

Neocleous, M. (2003). *Imagining the state*. Maidenhead: Open University Press.

Neu, D., Cooper, D., & Everett, J. (2001). Critical accounting interventions. *Critical Perspectives on Accounting, 12*(6), 735–762.

Nicholls, A. (2010). The legitimacy of social entrepreneurship: Reflexive isomorphism in a pre-paradigmatic field. *Entrepreneurship: Theory and Practice, 34*, 611–633.

Nichols, T. (1969). *Ownership, control and ideology*. London: George Unwin.

Nietzsche, F. (1968). In W. Kaufman (Ed.), *The will to power*. New York: Vintage Books.

Norreklit, H. (2000). The balance on the balanced scorecard- A critical analysis of some of its assumptions. *Management Accounting Research, 11*, 65–88.

Norreklit, H. (2003). The balanced scorecard: What is the score? A rhetorical analysis of the balanced scorecard. *Accounting, Organizations and Society, 28*(6), 591–619.

Norris, G., & O'Dwyer, B. (2004). Motivating socially responsive decision making: The operation of management controls in a socially responsive organisation. *British Accounting Review, 36*(2), 173–196.

Nussbaum, M. (2000). *Women and human development: The capabilities approach*. Cambridge: Cambridge University Press.

O'Grady, W., Rouse, P., & Gunn, C. (2010). Synthesizing management control frameworks. *Measuring Business Excellence, 14*(1), 96–108.

Oakes, L., & Young, J. (2008). Accountability re-examined: Evidence from Hull House. *Accounting Auditing and Accountability Journal, 21*(6), 765–790.

Oakes, L., Townley, B., & Cooper, D. (1998). Business planning as pedagogy: Language and control in a changing institutional field. *Administrative Science Quarterly June, 43*, 257–292.

OECD. (2012). *Closing the gender gap: Act now*. Paris: OECD Publishing. doi:10.1787/9789264179370-en.

Ojha, D., White, R., & Rogers, P. (2013). Managing demand variability using requisite variety for improved workflow and operational performance: The role of manufacturing flexibility. *International Journal of Production Research, 51*(10), 2915–2934.

Ollman, B. (1976). *Alienation: Marx's concept of man in capitalist society* (2nd ed.). Cambridge: Cambridge University Press.

Olve, N.-G., Petri, C.-J., Roy, J., & Roy, S. (2003). *Making scorecards actionable.* London: John Wiley.

Organization for Economic Cooperation and Development (OECD) Steering Group on Corporate Governance. (2004). *OECD principles of corporate governance 2004.* Paris: OECD Publishing.

Otley, D. (1980). The contingency theory of management accounting: Achievement and prognosis. *Accounting, Organizations and Society, 5*(4), 413–428.

Otley, D. (1999). Performance management: A framework for management control system design. *Management Accounting Research, 10,* 363–382.

Otley, D. (2015, April). The contingency theory of management accounting and control: 1980–2014. *MAR 25th anniversary conference*, LSE.

Ouchi, W. (1979). A conceptual framework for the design of organizational control mechanisms. *Management Science, 25*(9), 833–848.

Ouchi, W. (1981). Theory Z: How American business can meet the Japanese challenge. *Business Horizons, 24*(6), 82–83.

Overbeek, H., Van Apeldoorn, B., & Nölke, A. (2007). *The transnational politics of corporate governance regulation.* New York: Routledge.

Owen, D. (2008). Chronicles of wasted time? A personal reflection on the current state of, and future prospects for, social and environmental accounting research. *Accounting Auditing and Accountability Journal, 21*(2), 240–267.

Pacter, P. (2015). *IFRS as global standards: A pocket guide.* London: IFRS Foundation.

Palan, R., Murphy, R., & Chavagneux, C. (2010). *Tax havens: How globalization really works.* Ithaca: Cornell University Press.

Paranque, B., & Willmott, H. (Working Paper). Cooperatives—Saviours or gravediggers of capitalism? The ambivalent case of the John Lewis partnership.

Parker, L. (2008). Strategic management and accounting processes: Acknowledging gender. *Accounting Auditing and Accountability Journal, 21*(4), 611–631.

Parkinson, J. (2003). Models of the company and the employment relationship. *British Journal of Industrial Relations, 41*(3), 481–509.

Paton, W. (1922). *Accounting theory.* New York: Ronald Press.

Paton, W., & Littleton, A. (1940). *An introduction to corporate accounting standards.* New York: American Accounting Association.

Penn, S., & Massino, J. (2009). *Gender politics and everyday life in state socialist Eastern and Central Europe*. New York: Palgrave Macmillan.

Pepper, S. (1948). *World hypotheses: A study in evidence*. Berkeley: University of California Press.

Perrow, C. (2002). *Organizing America: Wealth, power, and the origins of corporate capitalism*. Princeton: Princeton University Press.

Pickering, A. (2004). The science of the unknowable: Staffor Beer's cybernetic informatics. *Paper presented at The History and Heritage of Scientific and Technological Information Systems: Proceedings of the 2002 conference*, Melford, New Jersey.

Plantin, G., Sapra, H., & Shin, H. S. (2008). Marking to market: Panacea or Pandora's box? *Journal of Accounting Research, 46*(2), 435–460.

Pollard, S. (1968). *The genesis of modern management: A study of the industrial revolution in Great Britain*. Middlesex: Penguin.

Pollitt, K. (2005). Marooned on Gilligan Island: Are women morally superior to men? *Good News of the Twentieth Century*. academic.evergreen.edu

Porter, T. (1995). *Trust in numbers*. Princeton: Princeton University Press.

Post, G. (1934). Parisian masters as a corporation, 1200–46. *Speculum, 9*(4), 421–445.

Power, M. (1991). Auditing and environmental expertise: Between protest and professionalisation. *Accounting Auditing and Accountability Journal, 4*(3), 30–42.

Power, M. (1994). Constructing the responsible organisation: Accounting and environmental representation, Chapter 16. In G. Teubner, L. Farmer, & D. Murphy (Eds.), *Environmental law and ecological responsibility: The concept and practice of ecological self-organisation* (pp. 370–392). London: John Wiley.

Power, M., & Laughlin, R. (1996). Habermas, law and accounting. *Accounting, Organizations and Society, 21*(5), 441–465.

Prokhovnik, R. (1999). *Rational woman: A feminist critique of dichotomy*. London: Routledge.

Puxty, A. G., Willmott, H. C., Cooper, D. J., & Lowe, T. (1987). Modes of regulation in advanced capitalism: Locating accountancy in four countries. *Accounting, Organizations and Society, 12*(3), 273–292.

Qu, S. Q., & Cooper, D. (2011). The role of inscriptions in producing a balanced scorecard. *Accounting, Organizations and Society, 36*(6), 344–362.

Ramirez, C. (2001). Understanding social closure in its cultural context: Accounting practitioners in France (1920–1939). *Accounting, Organizations and Society, 26*(4–5), 391–418.

Reed, M. (2005). Reflections on the 'realist turn' in organization and management studies. *Journal of Management Studies, 42*(8), 1621–1644.

Robé, J. (2011). The legal structure of the firm. *Accounting Economics and Law,* *1*(1), 1–86.

Roberts, J. (1991). The possibilities of accountability. *Accounting, Organizations and Society, 16*(4), 355–368.

Roberts, J., & van den Steen, E. (2001). Human capital and corporate governance. In H. Albach & J. Schwalbach (Eds.), *Corporate governance* (pp. 128–144). Berlin/Heidelberg: Springer.

Rorty, R. (1980). *Philosophy and the mirror of nature.* Oxford: Blackwell.

Rorty, R. (1992). *The linguistic turn.* Chicago: The University of Chicago Press.

Rorty, R. (2006). Is philosophy relevant to applied ethics? *Business Ethics Quarterly, 16*(3), 369–380.

Rose, H., & Rose, S. (1970). *Science and society.* New York: Penguin.

Rosenberg, T. (2002, August 18). Globalization: The free trade fix. *The New York Times Magazine.*

Roslender, R. (2013). Stuck in the middle with who? (Belatedly) engaging with Laughlin while becoming re-acquainted with Merton and middle range theorising. *Critical Perspectives on Accounting, 24*(3), 228–241.

Roslender, R. (2015). Accountancy. In M. Bevir & R. Rhodes (Eds.), *Routledge handbook of interpretive political science.* London: Routledge.

Rostain, T., & Regan, C., Jr. (2014). *Confidence games: Lawyers, accountants, and the tax shelter industry.* Cambridge, MA: MIT Press.

Roy, W. (1999). *Socializing capital: The rise of the large industrial corporation in America.* Princeton : Princeton University Press.

Runyan, A. (1999). Women in the neoliberal frame. In Meyer & Prügl (Eds.), *Gender politics in global governance.* New York: Rowman & Littlefield.

Schaltegger, S., & Burritt, R. (2000). *Contemporary environmental accounting: Issues, concepts and practice.* Sheffield: Greenleaf.

Schaltegger, S., Bennett, M., Burritt, R., & Jasch, C. (Eds.). (2008). *Environmental management accounting for cleaner production.* Dordrecht: Springer.

Schneider, R. (2015, September 18). ACCA and IMA explore future challenges facing the accounting profession. *AccountingEducation.com.* http://www.accountingeducation.com/index.cfm?page=newsdetails&id=153571

Schrader, D. (1993). *The corporation as anomaly.* Cambridge: Cambridge University Press.

Scott, D. (1931). *The cultural significance of accounts.* New York: Harold Holt.

SEC. (2000, February 16). *International accounting standards,* Release Nos. 33–7801, 34–42430. Securities and Exchange Commission, Washington, DC.

Sen, A. (2003). Missing women: Revisited. *Brigit Medical Journal, 327,* 1297.

Shearer, T., & Arrington, C. (1993). Accounting in other wor(l)ds: A feminism without reserve. *Accounting, Organizations and Society, 18*(2–3), 253–272.

Shenkin, M., & Coulson, A. (2007). Accountability through activism: Learning from Bourdieu. *Accounting Auditing and Accountability Journal, 20*(2), 297–317.

Sikka, P. (2000). From the politics to fear to the politics of emanicipation. *Critical Perspectives on Accounting, 11*(3), 369–380.

Sikka, P. (2006). The Internet and possibilities for counter accounts: Some reflections. *Accounting Auditing and Accountability Journal, 19*(5), 759–769.

Sikka, P. (2008). Enterprise culture and accountancy firms: New masters of the universe. *Accounting Auditing and Accountability Journal, 21*(2), 268–295.

Sikka, P. (2009). Financial crisis and the silence of the auditors. *Accounting, Organizations and Society, 34*(6–7), 868–873.

Sikka, P. (2010). Smoke and mirrors: Corporate social responsibility and tax avoidance. *Accounting Forum, 34*(3/4), 153–168.

Sikka, P., & Willmott, H. (1997). Practising critical accounting. *Critical Perspectives on Accounting, 8*(1/2), 149–165.

Sikka, P., & Willmott, H. (2013). The tax avoidance industry: Accountancy firms on the make. *Critical Perspectives on International Business, 9*(4), 415–443.

Sikka, P., Willmott, H., & Lowe, E. A. (1989). Guardians of knowledge and the public interest: Evidence and issues of accountability in the UK accountancy profession. *Accounting Auditing and Accountability Journal, 2*(2), 47–71.

Sikka, P., Willmott, H., & Puxty, T. (1995). The mountains are still there: Accounting academics and the bearings of intellectuals. *Accounting Auditing and Accountability Journal, 8*(3), 113–140.

Simon, H. (1964). On the concept of organization goal. *Administrative Science Quarterly, 9,* 1–22.

Simons, R. (1994). *Levers of control: How managers use innovative control systems to drive strategic renewal.* Boston: Harvard Business School Press.

Simons, R. (1995). Control in an age of empowerment. *Harvard Business Review, 73*(2), 80–88.

Simons, J. (Ed.). (2004). *Contemporary critical theory.* Edinburgh: Edinburgh Press.

Singh, G. (2008). Research assessments and rankings: Accounting for accountability in "higher education ltd". *International Education Journal: Comparative Perspectives, 9*(1), 13–25.

Söderbaum, P., & Brown, J. (2010). Democratizing economics: Pluralism as a path towards sustainability. *Annals of the New York Academy of Sciences, 1185,* 179–195.

Soederberg, S. (2004). *The politics of the new international financial architecture: Reimposing neoliberal domination in the global south.* London: Zed Books.

Solomons, D. (1974). Corporate social performance: A new dimension in accounting reports? In H. Edey & B. Yamey (Eds.), *Debits, credits, finance and profits* (pp. 131–141). London: Sweet and Maxwell.

Spencer, S., Adams, C., & Yapa, P. (2013). The mediating effects of the adoption of an environmental information system on top management's commitment and environmental performance. *Sustainability Accounting Management and Policy Journal, 4*(1), 75–102.

Spivak, G. (1996). 'Woman' as theatre: United Nations conference on women, Beijing 1995. *Radical Philosophy, 75,* 2–4.

Spivak, G. (2010). Situating feminism, Beatrice Bain Research Group (BBRG). *Annual Keynote Talk, February.* Accessed Oct 2010: http://crg.berkeley.edu/content/spivak

Starik, M. (2013). Sustainability management academics: How's that going? *Organization & Environment, 26*(2), 135–138.

Starik, M., & Kanashiro, P. (2013). Toward a theory of sustainability management: Uncovering and integrating the nearly obvious. *Organization & Environment, 26*(1), 7–30.

Starik, M., & Turcotte, M. (2014). With a little (Urgent) help from our friends management academic leadership for a sustainable future. *Organization & Environment, 27*(1), 3–9.

Steier, F. (Ed.). (1991). *Research and reflexivity.* London: Sage.

Stewart, R. (1992). Pluralizing our past: Foucault in accounting history. *Accounting Auditing and Accountability Journal, 5,* 57–74.

Stiglitz, J. (2012). *The price of inequality.* London: Allen Lane.

Stout, L. (2012). *The shareholder value myth: How putting shareholders first harms investors, corporations and the public.* San Francisco: Berrett-Koehler Publishers.

Strier, R. (2010). Women, poverty, and the microenterprise: Context and discourse. *Gender, Work and Organization, 17*(2), 195–218.

Stubbs, W., & Cocklin, C. (2008). Conceptualizing a 'sustainability business model'. *Organization & Environment, 21*(2), 103–127.

Tanima, F. (2015, October). *Microfinance and women's empowerment in Bangladesh: A study of 'competing logics' and their implications for accounting and accountability systems.* PhD dissertation, Victoria University of Wellington.

Tayler, W. (2010). The balanced scorecard as a strategy-evaluation tool: The effects of implementation involvement and a causal-chain focus. *The Accounting Review, 85*(3), 1095–1117.

Thielemann, U. (2000). A brief theory of the market – Ethically focused. *International Journal of Social Economics, 27*(1), 6–31.

Tiessen, P., & Waterhouse, J. (1983). Towards a descriptive theory of management accounting. *Accounting, Organizations and Society, 8*(2), 251–267.

Tinker, T. (1984). Accounting for unequal exchange: Wealth accumulation versus wealth appropriation. In T. Tinker (Ed.), *Social accounting for corporations: Private enterprise versus the public interest*. New York: Markus Wiener.

Tinker, T. (1985). *Paper prophets: A social critique of accounting*. London/New York/Eastbourne: Holt, Rinehart and Winston/Praeger/Holt Saunders.

Tinker, T. (2001). Paper prophets: An autocritique. *British Accounting Review, 33*(1), 77–89.

Tinker, T., & Lowe, E. A. (1978). Some empirical evidence related to the case of the superordinate integrator. *The Journal of Management Studies, February, 15*, 88–105.

Tinker, T., & Lowe, E. A. (1980). A rationale for corporate social reporting: Theory and evidence from organizational research. *Journal of Business Finance and Accounting, 7*(1), 1–17.

Tinker, T., & Lowe, E. A. (1982). The management science of the management sciences. *Human Relations, 35*(4), 331–347.

Tinker, T., & Lowe, E. A. (1984). One-dimensional management science: The making of a technocratic consciousness. *Interfaces, 14*(2), 40–56.

Tinker, T., & Puxty, A. (Eds.). (1995). *Policing accounting knowledge: The market for excuses affair*. London: Paul Chapman.

Tinker, T., Neimark, M., & Lehman, C. (1991). Falling down the hole in the middle of the road: Political quietism in corporate social reporting. *Accounting Auditing and Accountability Journal, 4*(2), 28–53.

Tomkins, C., & Groves, R. (1983). The everyday accountant and researching his reality. *Accounting, Organizations and Society, 8*, 361–374.

Townley, B. (1995). Managing by numbers: Accounting, personnel management and the creation of a mathesis. *Critical Perspectives on Accounting, 6*(6), 555–575.

Townley, B., Cooper, D., & Oakes, L. (2003). Performance measures and the rationalization of organizations. *Organisation Studies, 24*(7), 1045–1071.

Tregidga, H., & Milne, M. (2006). From sustainable management to sustainable development: A longitudinal analysis of a leading New Zealand environmental reporter. *Business Strategy and the Environment, 15*(4), 219–241.

Tricker, R. (1979). Research in accounting—Purpose, processes and potential. *Accounting and Business Research, 10*(37), 3–15.

Tsagas, G. (2014). A long-term vision for UK firms? Revisiting the target director's advisory role since the takeover of Cadbury's PLC. *Journal of Corporate Law Studies, 14*(1), 241–275.

Tsuk, D. (2003). Corporations without labor: The politics of progressive corporate law. *University of Pennsylvania Law Review, 151*(6), 1861–1912.

Tuomela, T.-S. (2005). The interplay of different levels of control: A case study of introducing a new performance measurement system. *Management Accounting Research, 16*(3), 293–320.

Tweedie, D., & Whittington, G. (1984). *The debate on inflation accounting.* Cambridge: Cambridge University Press.

UK House of Commons Committee of Public Accounts. (2011). *HM revenue & customs 2010–11 accounts: Tax disputes.* London: TSO.

UK House of Commons Committee of Public Accounts. (2013a). *Tax avoidance: The role of large accountancy firms.* London: The Stationery Office.

UK House of Commons Committee of Public Accounts. (2013b). *HM revenue & customs: Progress in tackling tobacco smuggling.* London: TSO.

UK House of Commons Committee of Public Accounts. (2015). *Tax avoidance: The role of large accountancy firms (follow–up).* London: The Stationery Office.

UNIFEM. (2006). *United Nations study on violence against women.* United Nations Fund for Women (UNIFEM), http://www.un.org/en/women/endviolence

US Census Bureau. (2013). http://www.census.gov/population/race/. Accessed 26 Sept.

US Senate Permanent Subcommittee on Investigations. (2003). *US tax shelter industry: The role of accountants, lawyers, and financial professionals – four KPMG case studies: FLIP, OPIS, BLIPS and SC2.* Washington, DC: USGPO.

US Senate Permanent Subcommittee on Investigations. (2005). *The role of professional firms in the US tax shelter industry.* Washington, DC: USGPO.

Vaivio, J. (2004). Mobilising local knowledge with 'provocative' non-financial measures. *European Accounting Review, 13*, 39–71.

Valente, M. (2012). Theorizing firm adoption of sustaincentrism. *Organization Studies, 33*(4), 563–591.

Van Gusteren, H. (1976). *The quest for control.* New York: Wiley.

Van Horn, R. (2009). Reinventing monopoly and the role of corporations: The roots of Chicago law and economics. In P. Mirowski & D. Plehwe (Eds.), *The road from Mont Pèlerin: The making of the neoliberal thought collective* (pp. 204–237). Cambridge, MA: Harvard University Press.

Veldman, J. (2011). Governance Inc. *Business Ethics: A European Review, 20*(3), 292–303.

Veldman, J., & Parker, M. (2012). Specters, Inc: The elusive basis of the corporation. *Business and Society Review, 117*(4), 413–441.

Veldman, J., & Willmott, H. (2015 (in press). The cultural grammar of governance: the UK code of Corporate Governance, reflexivity and the limits of 'soft' regulation. *Human Relations.*

Veldman, J., & Willmott, H. (forthcoming). Management and the corporate form. In *Critical corporation handbook.* Cambridge: Cambridge University Press.

Vogus, T., & Sutcliffe, K. (n.d.). Requisite variety and firm performance: An empirical exploration. *Working Paper: University of Warwick.*

Von Bertalanffy, L. (1955). General systems theory. *Main Currents in Modern Thought, 11*, 75–83.

Von Bertalanffy, L. (1968/1976). *General systems theory: Foundation, development, applications.* New York: George Braziller.

Wacquant, L. (1992). The structure and logic of Bourdieu's sociology. In P. Bourdieu & L. Wacquant (Eds.), *An invitation to reflexive sociology.* Chicago: The University of Chicago Press.

Walker, S. (2008). Accounting histories of women: Beyond recovery? *Accounting Auditing and Accountability Journal, 21*(4), 580–610.

Waring, M. (1988). *If women counted: A new feminist economics.* London: Macmillan.

Waterhouse, J., & Tiessen, P. (1978). A contingency framework for management accounting systems research. *Accounting, Organizations and Society, 3*(1), 65–76.

Watts, R., & Zimmerman, J. (1979). The demand for and supply of accounting theories: The market for excuses. *Accounting Review, 54*(2), 273–305.

Weick, K. (1979). *The social psychology of organizing.* Reading: Addison Wesley.

Wells, C. (2005). *Corporations and criminal responsibility.* Oxford: Oxford University Press.

Whiteman, G., Walker, B., & Perego, P. (2013). Planetary boundaries: Ecological foundations for corporate. *Sustainability Journal of Management Studies, 50*(2), 307–336.

Whitley, R. (1999). Firms, institutions and management control: The comparative analysis of coordination and control systems. *Accounting Organizations & Society, 24*(5/6), 507–524.

Whittington, G. (2005). The adoption of international accounting standards in the European Union. *European Accounting Review, 14*(1), 127–153.

Whittington, G. (2008). Fair value and the IASB/FASB conceptual framework project: An alternative view. *Abacus, 44*(2), 139–168.

Widener, S. (2006). Associations between strategic resource importance and performance measure use: The impact on firm performance. *Management Accounting Research, 17*(4), 433–457.

Wiener, N. (1948). *Cybernetics: Or control and communication in the animal and machine.* New York: ffiley.

Wiersma, E. (2009). For which purposes do managers use balanced scorecards: An empirical study. *Management Accounting Research, 20,* 239–251.

Wilks, S. (2013). *The political power of the business corporation.* Cheltenham: Edward Elgar.

Williams, C., & Zumbansen, P. (2011). *The embedded firm: Corporate governance, labor, and finance capitalism.* Cambridge: Cambridge University Press.

Williams, K., Haslam, C., Cutler, T., Johal, S., & Willis, R. (1994). Johnson 2: Knowledge goes to Hollywood. *Critical Perspectives on Accounting, 5*(3), 281–293.

Williston, S. (1888). History of the law of business corporations before 1800. *Harvard Law Review, 2*(3), 105–124.

Wilmott, H. (1983). Paradigms for accounting research: Critical reflections on Tomkins and Groves' 'everyday accountant and researching his reality'. *Accounting, Organizations and Society, 8,* 389–405.

Wilson, R., & Sikka, P. (2014). In memoriam: Emeritus Professor E.A. Lowe *British Accounting Review, 46*(2), 213–214.

Winch, P. (1958). *The idea of a social science and its relation to philosophy.* London: Routledge & Kegan Paul.

Yeats, W. B. (1965). *Collected poems of W B Yeats.* London: Macmillan.

Young, W., & Tilley, F. (2006). Can business move beyond efficiency? The shift toward effectiveness and equity in the corporate sustainability debate. *Business Strategy and the Environment, 15,* 402–415.

Zeff, S. (2002). 'Political' lobbying on proposed standards: A challenge to the IASB. *Accounting Horizons, 16*(1), 43–54.

Žižek, S. (2000). Class struggle or postmodernism? Yes, please! In J. Butler, E. Laclau, & S. Žižek (Eds.), *Contingency, hegemony, universality: Contemporary dialogues on the left* (pp. 90–135). London: Verso.

Žižek, S. (2006). *The universal exception: Selected writing* (Vol. 2). London: Continuum.

Žižek, S. (2014). *Trouble in paradise: From the end of history to the end of capitalism.* London: Allen Lane, Penguin.

Zollo, M., Cennamo, C., & Neumann, K. (2013). Beyond what and why understanding organizational evolution towards sustainable enterprise models. *Organization & Environment, 26*(3), 241–259.

Zuboff, S. (1988). *In the age of the smart machine.* London: Heinemann.

Zukav, G. (1989). *The dancing Wu Li masters: An overview of the new physics.* New York: Bantam New Age Books.

Index

© The Author(s) 2016
J. Haslam, P. Sikka (eds.), *Pioneers of Critical Accounting*,
DOI 10.1057/978-1-137-54212-0

Printed by Printforce, the Netherlands